J500

# THE ROMANTICS OF SPAIN

STUDIES IN HISPANIC LITERATURES

*General Editor :* E. ALLISON PEERS

# THE ROMANTICS OF SPAIN

*Translated from the Spanish of*

*ENRIQUE PIÑEYRO*

*With an Introduction and Bibliography*

BY

## E. ALLISON PEERS

LIVERPOOL

INSTITUTE OF HISPANIC STUDIES

1934

*Made and Printed in Great Britain by William Clowes and Sons, Limited,
London and Beccles*

# TRANSLATOR'S PREFACE

It is now almost thirty years since Enrique Piñeyro published his studies of the principal figures in the Romantic era of Spanish literature, in the volume here translated, entitled *El Romanticismo en España*. Though as a Hispano-American living in Paris he modestly disclaimed any idea of teaching Spaniards their own literature and professed to be writing solely for Spanish Americans, his book at once became a standard work of reference on its period wherever Spanish is spoken, and, together with Blanco García's *Literatura Española en el Siglo XIX* and a single valuable chapter of Sr. Alonso Cortés' study of Zorrilla, the principal authority on the Spanish Romantics. Like D. Andrés Bello and D. Rufino José Cuervo, whom he eulogizes in his original preface, Piñeyro has thoroughly merited his election, by common consent, into that ideal and invisible Academy which recognizes no distinction between Spaniard and Spanish American and judges the critic solely by the services he has rendered to literature. His book reveals a profound knowledge of the great literary figures of the early nineteenth century, a keen insight into their genius, a just appreciation of their failings as well as their merits, and a complete and fearless independence of judgment and expression. He has also another quality too rare among Spanish-speaking critics—a wide acquaintance with other literatures than that of Spain, and particularly with English literature, for which, as he very clearly shows, he has the greatest admiration. This has made it the more welcome task to translate the book into English, students of Spanish literature who read that language being now so numerous that one may safely predict as long a life for it, in this new and revised form, as it has had in its original Spanish.

Considerable progress has been made in the study of the Romantic Movement in Spain during the last generation.

When Piñeyro wrote, Sr. Lomba y Pedraja had published
none of his valuable work on Larra, M. Sarrailh had not
begun his researches on Martínez de la Rosa, and neither
M. Le Gentil's study of Bretón de los Herreros nor Sr.
Alonso Cortés' critical biography of Zorrilla was as yet
written. And, difficult though it may be to believe, the
treatment of individual authors was that part of the work
which had been covered the least inadequately. There was
no bibliography of the period ; its reviews and newspapers
lay unstudied in dusty libraries ; no investigations had been
made either into the nature of nineteenth-century romanticism or into its history ; and the important though intricate
question of the influence on Spanish literature of such
authors as Byron, Scott and Hugo had been pontifically
pronounced upon but never seriously examined. Small
wonder if historians of literature were content with vague
generalizations about romanticism, many of which, in the
light of the studies that have since been pursued, are now
discovered to have been erroneous.

The legends of a Romantic "school" (which issued no
prospectus and had no single aim and no leader) and of a
Romantic "triumph" (which proves, on investigation, to
have lasted for about three years) are referred to frequently
in Piñeyro's work, but fortunately, since he made no
attempt to write a history of the Romantic movement,
they figure only as allusions. It is now clearly seen that,
almost as soon as it reached its climax, which was approximately coincident with the production of *El Trovador* in
1836, this vague, formless movement dissolved readily into
its component elements, some of which continued to pervade
Spanish literature till late in the century. The so-called
"Romantic battle" (culminating, according to the legend,
in the Romantic "triumph") lasted only for a matter oi
months, and was brought to an end, not so much by the
rout of the Classicists as by the desertion of the Romantic
generals, though the issue was really decided by the appearance of the Eclectic army, which charged at full strength with
its battle-cry of "¡ Viva el justo medio !" and within a very
short time had carried all before it.*

Since all this has now been documentarily proved, it

---

* I hope to treat the critical years 1833-7 with all necessary fullness in my
forthcoming historical study of the Spanish Romantic Movement.

suffices merely to state these essential facts, which throw much light on the literary figures to be studied in the following pages. No attempt has been made to add to Piñeyro's studies themselves, for, though it would have been easy to re-write the book in a greatly enlarged form, to do this would have been to destroy its individuality and much of its unity. I have translated freely, altered the few passages which "date" (as on p. 208), and curbed some of the author's rhetorical flights in conformity with our more restrained habits, my aim being to produce a book as acceptable in England and English-speaking America as the original was in Spanish America and Spain. Errors of fact and date, which are somewhat numerous, have been corrected, a very few necessary footnotes added in square brackets, and slight modifications made in the arrangement of the chapters dealing with the lesser writers of the period. The only addition of any substance, apart from this preface, is that of some bibliographical notes, without which, now that the Spanish Romantics have become a subject of serious study, the book would be markedly incomplete. It should be emphasized that the opinions expressed throughout the following pages are not mine but the author's. This applies especially to the chapters on La Avellaneda, Campoamor, and Estébanez Calderón.

The most grateful acknowledgments are due to the author's daughter, Mlle. Piñeyro, of Paris, for her kindness in granting me permission to make and publish this translation. The labour of checking facts has been lightened, and the translation greatly improved, by the help of my former pupil, Miss I. L. McClelland, Lecturer in the University of Glasgow, who read the entire book in manuscript. I also owe some valuable suggestions to my friend, Professor F. Courtney Tarr of Princeton University, U.S.A.

E. A. P.

UNIVERSITY OF LIVERPOOL,
    *July 15th, 1934.*

# CONTENTS

ix

# THE ROMANTICS OF SPAIN

## INTRODUCTION

The aim of this book, as its title indicates, is not to write
the history of Spanish literature during the Romantic period,
but to study in turn the chief writers who flourished in Spain
during the first half of the nineteenth century, which in
general terms may be described as the age of romanticism.
These writers are discussed in a series of biographical and
critical essays and arranged according to their relative
importance, and according to the *genre* in which each chiefly
shone, rather than in strictly chronological order. The
principal authors of the second rank are grouped together in
two separate chapters. Not all the writers studied were pure
Romantics ; all of them, however, illustrate in some way or
other the development of the new ideas generally known, in
Spain and elsewhere, as Romantic, and the application of
these ideas to literature.

It will be observed that a large proportion of the work
under consideration is written in verse. Prose was less
popular and less successful than verse during this period.
Spain, in the early nineteenth century, had no Macaulay or
Carlyle, no Michelet or Sainte-Beuve ; even the novel,
which in other countries, in the hands of Scott, Hugo,
Balzac, Manzoni or Mérimée, did so much to enlarge the
domain of prose and awaken a new interest in it, seemed
incapable here of more than bare existence as a parasite of
Sir Walter Scott's Waverley Novels. It is therefore no
undue disparagement of an important type of literature to
have grouped some of the minor *prosistas* with a number of
poets in a final chapter.

The peculiar situation in which the country found itself
between the French invasion of 1808 and the death of
Ferdinand VII in 1833 makes it possible to delimit the stages
in the development of Spanish romanticism with some
precision. With Ferdinand and his justly loathed political
*régime* there disappeared a whole system of abuses and

iniquities, never to return, and in literature, as in politics, a new era began. Writers who were clearly marked out to inaugurate this new era and to lead the literary revolution which at once declared itself upon the removal of the suffocating oppression of Ferdinand's tyranny had now arrived at varying stages of maturity. Some had lived abroad as exiles, with no public for their original literary ideas and creations; others had remained in their own country, but in semi-retirement, able to publish only what foolish or malicious censors deigned of their charity to permit. To the latter group belonged Larra, Bretón, Vega, Escosura, Gil y Zárate and many others; to the former, such men as Martínez de la Rosa, Ángel de Saavedra, Alcalá Galiano and Espronceda. Once the curtain went up on a fresh scene in Spain's political life, these writers appeared on the stage in shining armour, ready to defend and propagate the new ideas, each according to his temperament and the degree of completeness of his literary education. In the preface to *Hernani*, Victor Hugo had defined romanticism as "liberalism in literature." The description was correct enough as applied to Spain. All the Spanish Romantics were liberals, and, in the first years of the new epoch, at least, they unanimously demanded freedom for art as much as freedom in politics.

At about the middle of the nineteenth century, fresh tendencies began to appear in drama, in lyric poetry and above all in prose fiction. Young writers started to strike out for themselves from the paths followed by their predecessors and once more both literature and politics saw the inauguration of a new era. That Spain which had endured the agitations and convulsions of a fierce civil war, the regency of Espartero and the violent, implacable reaction of the *moderados*, under their long-needed leader Narváez, began a slow transformation which fitted it to pay increasing attention to the arts of peace in preparation for a great future. Romanticism did not, of course, immediately and entirely disappear; a few of the best-known Romantics continued writing; but gradually they grew fewer and less productive. The last of them, Zorrilla, lived until 1893, by which time the Romantic movement had long passed into history, having lost practically all its influence and almost its entire prestige.

The writers studied or referred to in this book were born either at the end of the eighteenth century or during the first quarter of the nineteenth ; those who came later found the Romantic battle ended. This battle was neither as fierce nor as prolonged in Spain as in France ; there were no organized forces to defend Classical precepts and oppose Romantic innovations, nor was the public particularly interested in literary warfare. The Classicists themselves, moreover, were less formidable. In France the eighteenth century had been marvellously fruitful ; in Spain the little that had grown in the literary soil had been transplanted, through Bourbon influence, from France and had never become deeply rooted. Only in the latter years of the century, with such writers as Meléndez Valdés, Cienfuegos and Quintana, did a truly national inspiration return to Spain. Meléndez Valdés, Cienfuegos and most of their contemporaries, however, barely survived the beginning of the nineteenth century, while Quintana, in collecting and editing old Spanish ballads and lyrics in the *Cancionero* of 1796 and in his first *Parnaso*, directed the gaze of his fellow-countrymen to more distant horizons, and, however unconsciously, prepared the way for the Romantics. Golden Age drama, again, had been neglected and looked down upon during the eighteenth century, but that century had produced nothing even faintly comparable with it, and it had little difficulty in recovering its popularity. This was partly—though only partly—due to German critics, who eulogized it as one of the great monuments of Romantic art, gave Calderón a place near Shakespeare and sought in Spain's Golden Age argument and inspiration for the Romantic reform in their own country. The lectures on dramatic literature given by the brothers Schlegel were widely read in Spain, in their French translation ; some of them, at a later date, were translated into Spanish. In the Peninsula itself, a German, Böhl von Faber, defended Calderón against two prominent Spaniards, José Joaquín de Mora and Antonio Alcalá Galiano, the latter of whom afterwards became a convert to romanticism and wrote the important preface to the Duque de Rivas' narrative poem *El Moro Expósito*.

The ease with which romanticism made its way into Spanish literature may be illustrated by the critical essays of Alberto Lista (1775–1848), an eminent professor, a distinguished poet and a convinced Classicist both by temperament and by education. Far from showing the irreconcilable enmity to romanticism that marked Classical criticism in France, he did his utmost to understand and appreciate its principles. A number of his old pupils, such as Espronceda and Escosura, to whom he was deeply attached, had been attracted by the new doctrines, and he himself, in the well-known lectures which he gave at the Madrid Ateneo, as early as 1822, attempted to legitimize the origins of these doctrines, which many considered of foreign importation, and to relate them with Golden Age drama—especially with that of Calderón, for as regards Lope de Vega he was more reactionary. These lectures were discontinued on Ferdinand VII's resumption of absolute power in 1823, but were recommenced upon the re-founding of the Ateneo in 1835, when the Romantic revolt was at its height and such audacious dramas as Larra's *Macías* and Rivas's *Don Álvaro* were being discussed by all. Typical of Lista's criticism in this period was his somewhat pathetic plea that the Romantics "would respect the unities of time and place as far as possible." Things might have been different had he been able, twelve years earlier, to continue his defence of Golden Age drama, for this drama played an important part in the native development of the Romantic movement with which he had much in common.

Mention may here be made of another critic, a man of less note but a patient and learned researcher into the past, whose work had a considerable formative influence on the Romantic movement—Agustín Durán (1789–1862). A "Discourse" which he wrote in 1828 on old Spanish drama and "the way in which it should be considered if we are to arrive at a fit estimate of its peculiar merit" exercised a great influence when it first appeared, though it was somewhat quickly forgotten and was not reprinted until the Spanish Academy inserted it in the second volume of its *Memorias* in 1870. Even to-day it can be read with profit and one can well imagine the effect upon thoughtful readers, when it first appeared, of its insistence that the youth of Spain "has no idea of what romanticism is, despite the fact that in Germany, France and England the discussion of the subject is nearly at an end." Could it have been more widely read, and had Spain in 1828 not been overborne by intellectual oppression, it might well have marked the exact date of the outburst of the Romantic revolt.

It is of less importance to attempt to fix the end of the Romantic movement than its beginning, for although when Zorrilla published his *Granada* in 1852 its influence was all but exhausted and the days of its dominance had long passed, it continued to permeate all kinds of art—poetry and prose, painting, sculpture, architecture and music. Individual Romantics continued to appear, and have never ceased to appear : Echegaray, for example, is as much a Romantic as Rivas and Zorrilla. But to pursue the history of romanticism considered as a tendency and an influence would carry us so far beyond the limits of this book that it would be unjustifiable to embark upon it.

# CHAPTER I

## MARIANO JOSÉ DE LARRA

### I

The Romantic movement, which began to impose its formulas and dogmas upon Spain about the year 1830, which gave a new and brilliant form to literary art, and among many lyric and dramatic poets produced writers of the calibre of Espronceda, Rivas, García Gutiérrez, Hartzenbusch and Zorrilla, can only claim one single first-class writer of prose : Larra. And unhappily the life of that single writer was a short one, for, after spending the best of his talent in journalistic improvisations on literature or society, he died at the early age of twenty-eight. The importance ascribed to his work by posterity is based upon these articles, which enshrine the greater part of a well-merited reputation. Only Donoso Cortés, who was born in the same year as Larra, could be placed beside him as an eminent prose writer of the same period, and Donoso Cortés, as we shall see, was a jurisconsult, a publicist and a philosopher rather than purely and simply a man of letters.

Larra occupies an important period in the history of the Romantic movement—a period of which the output is largely supplied by his own writings. He was a precursor, a pioneer ; and the roads which he opened up were soon followed by others. His *Macías* was the first Romantic drama in verse, with varied metres, to appear in Spain, and it had a long period of success in the theatres of his own country and of Spanish America. His novel, *El Doncel de Don Enrique el Doliente*, in which Macías reappears as the protagonist, is the most interesting and perhaps the best wrought imitation of Sir Walter Scott in Spanish. As a dramatic critic, in his own time, he had no rival, nor since then has there been any other who can fairly be said to have surpassed him. His critiques of García Gutiérrez' *Trovador* and Hartzenbusch's *Amantes de Teruel* are the fullest, fairest and most exact that have been written upon two works of

6

capital importance in the development of Spanish romanticism. Finally his *artículos de costumbres*, the satirical pictures in which he so vigorously describes the men and the political events of his time, are little masterpieces. Rivalling the sketches of Cervantes in their apt and penetrating observation and strongly tinctured with a bitter frankness of speech, they represent the public and the private life of Spain during that highly critical period in which, under Ferdinand VII, the despotic *régime* of absolutism and theocratic domination drew to its close, and, under his infant daughter Isabel, there grew in strength and experience a new *régime* of limited monarchism and comparative freedom. But before the old *régime* had completely died away, and the new *régime* had begun to make itself felt, there was an interregnum of confusion, uncertainty and unrest, a period of infinite weariness and disillusionment. It is within this period, during its seven or eight darkest and most troubled years, that the literary life of Mariano José de Larra began and ended.

Born in Madrid, in 1809, he was the son of an army doctor who, despite the strong feeling in Spain against the invader, served in the troops of the Emperor Napoleon. When in 1812 the French army began its final withdrawal from the Peninsula, both father and son accompanied it to France. Not until 1817 did Larra return to his own country, and at that time he was unable to speak either French or Spanish well, though his French was a little better than his Spanish. At first he went about with his father, whose profession prevented him from establishing a fixed abode. Later, according to one of his biographers, he studied law, with the idea of becoming an *abogado*.* But his slender means, his intractable character and his precocious literary inclinations combined to divert him from this first intention. He soon established himself in the capital, with a small government post which was insufficient to bring him in a livelihood, the more so since he was rash enough to marry, against the wishes of his family, at twenty. In Madrid he devoted himself to writing—the almost invariable resource, as he

---

* Cf. the biography prefixed to the so-called *Obras completas* (Madrid, 1843). According to Mesonero Romanos' *Memorias de un Setentón* (Madrid, 1881, Vol. II, pp. 53, 85), the subject of his study was medicine. I believe this, however, to be an error.

says in one of the numbers of the *Pobrecito Hablador*, of a person who has no other.

Immersed in the literary life of the capital, he had now begun a career which was to take him continually to editorial office, café and theatre. He wrote incessantly, adapting comedies and dramas from the French for the Spanish stage, and attending the meetings of the so-called "Parnasillo" in the Café del Príncipe, where he mixed with the principal writers and artists of his day, although he never became really popular with them, on account (says Mesonero Romanos) of his "innate mordacity." As his reputation grew and his work became better paid, he entered more and more into Madrilenian society, where his youth, his talent, his elegance of demeanour and his polished manners all lent him attraction. He formed personal relations of many kinds, among them love intrigues, one of which was so violent and so unhappy that it drove him to suicide ; he shot himself in his own room, on February 13, 1837, while his wife and his three children were in the room adjoining it. A painful and a tragic ending to so short a life, but one which may well have been tragically inevitable, and was only precipitated by the interview with his mistress which was the direct cause of the catastrophe. The mere perusal of Larra's brilliant articles written during the last six months of his life is sufficient to convince one that, humanly speaking, nothing could have saved him from some such tragedy.

These few lines tell as much of the story of Larra's life as we need know for an understanding of his writings, which we may now examine in order.

He was only nineteen years of age when, in 1828, he published his first piece of journalism, which was a complete failure. He himself showed that he realized the weakness of this juvenile work, which he brought out in parts, and at irregular intervals, under the name of *El Duende satírico*, by omitting it from the first collected edition of his articles, published in 1835. When, barely more than twenty, he found himself in straits—unknown, with family obligations and forced to write for his living—he naturally set his first and principal hopes of making a fortune on the theatre. Dramatists, at that time, though by no means well remunerated, were at least in a better position than any other type of writer. Bretón de los Herreros and Gil y Zárate, both older than Larra, were living on the proceeds of plays which, if not the worst they ever wrote, were certainly of no great excellence : Bretón's *A Madrid me vuelvo* and Gil's *Un Año después de la boda* will serve as examples. Ventura de la Vega, too, who was almost exactly of Larra's age, was already working at those translations and adaptations from the French in which he was so particularly to distinguish himself. To earn anything at all, of course, hard work was necessary, rates of remuneration being extremely low. The best paid authors received from their managers only a total fee of from 300 to 400 pesetas per play, with perhaps a further sum not exceeding 125 pesetas if they disposed of their copyright to their publishers. This, according to Mesonero Romanos, was all that Bretón and Gil received for the two plays named above, in spite of the excellence of the reception given to both. Managers and publishers, like the public itself, attributed so little importance to art and had so little confidence in the imagination and merit of their authors, that they paid the same fee for an original work as for a translation.* We can understand, therefore, why Ventura de la Vega had been toiling for twenty years, and had translated more than seventy plays from the French, before he wrote his first completely original play, *El Hombre de mundo*, produced in 1845.

On April 27, 1831, there was given in Madrid a successful five-act play entitled *No más mostrador*. By many it has always been supposed to be an original work of Larra's ; his personal friend, the Marqués de Molíns, held this view half a century after its production and affirms it in his biography of Bretón de los Herreros.† In reality, though there are some entirely original passages in the play, and though the framework was ably filled out, co-ordinated and adjusted by Larra, *No más mostrador* is based upon Scribe's one-act vaudeville *Les Adieux au comptoir* and a comedy by Michel Dieulafoy, entitled *Le portrait de Michel Cervantès*, which had been produced in Paris, at the Théâtre Louvois, on the 2nd Fructidor of the year X of the French Republic.

* Mesonero Romanos, *op. cit.*, Vol. II, p. 65.
† *Bretón de los Herreros* (Madrid, 1883), p. 155.

Scribe's brief comedy gave Larra the material for his first act and for half of his second ; he probably also took his *dénouement* from Scribe's, the two being identical. The chief characters in *No más mostrador* are a prosperous business man, Don Deogracias, and his wife, Doña Bibiana. The wife, full of aristocratic yearnings and affectations, insists that her husband shall leave the shop, go with her into society and seek a brilliant match for their daughter Julia. The husband, an honest fellow, prefers that she should marry the son of one of his own agents, a plan which the obstinate and domineering wife stubbornly opposes. This is quite a commonplace situation, which has been exploited in drama times without number, but Scribe develops and resolves it with his accustomed skill, and produces quite a light and agreeable *vaudeville à couplets*. Don Deogracias arranges that the suitor of his own choice shall be introduced to Doña Bibiana as a Count with a well-known title, and endowed with Madrilenian elegance. In due course matters are cleared up and all ends happily.

Larra, anxious to enlarge the field of his play and extend it from one act to five, borrows from Dieulafoy* the idea of bringing the Count himself on the stage in flesh and blood, and causing him, after a series of events that need not here be specified, to assume the name and situation of the first claimant. By means of one *quid pro quo* after another, some of them forced and improbable, the action progresses in languid fashion till it reaches the end of the fifth act. Here Doña Bibiana abandons her ridiculous ideas and asks pardon of her husband, who, before the curtain falls, sums up the homely moral of the play in these words :

Casaremos a nuestra hija y nos honraremos con el trabajo, que si algo hay vergonzoso en la vida, no es el ganar de comer, sino el no hacer gala cada uno de su profesión, cuando es honrosa.

* *Le Portrait de Michel Cervantès* is an adequately written comedy, the action of which is supposed to take place on the day of Cervantes' death. Towards the end of the second act the proposal is made to the protagonist, a painter named Morillos, that as a speculation he should paint a portrait of the "poor devil" who has just died, since, though they disdained him in life, men will certainly be glad to purchase his portrait now that he is dead, and there is no other portrait of him in existence. Hence the title of the play, which has no further connection with Cervantes himself than this.

[While leaving this note as the author wrote it, the translator would refer students to Miss McGuire's study of the subject (Bibliography, p. 238, below).]

The lesson is an ordinary and an uninspiring one, but not more so than the moral declaimed by Don Diego at the end of *El Sí de las Niñas :*

> Esto resulta del abuso de la autoridad, de la opresión que la juventud padece. . . .

The argument of *No más mostrador*, as we have seen, is neither of any great interest nor in the least degree original ; and, after the second act, the piece makes none too rapid progress. The success which it achieved is explicable only by its formal merits—the transparent elegance of its language and the vivaciousness of its dialogue. It was no doubt for this reason that for a long time it figured in the regular repertory of touring companies, both in Spain and in Spanish America.

Before Moratín, it had been long since a Spanish comedy of any merit had appeared in prose. The truth is that Spanish prose hardly lends itself to comedy. Various authors, following the example of Diderot or Sedaine, had published some well-written prose dramas of the type of Jovellanos' *Delincuente Honrado*. But in comedy, the great French tradition of the eighteenth century, beginning with Le Sage's *Turcaret* and continuing by way of Marivaux down to the ingenious Beaumarchais, had hardly any Spanish followers. Bretón, it is true, wrote the first of his comedies, *A la vejez, viruelas*, in prose, and translated others from the French into the same medium, all of them before the time of Larra ; nevertheless, it is only in verse that Bretón achieves brilliance. His prose is always indifferent ; it is his facility as a versifier that is a perennial marvel.

Moratín is an avowed disciple of Molière. Four of his comedies—two of them original and two translations—are written in prose, and in a prose of an excellence and a correctness almost without blemish, often combined with the wit of true comedy. Yet there is little to laugh at in *El Sí de las Niñas ;* except in its *dénouement*, the play is a comedy of sentiment, almost a drama. Of the two acts of *El Café*, or *La Comedia Nueva*, the second is completely devoid of dramatic interest ; and the effect of the first, despite the vigour of the satire with which it ridicules contemporary poetasters, is weakened by the tirades of Don Pedro, the mouthpiece of Moratín himself, a character always tedious and disagreeably severe, though it was clearly not the author's intention to make him so. Of Moratín's two translations from Molière, only *El Médico a palos* has attained general popularity, and the original of this, *Le Médecin malgré lui*, is not a true comedy, but a three-act *sainete*, a *fin de fiesta*—"a farce," to use the words of Voltaire, "both gay and comic, as the vulgar taste demands."

The disciples or followers of Moratín—first Gorostiza and Martínez de la Rosa and then the fertile Bretón—wrote their principal plays, if not all of them, in verse. The idea of writing good prose comedies was apparently relegated to oblivion, and no single work of the time in Spain can be found which showed any serious attempt to cultivate a *genre* that has covered France with such glory throughout the nineteenth century.

Larra, who does not aspire to the heights of Molière, but has a much closer resemblance to the Beaumarchais whose Figaro provided him with a pen-name, is certainly far from attaining that perfection of form which characterizes Moratín ; but neither, it must be allowed, does he make any attempt to achieve it. His freer and livelier style conveys none of that impression of frigidity, hardness and excessive polish which we get from the prose of Moratín. In his hands the Spanish language is capable of greater dramatic effect, and lends itself to a profound study of character and a sharp and bitter satire which penetrates much deeper than the satire of his illustrious predecessor. Moratín has few passages as full of brief, expressive, transparent phrases producing the maximum effect upon the spectator as are these few lines, taken from the exposition (Scene I) of *No más mostrador*, which have no kind of parallel in Scribe's vaudeville :

Mira, mujer. Bibiana Cartucho eras cuando me enamoré de ti, por mi mala estrella ; con Bibiana Cartucho me casé, que ojalá fuera mentira, para purgar mis pecados en este mundo ; y para mí Bibiana Cartucho has sido, eres y serás hasta que me muera ; y si te mueres tú antes, en tu lápida he de poner 'Aquí yace Bibiana Cartucho,' y nada más.

There were once many theatre-goers who knew these lines by heart, though to-day they are quite forgotten.

It was with greater confidence in his own powers, and with the encouragement given him by the fame which his comedy had won him, that in August 1832 Larra began to publish *El Pobrecito Hablador, Revista satírica de costumbres, etc., por el bachiller don Juan Pérez de Munguía*. This publication, like the earlier *Duende satírico*, appeared at irregular intervals, and continued until March 1833. Larra's assurance was not excessive, as befitted a youth of twenty-three who was about to constitute himself a censor of society. He aims, in his own words, at "la sátira de los vicios, de las ridiculeces y las cosas" ; and in the article which serves as a prospectus he announces that his publication will not always be original, but will include material translated, adapted or completely recast—"una capa," as it were, "con embozos nuevos." The first article of the first number, following this convenient rather than attractive programme, is simply the adaptation to a Spanish *milieu* of an article by the French writer Jouy, who, at the time of the First Empire, was famous under the name "L'Hermite de la Chaussée d'Antin." But the *Pobrecito* soon shakes itself free from such influences, and almost the whole of the rest of the series is original.

Mesonero Romanos, in his *Memorias*,\* shows a particular anxiety to set it on record that Larra's publication appeared in August 1832, whereas his own *artículos de costumbres*, afterwards collected under the title of *Panorama Matritense*, had begun in *Cartas Españolas* in the January of the same year. He might, however, have spared himself this anxiety. As far as form was concerned, *artículos de costumbres* inserted in periodicals could not be held to constitute a new literary *genre* simply because the *costumbres* depicted in them were Spanish, for, both before and after Jouy, who published the "Observations" of his "Hermite" at the beginning of the century, satirical pictures had been drawn in exactly the same manner. As to content, there have never been two things of one kind more unlike one another than Larra's articles and the *Escenas Matritenses*. To compare these only with the *Pobrecito Hablador*, which is inferior to many of Larra's later productions written over the pseudonym of "Fígaro," Mesonero was never capable of rising to the degree of wit and vigour which are found in such noteworthy articles as "El Castellano viejo," "Empeños y desempeños" or "Vuelva usted mañana," and these have neither the loftiness of thought of Larra's later writings nor their tragic and

\* *Op. cit.*, Vol. II, p. 84.

eloquent misanthropy. Both the style and the matter of the
"Curioso Parlante" are borne down by their own weight and
are thus excessively pedestrian, whereas the phraseology of
"Fígaro" soars aloft as on its own wings and takes on colours
of the highest brilliance.

Wearied by his strife with the censorship, Larra at length
suspended the publication of his pamphlets, in spite of the
favourable reception given them by the public, a success the
more appreciable in days when, as the *Pobrecito Hablador*
itself tells us, it was hard to say whether no one in the
country read because no one wrote, or no one wrote because
no one read. In 1832, thanks to Ferdinand VII's last consort, an unexpected ray of light pierced the darkness of his
gloomy reign, and, for the short time it illumined the
horizon, encouraged writers to hope for a little freedom—for
permission, at the least, to write anything that in no way
prejudiced the vested interests of the Throne and the Church.
With the aim of conciliating the censor, Larra had already,
in one of the first numbers of the periodical, burned an im-
moderate quantity of incense at Ferdinand's feet, in gratitude
for a list of favours which he enumerates : a typical example
of these is the substitution of the *garrote* for the gibbet as a
means of carrying out the executions which at this time were
of such frequent occurrence.

But Larra's incense proved to be of no great potency : if it
had never been offered at all the result would have been the
same. The gleam of hope soon departed. The *régime*
loosened none of the fetters which it had imposed, and the
*Pobrecito Hablador* came to an end because wherever it turned
its gaze it found only "a wall which to attempt to break
down would be madness." In suspending publication, it
eased its conscience by declaring that "if whole numbers
have been devoted to matters of small importance, this was
not because such was our intention, but because of the nature
of the circumstances which surround us." This allusion
to the inexorable censorship is made in suitably veiled
language—the only language in which such an allusion was
possible.

II

One of the earliest manifestations of romanticism in Spain was the popularity of Sir Walter Scott—or, one should rather say, of his French translators.

A few lines, attributed by the *Pobrecito Hablador* to an author "known to all and a man of great merit," describe the means by which Scott first entered the Peninsula :

Me he ajustado con un librero para traducir del francés al castellano las novelas de Walter Scott, que se escribieron originalmente en inglés, y algunas de Cooper. . . . Doce reales me viene a dar por pliego de imprenta, y el día que no traduzco, no como.

There is a direct and a legitimate filiation in this proceeding. Scott, in his youth, translated into English Goethe's first drama and also Bürger's famous ballad *Leonora*—both of which works may be said to have stimulated his poetic ardour and to have led his genius along new literary paths.   France translated both Sir Walter Scott and Fenimore Cooper, and from France their works passed into Spain, there likewise to awaken love for the new literature. We are not, of course, forgetting that France had other points of contact with Germany, or that Spain drew its romanticism from other and deeper sources than either of these countries. This is only one line of literary descent, but it is an important one, and it must be remembered that neither Mme de Staël, on the one hand, nor Goethe and Schiller on the other, had any considerable vogue in Spain till later in the century.

During the last part of Ferdinand's reign, and until the very time of his death in 1833, the rigours of the censorship weighed not only upon original Spanish works but also upon works imported from abroad.   Thus the first productions of the French Romantics did not easily penetrate as far as Madrid, being open to suspicion on account of their foreign origin, the innovations which they represented and the lack of respect which they showed for the dignity of the throne, in the peculiar sense in which this was understood in Spain. Larra, no doubt, with his perfect understanding of French, would have found opportunities of reading these latest French novelties ; but it is certain that very few Spaniards would be able to obtain and sample for themselves the works of Victor Hugo and his fellow-Romantics until the King's death began to dissipate the dense mist which had for so long covered the entire country. It was in the last dismal year of Ferdinand's life that Larra collected the materials for his novel *El Doncel de Don Enrique el Doliente*, which he wrote in the same year and published at the beginning of 1834.

Superficially, the *Doncel* bears a close resemblance to one of Scott's novels : we recognize the same method of construction, the same slow movement of the narrative, the long dialogues, chapters without titles, verse epigraphs introducing the chapters and taken as a rule from old ballads, and, at the beginning of the work, a rapid survey of the history and the customs of the age in which the action takes place. But with these characteristics the resemblance may be said practically to end : argument, characters, episodes and all the other features of the novel are wholly Spanish, though there is a "Judgment of God" as in *Ivanhoe*, and various details recall *Kenilworth* and other of the Waverley Novels.

The legend of the life and the tragic death of Macías el Enamorado was extremely popular all over Spain—from Galicia, the birthplace of that importunate lover whose name has attracted to itself such a wealth of fable, to the very opposite end of the Peninsula. In the fifteenth century, that age in which Dante inspired a whole province of Spanish letters, there was hardly any writer who failed to compose an *Inferno*, more or less directly imitated from the *Divine Comedy*, and bewailing his fate. The Marqués de Santillana, author of the *Infierno de los Enamorados*, puts into the mouth of Macías a weak reproduction of Francesca's "Nessun maggior dolore" :

> La mayor cuyta que aver
> Puede ningún amador,
> Es membrarse del placer
> En el tiempo del dolor.

But Larra had no interest in making an exact reproduction of all the details of the legend, as they first appear, in collected and completed form, in Argote de Molina's *Nobleza del Andaluzia*. The argument evidently had a special attraction for him, since he treated it twice—in a novel and in a drama. These two works, however, have little in common save the name of the protagonist, the theme of adulterous passion and the sanguinary *dénouement* of the action ; and even these features differ in details. The other parallel scenes in the novel and the drama vary greatly.

The author makes it evident that, in sketching the background of his picture, he has studied with some care both the general history of Spain and that of Europe in the last years of the fourteenth century and the first years of the fifteenth. He makes a real effort to reproduce with approximate exactness the special period to which his picture belongs. It is true that about Macías, the protagonist, hardly anything is known with certainty—neither the date of his birth nor that of his death : little more, indeed, than that he was consumed by an ardent passion and that five compositions of small artistic merit are attributed to him by the Cancionero de Baena. The other characters who play an important part in the novel—notably Don Enrique de Villena, and his wife María de Albornoz—were in reality, according to chronicle and history, very different from Larra's presentations and descriptions of them ; he very properly considered that he had a perfect right to adapt them according to his fancy.

Customs, dresses and the thousand and one details of the private life of the time are not, according to the general opinion of the critics, presented in conformity with strict truth. "El que buscara en su obra colorido arqueológico," writes Menéndez y Pelayo, for example, "se llevaría solemne chasco."* This judgment seems to us unduly severe. Larra was certainly not, like Scott, a lover of archæology or a curiosity-collector, but he gives proof of having sought carefully for details in the poets, chroniclers and other writers of the age he describes, of having visited and studied in museums of armour and antiquities, of having followed with scrupulous precision such old texts as the *Libro de Montería :* the ordinary reader, on laying down the novel, finds that he has learned a multitude of things unknown to him, and, unlike the critics, is duly grateful. What we miss in the novel, from the antiquarian point of view, is what Larra probably considered unnecessary—the notes and references which he deliberately refrained from adding to his story, after the fashion set by Scott and other contemporaries, in order to make a parade of erudition. This the Duque de

* *Obras de Lope de Vega*, Vol. X (Madrid, 1899), p. lviii.

2

Rivas did in his *Moro Expósito*, a verse narrative something in the style of Scott's lays, and he succeeded thereby in convincing critics of the type of Alcalá Galiano and Enrique Gil that his poem was full of the most exact and admirable local colour. But to-day we can no longer trust the Duke's erudition : so notable an authority as Sr. Menéndez Pidal assures us that the Middle Ages were a closed book to him.* Nor can we even rely wholly on the lists of authorities in the two long final notes of the *Moro Expósito*, since among them Rivas includes authors who make no mention of the questions referred to.†

*El Doncel de Don Enrique el Doliente* may still be read with profit and even with enjoyment. If it has not the thrilling interest of *Ivanhoe* or *Quentin Durward*, it is not on the whole greatly inferior, for example, to Alfred de Vigny's *Cinq Mars*, one of the three best novels of the Romantic period in France.‡ Vigny imitates Scott very frequently and very closely ; he is a far greater poet than Larra ; and his characters—Richelieu, Louis XII, Anne of Austria, Père Joseph—have a popular interest incomparably greater than that of the dismal and shadowy period of Spanish history inhabited by Macías. In *Cinq Mars*, as in those great novels of Scott which we have just mentioned, the nature of the argument "causes particular and individual passions to pale before wider interests of greater importance."§ But Larra's novel has one living spring of interest, which attracts and even fascinates his readers. The love intrigue, weak and artificial in *Cinq Mars*, constitutes the whole theme of the *Doncel*, and the passion of Elvira and Macías has sincerity enough to be intensely moving. The final chapter, with its epigraph from the Conde Claros arranged so as to convey a mysterious effect which is certainly not present in the original ballad, is characterized by a melancholy at once profound and affecting.

Further, the position of this work in Spanish literature of the last century is unique. Anyone wishing to read an

---

* Ramón Menéndez Pidal, *La Leyenda de los Infantes de Lara* (Madrid, 1896), p. 169.
† *Obras completas de Don Ángel de Saavedra, Duque de Rivas* (Madrid, 1897), Vol. III, p. 546.
‡ The other two would be Hugo's *Notre Dame de Paris* and Mérimée's *Chronique du Règne de Charles IX.*
§ Louis Maigron : *Le Roman historique* (Paris, 1898), p. 255.

historical novel of the early nineteenth century for mere pleasure would find hardly anything but the *Doncel*, though historical novels were attempted by many authors, including men as well known as Martínez de la Rosa, Espronceda, Escosura, García de Villalta and Enrique Gil. The *Señor de Bembibre* (1844) of Gil is probably the best of the remainder ; but, though its argument is somewhat reminiscent of the *Bride of Lammermoor*, it has travelled a considerable distance from the path trodden by Scott and the more successful of his followers and lacks both the dramatic movement of their fiction and its virile eloquence.

### III

*Macías*, an "historical drama in four acts and in verse" given "with great applause," according to Hartzenbusch,* on September 24, 1834, is not, perhaps, as a work of art, as interesting as the novel on the same subject, but it occupies a much more important position in the history of Spanish literature and had a wider and more considerable influence.

Although a few attempts had already been made in Spain to follow the same road, *Macías* came as a great novelty. The new æsthetic ideas and the decreasing preoccupation with rule which for the preceding five years had been characterizing the French stage, so that almost all the fetters and limitations imposed upon classical tragedy were disappearing, first made a prominent appearance on the Spanish stage on that day in April 1834 which witnessed the *estreno* of Martínez de la Rosa's historical drama *La Conjuración de Venecia*. Larra, who by that time must certainly have completed the plan of his *Macías*, attended the performance as the dramatic critic of Carnerero's *Revista Española*, gave it his keen and sympathetic approval and wrote a highly favourable critique upon it in his review.

The success of this pleasant if somewhat timid attempt at acclimatizing the new drama pointed Larra to the road which he himself now proposed to follow. It is true that Martínez de la Rosa was less of a Dumas or of a Hugo than of a Delavigne. The general tone of his play, the meticulous care with which he steered a middle path and avoided

* *Obras escogidas de Don A. García Gutiérrez* (Madrid, 1866), Prólogo, p. xv.

excesses, the indeterminate colouring of scenes often weak in
the extreme inevitably recalled the author of *Marino Faliero*
and the *Vêpres Siciliennes*.  But at least he had produced a
well constructed play, with an historical narrative vigorously
sketched on broad and interesting lines, and such attractive
pictures as that of the pantheon of the Morosinis, or the
square of St. Mark attractively lit up and packed with
animated crowds, each character saying what the situation
required of him, in a perfectly straightforward way, without
either irrelevant wit or exaggerated lyricism.  Then there is
the conspiracy breaking out in the middle of Carnival,
ending in the triumph of the republic ; and, in the last act,
the *sala de audiencia* of the inexorable tribunal of the Ten, with
black hangings and funereal inscriptions ; Morosini, the
President, swooning as he recognizes in the accused man his
own son ; the other judges relentlessly condemning him, and
sentencing him to death in the presence of the woman he
adores.  Here we have the elements of the most harrowing
melodrama, unrelieved, unhappily, by beauties of versification, but occasionally enhanced by a splendid pathos, expressed in sober and eloquent language—the whole erection
resting upon an historical foundation conceived on a
grandiose scale.

Larra, who was less of a poet than Martínez de la Rosa,
and could only write verse at all with considerable labour,
was nevertheless aided by his own good taste and artistic
inspiration and felt himself capable of going farther than this
irresolute innovator who had preceded him.  He aspired to
the composition of an historical drama which should also
treat of love, and, like his seventeenth-century predecessors,
desired to avail himself of the completest freedom as regards
both plot and versification, while at the same time treating
his ideas and sentiments with the frankness, warmth and
energy of the plays of the French Romantics.  The idea
could not have been bettered ; but, though he set out
bravely in this new direction, he had, like Martínez de la
Rosa, insufficient energy for travelling a great way along the
road, and he was soon followed by others who advanced no
less boldly and attained more nearly to the desired goal.

The action of *Macías* is too arid and unadorned : it
entirely lacks that richness of incident, that lively and
picturesque actuality and that freshness in its art which were

the *raison d'être* of Romantic drama. Though in the poetic quality of its form and in the intensity of its feeling it improves notably upon Martínez de la Rosa's play, its historical canvas needs greater breadth and it has none of the variety of interest which we find in the *Conjuración de Venecia.* Not even *Porfiar hasta morir,* Lope de Vega's drama on the *Macías* legend, which has only three acts and which Larra nowhere imitated, can be said to contain less material, even if we take from it the superfluities belonging to the part of the *gracioso.*

The argument of *Macías* is very different from that of the *Doncel.* In the drama, the spectator is aware from the very first scene that Macías and Elvira know and love one another ; that they are betrothed ; that, as in the story of the lovers of Teruel, there enters into the plot a fixed limit of time ; and that, if Macías should present himself before it expires, the hand of his lady will perforce be granted him. This naturally disfigures and weakens the tradition, taking from the violent and adulterous love, and from the importunity—the *porfía*—of the lover, that element of fatefulness which they have in the legend, and also minimizing its terrible consequences. Macías is detained far from Andújar, the city where the action takes place, through the intrigues of a rival and the ill-will of his lord—who is Villena and not the "Rey Doliente"—and thus he is prevented from returning strictly within the time-limit, though he arrives post-haste at a later hour on the very day of its expiry. From an early stage in the story, the marriage of Elvira with Fernán Pérez has been hastened. When, about the middle of the second act, Macías appears, and demands of his lord the fulfilment of the promise, Villena delays it till the moment at which the bridal party is returning from the church, for his return has been anticipated and the ceremony performed early. Elvira, recognizing her lover, whom she had believed to be disloyal to his word, swoons away, and Macías, in despair, throws himself at Villena's feet, crying :

¡ Señor ! ¡ O muerte o venganza !

This is a scene of extraordinary rapidity, written with extraordinary vigour ; a few short phrases alone are needed to bring the act to a dramatic conclusion.

Macías succeeds in penetrating to the chamber of his fortunate rival, where he finds Elvira, still in her bridal array.

The impassioned dialogue which the poet puts into the lovers' mouths—the one asserting the rights of his love, the other representing the duties of her new estate—reminds one somewhat, both in its prose and in its ethical attitude, of *Antony* :

> Los amantes son solos los esposos.
> Su lazo es el amor : ¿ cuál hay más santo ?
> Su templo, el universo : donde quiera
> El Dios los oye que los ha juntado.
> Si en las ciudades no, si entre los hombres
> Ni fe, ni abrigo, ni esperanza hallamos,
> Las fieras en los bosques una cueva
> Cederán al amor . . .

Throughout this third act, indeed, the influence of Dumas is only too evident. The lovers are surprised during their meeting. Macías, in his desperate frenzy, and seeing Elvira humbly entreating pardon for him, while Don Enrique commands him to be thrown into prison, breaks into invective, violent and declamatory, it is true, but entirely in keeping with the situation and marked by an occasionally admirable energy of expression. For many years Valero's rendering of this scene could be relied upon to raise a furore of applause in any theatre in Spain.

This crisis is followed by a scene which appears to come directly from the elder Dumas' *Henri III et sa Cour*. Fernán Pérez, the bridegroom, mad with jealousy, flourishes his dagger and threatens to kill Elvira. She for her part calmly awaits the blow, but in her calmness he can see only the proof of the immensity of her love for his rival. "Le ama," he exclaims :

> Le ama, oh cielos, de tal modo,
> que ya prefiere a su olvido
> la muerte . . .
> ¡ Mal haya el que tan amado
> supo ser ! . . .

Just so Dumas' Duke of Guise, put to an identical proof, exclaims :

> Vous l'aimez bien, madame ! Malédiction sur lui qui est tant aimé !

Fernán Pérez, like Guise, endeavours to force her to make a tryst with her lover in order to ruin him, and, when she refuses, seizes her violently by the arm till she cries "¡ Por piedad, me lastimáis, señor !" In the same way the Duchess of Guise, feeling the steel gauntlet hurt her, exclaims : "Vous me faites bien mal, Henri, horriblement mal !"

Finally, Elvira's obstinacy drives Fernán to call a servant aside and say to him :

> Alvar, cuatro hombres buscadme. . . .
> ¿ Me entendéis ?

—less explicitly than Guise, who exclaims : "Saint-Paul, qu'on me cherche les mêmes hommes qui ont assassiné Dugast !" but with the same sinister intentions.

The fourth and last act of Larra's drama is a short one. Elvira, guessing her husband's schemes, runs to the prison to forestall him. There ensues a second love-scene, finer even than the first, in which both lovers are now at one in senti-ment. But by this time it is too late for Macías to escape from Fernán Pérez and his assassins. Hardly has he gone out to meet them than he re-enters mortally wounded. Elvira stabs herself with her lover's dagger, which he "holds out feebly to her," and, with these words on her lips,

> Llegad . . . ahora . . . llegad . . . y que estas bodas
> Alumbren . . . vuestras . . . teas . . . funerales,

she dies.

Though these lines, together with the nature of the catastrophe and its poetic colour, convey some suggestion of the conclusion of *Hernani*, the words of Fernán Pérez which follow send us back again to Dumas :

> Me vendían.
> Ya se lavó en su sangre mi deshonra.

Even Calderón, who often staged husbands wiping out their dishonour with blood, never concentrated in so short a final phrase the catastrophe of an entire tragedy. But it was Dumas who in 1831 had set the fashion for the somewhat gruesome tombstone epitaph : "Elle me résistait, je l'ai assassinée !"

We said just now that Larra was less of a poet than Martínez de la Rosa ; to realize the difference between them it suffices to compare the elegies which the two writers composed upon the death of the Duquesa de Frías. In

Larra's elegy we miss above everything else any expression whatever of his own feelings. There is an aridity, a hardness in his work which belongs to one who has been keenly wounded by men and things and in consequence is profoundly embittered. He can easily achieve eloquence, but, where the need is for tenderness, for words which read as though the writer was choked by tears, for an emotion that will communicate itself to others, he almost invariably fails. His passions are real and he expresses them with sincerity, but they usually contain at least as much of vanity and pride as of affection or fellow-feeling.

He could write good verse, and, with his quite considerable education, his cultured taste, the precision of his language and the natural vigour of his style, he reached a point approaching excellence in this art, as is frequently the case in *Macías*. The chief demands of the stage are energy and clearness of expression, and such a passage as this, which has both these qualities in abundant measure, will always gain applause and appreciation :

> Yo le maté, dirás :  tu esposo en celos
> Arderá, temeroso de que al cabo
> Le vendas como a mí, y hasta tus besos
> Mentiras creerá.   Cierto ;  y seránlo.
> Ella, Fernán, me amó, y volverá a amarme :
> Si constancia te jura es solo engaño ;
> También a mí me la juró, y mentía.

These lines may be deficient in both the content and the form of poetry, but there is compensation enough for this in their force and concise brilliance. And this is not only true of Larra's hendecasyllables ; again and again the octosyllabics of *Macías* are admirable, and we can find in it whole series of perfectly rounded *redondillas* which are worthy of all praise.

IV

*Macías* was the true precursor of Spanish Romantic drama —"historical or chivalric drama," as it was called at first— which soon came on parade in full panoply. García Gutiérrez's *Trovador* and Hartzenbusch's *Amantes de Teruel* were the rich firstfruits of the talent of men who were to be among the most favoured and famed of Spanish writers of the century, and the first production of these plays took place eighteen months and two years respectively after *Macías*. It is said* that Hartzenbusch, who, when Larra's play appeared, had already sketched his own, was forced to modify his plan on account of the fortuitous coincidences between them in essentials. This was hardly surprising, as Larra took for the antecedent of his argument that idea of the outrunning of a previously fixed period of time which plays so important a part in the legendary and historical narrative of Diego Marsilla.

It must not be forgotten that, during the interval which separates *Macías* from the two dramas already mentioned, there had appeared the Duque de Rivas' *Don Álvaro*, partly inspired by Mérimée's novel *Les Ames du Purgatoire*, which suggested to Dumas his *Don Juan de Marana*, and in this way also influenced Zorrilla's *Don Juan Tenorio*. *Don Álvaro*, which was written during its author's exile in France, is not in the least like Larra's drama. It gives the impression of having been written in order to defy all the rules and traditions of Classical art at once, without setting much in their place, for it is deficient in character-psychology and dramatic passion and has no great depth of poetry. Nevertheless it is always full of life and animation, sometimes even of fire ; and the broad sweeps of the brush by which Rivas the painter-poet thought to produce bold effects did in fact succeed in attracting and catching the enthusiasm of the masses. Most noteworthy are the popular scenes in prose, offering a welcome contrast with the terrible events of the principal action : the Sevilian *aguaducho* of the first act, the inn at Hornachuelos in the second and the *portería* of the convent in the fifth. These are all excellent of their kind—realistic, human pictures admirably reproduced and completely independent of the main story.

We do not possess Larra's critical opinion upon Rivas' drama, but we have two notable articles of his, one upon the *Trovador* and another upon the *Amantes de Teruel*. Never was the work of a critic-dramatist's fortunate rivals judged with greater skill and keener sympathy. All their merits are pointed out with real appreciation, while their defects are

---

* *Apuntes para una biblioteca de escritores españoles contemporáneos* (por D. Eugenio de Ochoa, Paris (n.d.) ), Vol. II, p. 80. See also : Ferrer del Río, *Galería de la Literatura Española* (Madrid, 1846), p. 163.

indicated with precision and sobriety. Both dramas were written in a combination of verse and prose. While not condemning this procedure, Larra considers that a dramatist who adopts it voluntarily adds one more difficulty to those with which he already has to contend, and that this difficulty is not surmounted when he has decided which scenes are more effective in the one form or the other. In their later editions García Gutiérrez and Hartzenbusch bowed to the opinions of their benevolent critic, and corrected the defects to which he had drawn attention. The revised form of the *Trovador* is on the whole inferior to the original version. The contrary is true, however, of the *Amantes de Teruel ;* and it is the later version of this play that its author includes in the definitive collection of his writings.

No Spanish critic, during the whole of the nineteenth century, wrote in the Press with the sustained excellence of Larra. None, either before or after him, succeeded in writing so authoritatively or so instructively and in maintaining such a high and unvarying level of impartiality. To read his articles to-day provokes an instinctive feeling of regret, when one realizes that, though they were frequently improvised between one night and the following morning, their writer had such taste and enlightenment that they have lost practically none of their value. What magnificent pieces of criticism would they not have been had he but had the time and opportunity to complete them at his leisure ! The majority of them—the best—were collected in one volume after his death, and not even the most superficial of their original *errata* were corrected. In all of them we catch the unmistakable accent of bitterness and desolation. They bear the stamp, as it were, of their author's conviction of the uselessness of his task, confronted as he was with the supine ignorance of a public which, in those troubled days of the Carlist War and the ill-fated Statute or Constitution of 1812, would read hardly anything but politics.

Larra consistently showed the keenest interest in dramatic art and made the most strenuous efforts to raise it to a high level and keep it there. This favourite *genre*, which so readily becomes popular in Spain, was at that time wearing itself out through the sheer indifference that was all but universally felt for it. "Without actors and without a public," as Larra said in one of the last of his articles, the theatre was simply an "appendage of the Opera." He himself, he confessed, shared the general indifference to it, despairing of the future when he considered the present—"the dark and stormy night through which we are journeying, wrestling vainly with the gale that in the end will unmast our vessel."

But Larra by no means confined his critiques to the drama of his own country. He frequently dealt with the latest products of French dramatic art as they came to be translated into Spanish ; and these later articles show how perfect was his knowledge of contemporary French literature.* If the Madrilenian public had but helped him by displaying a more intelligent appreciation of literary criticism and the art of the theatre, he would have attained to something more than being a Spanish Sarcey or Janin, for to his great knowledge he added rare artistic talent. His collected articles would in such a case have had something of the excellence and the usefulness of Lessing's *Hamburgische Dramaturgie*. But fate had not willed it so.

Imbued as he was with the spirit of his time, Larra was a constant student of the brilliant Spanish literature of past ages. This he was able to appreciate with complete independence, for he neither clung to the opinions of others nor allowed himself to be blinded by false patriotism, so productive of error, and handed down almost mechanically from one generation and from one critic to another. His chief anxiety was to lighten the excessive weight of tradition which was hindering the new literature from being safely steered into new directions. It is useful, and indeed essential, he considers, to study the writers of the Golden Age in order to understand and admire the great genius and the marvellous history of the Spanish nation and to experience the keen delight of analyzing and sampling a beauty which is not only of an age but for all time. Yet few writers of that period, he thinks, should be imitated by modern authors. In a noteworthy article entitled "Literatura"—a rapid survey of the history of literature in Spain and its general tendency—he

* He greatly esteemed Dumas as a dramatist and in five lengthy articles analyzes four of his works : *Thérèse, La Tour de Nesle, Catherine Howard* and *Antony*. Of Victor Hugo, on whose *Hernani* he wrote a striking article *à propos* of Ochoa's verse translation of it, he says : "He is one of the greatest poets that the ages have seen," an opinion which in the France of his day was very far from being generally held, most literary men placing Béranger and Lamartine above Hugo.

recognizes that, political tyranny having succeeded religious
tyranny since the loss of what national liberty remained in
the first quarter of the sixteenth century, the literature which
flourished immediately afterwards had been condemned at
its birth to be a prodigious phenomenon, but an essentially
transitory one, without any possibility of wide and fruitful
development. He explains why Spain did not at that time
possess what he calls "escritores razonados" and why the
only arts that blazed with dazzling brilliance were those of
the novel and the drama, both of them results of the powerful
imagination of the race. Serious prose, on the other hand,
was confined to mysticism and theology, in which fields (he
adds) "we can unhappily present a catalogue more complete
than that of any other nation," and to history, as represented
by Mariana and Solís, who, rather than historians, should be
called "monuments of our language," for they wrote what
are really historical novels devoid of all critical spirit, resolutely abstaining from paying any heed to the "movement of
their age" and catching not the faintest echo of the events
going on outside Spain which were transforming the progress
of civilization. This literature soon declined, and was
succeeded in the eighteenth century by imitations from the
French, produced and eulogized by a small group of literary
men who, without having the necessary qualifications,
"joined the literary movement of the neighbouring country,
and took over its ideas exactly as they found them, so that we
discovered we were at our journey's end without ever having
made the journey." As Spain's national misfortunes made
such little inspiration as this reform movement had brought
with it ineffective, it remained entirely without result.

With no less energy Larra rejected that conception of art
which in his days was crippling a literature "now reduced to
the trappings of language and the jingle of rhyme." He
fought for the advent of another type of literature altogether :

hija de la experiencia y de la historia, estudiosa, analizadora,
filosófica, profunda, pensándolo todo, diciéndolo todo, en
prosa, en verso, expresión en fin de la ciencia de la época, del
progreso intelectual del siglo.

He was particularly impatient with the mania for using
archaic language and with the puristic fever which had come
into fashion during the preceding century—partly through

the popularization of satires like those of Iriarte and Cadalso, partly through the examples set by García de la Huerta and Moratín. "To make progress in ideology," said Larra, "in metaphysics, in science, in politics, to increase the number of new ideas, and yet to seek to remain at a standstill in the language in which this progress must be expressed is (if my purist critics will pardon me the expression) to have lost one's head." It is one thing, he added, to fall into the affectation of imitating what is old, and quite another to respect, as far as is possible, "the type, the nature, the sources and the analogies of one's own language." This Larra wrote in 1835, and this same dictum may be repeated to-day, for there are still purists in Spain who use words and phrases which they term *castizos* with the reverence of men uttering a spell. This is bound to happen with an idiom the elements of which are not yet completely fixed, in which no lexicons of the language of its great writers (not even of that of Cervantes) have been compiled, and whose supreme and official authority is a dictionary that omits many words, both old and new, contains faulty definitions, and, worse still, lacks examples, which are infinitely more necessary to a dictionary than etymologies printed in mysterious characters and quite incomprehensible to the vast majority of those who most need to consult it. Even Littré, in the body of his most useful dictionary, so rich in examples and in other data, and giving far more detailed etymologies than the dictionary of the Spanish Academy, abstained from pedantic transcription of the characters of Arabic, Hebrew and Sanskrit.

Despite the little love which he bore the purists, Larra had a good knowledge of his own language, and studied it constantly. He had, indeed, composed for his own use a work on synonyms. Speaking of the Academy dictionary, he once remarked, with his customary wit, that "we must all respect it when it hits the mark ; in other words, it is just as authoritative as anyone who is correct—when it is itself correct !"

v

During the last years of the reign of Ferdinand VII, his younger brother, Don Carlos, fled to Portugal. The silence he preserved, the threatening attitude he maintained and the type of person that surrounded him all gave the clearest indications of his design to assert his claim to the throne, to dispute the succession by the employment, if necessary, of force and to disregard the King's testament, invoking the ancient Salic law and that Bourbon tradition which had been put forward of old, more than once, by Ferdinand himself, as a dogma of the monarchy. The King's daughter, a child of three, was proclaimed queen in Madrid immediately after her father's death. Almost at the same time the cloud which had been forming on the French frontier gathered and burst, and the civil war began which for seven years was to rage over the north of the Peninsula.

Although at first Carlism was very far from having the military power which it was to acquire later, and for a long time many people failed to realize the gravity of this rebellion carried on under the banner of the absent Pretender, everyone trembled at the remembrance of the horrors and atrocities which had been committed on both sides during the six years of the struggle against the Emperor Napoleon. The same men, engaged in a conflict which roused within them no less profound and firmly rooted passions, had now perforce to behave in the same way. It would have been a miracle if, at the end of so violent a convulsion, the country had not been permanently split up into two irreconcilable parties.

The miracle happened. Behind the hurricane that descended upon Spain brighter horizons and a more placid sky awaited those who were preparing to do battle, with indefatigable energy, both for the more or less disputable claims of the King's daughter Isabel, and for the regeneration of the country, and were also eager to uproot from its soil the organized despotism which for three hundred or more years had caused one disaster after another, and had brought the nation to the miserable state in which Ferdinand VII left it.

From the very first there were many in Spain who realized how fundamental for the future was the political problem which circumstances had now brought to a head. One of these was Larra.

Through the strangest mingling of cause and effect, this civil war, stirred up by the fanatical brother of the late king, proved to be a blessing in disguise. When it began, the legitimists were, of course, convinced that there was no

possible means of settlement, that the struggle was one between liberty and slavery, and that for the first time the
defenders of theocracy and political absolutism would inevitably succumb, before a younger generation determined to
implant in the country a *régime* in which the voice of the
people legitimately expressed would have greater virtue than
the will of a monarch.

When the War of Independence had broken out in 1808,
all the most liberal and enlightened Spaniards (whether old
men like Jovellanos or young men like Quintana, Antillón
and Argüelles) had joined ranks with the clergy, the bulk of
the nobility and the people, and thus the struggle had
acquired an indisputably national character. But, in the
hour of triumph, people, clergy, nobility and soldiery had
acclaimed Ferdinand as an absolute monarch, treated their
Liberal allies as though they had been conquered foes and
allowed them to purge their patriotism in prison or in exile.
The country returned, in fact, to what it had been in the
past, without having taken a single step upward upon the
ladder of civilization.

But this time the progress of events led to a very different
kind of settlement. The eternal enemies of freedom hastened
to the side of Don Carlos ; a good third of the Peninsula
hailed him as king ; the clergy in a body wished him
victory. The Liberals, therefore, were free to declare themselves defenders of the throne of Isabel II, and to make its
existence conditional upon the concession of political rights.
Once that compact had been sealed with blood and carried
through by vigorous effort, it was clear that the victory
would not be followed by a repetition of the indescribable
scenes of perfidy and cruelty that had dishonoured the return
of Ferdinand in 1814.

For Larra more than for most writers, the death of the
monarch meant redemption. All the best of his talents, all
the noblest of his ideas and sentiments would have remained
undiscovered had Ferdinand's cruelly oppressive *régime* continued for but a few years longer. He was a Liberal, and a
deep and sincere one. He maintained that the people should
have all their political rights, and, as he declared in the
preface to his translation of Lamennais' *Paroles d'un croyant*,
entitled *El dogma de los hombres libres*, he had an indestructible
faith in human progress and social perfectibility. This

famous book, the gospel of Christian socialism, which has fallen into oblivion in the literary world because of the somewhat affectedly Biblical nature of its style, was considered in its own day to be an instrument for the demolition of society. But this was not the view of Larra, who saw in it only that ardent love for the people, and for justice, which so vividly illumines it. He translated it lovingly and with striking skill. Yet he well knew that the Spanish nation was as yet insufficiently prepared for the exercise of certain rights which were its due, nor was he unmindful of the fact that those who have been born and educated as slaves need to learn how to use liberty before it is granted them. When, therefore, in 1836, he beheld the uprising of the monster of militarism with all its horrors, he took affright and despaired of the future of his country much in the same way as a few months later he was to despair of life.

In 1834, the problem had not yet become the avoidance of a possible abuse of liberty. Another phantom, at the moment a more terrible one still, had arisen in the northern provinces, and kept men's minds in an anguish of uncertainty. Larra did not, like certain others, feel that he was becoming hypnotized by the yawning abyss of civil war, and he set to work on what was to him a task imposed by duty— that of stripping the monster and exhibiting it as it was in actual fact, and not as imagination or terror might portray it. All the grotesqueness, as well as all the mistakenness and fanaticism of this insurrection, begun in order to set upon the throne a man cut out, in Lafuente's words, "for a monk rather than for a monarch," is skilfully portrayed in that wonderful series of sketches of Carlism which Larra contributed to the *Revista Española* over the pseudonym "Fígaro." To this pseudonym, it may be remarked, he adhered from that time until his death ; it came to be so much better known and more popular in Spain than his own name that all the collections of his writings bear the words "Obras de Fígaro" on their title-page. These articles, written for the most part in dialogue form, recall the comedies of Aristophanes in the vigour and energy with which they penetrate to the very heart of the pretensions they set out to ridicule, destroying appearances and tearing into shreds false pretences of legitimacy and piety invented to cover sordid passions, just as the Greek dramatist destroyed the false idols of Athenian demagogism. Larra's satire is more decent and more prudent than Aristophanes', and also, of course, is fettered by the censorship, but the power and efficacy of the two writers are not dissimilar, although it is clearly impossible to make accurate comparisons between articles which appeared in Spanish newspapers of the nineteenth century and plays written in verse by a poet of genius in the Golden Age of Greek literature.

To ridicule the Carlist War during the first years of the new reign was permitted and even encouraged by authority. But the complete freedom of the Press was still very far from being a fact and Larra had for some time to confine himself principally to *artículos de costumbres* and literary criticism. His judgments, like his style, gradually became weightier and more varied as he subjected one after another of the traits and characteristics of society to his caustic ridicule. He grew to acquire such flexibility, grace and elegant sobriety as were never again found together in any writer cultivating the same *genre*. The pity was that, at that time, there were appearing very few books other than plays which afforded a critic adequate opportunities to display his talent and to interest his public. Even when dealing with plays, Larra more than once measured his steel against authors unworthy of his efforts.

Meanwhile, the political situation grew worse from day to day. Carlism, though increasingly recognized as having no future, continued to exist and seemed even to be growing stronger, by reason of the incapacity of the generals who were first entrusted with the task of defeating it and of the lack of resources in the Queen's government. The power was in the hands of well-intentioned men, somewhat of the type of Martínez de la Rosa—irresolute by nature, that is to say, and intimidated with the greatest ease. Though convinced that it was only by means of liberal institutions and ideas that an impregnable barrier could be raised against Don Carlos' supporters, they curtailed reforms, and prescribed them in small doses like dangerous medicine, little realizing that in the end these reforms might be extracted from them by force and under conditions disadvantageous to themselves, whereas, had they conceded them of their own free will, they would have proved an effective and satisfying remedy.

3

As though depressed or wearied by his disappointment, Larra decided to go abroad for a time and spent the greater part of the year 1835 in France. He left Spain in May, by way of the Portuguese frontier, as the Carlist forces were holding the route through Vizcaya. The state of his mind at the time of his departure may be inferred from the following passage :

El Caya, arroyo que divide la España del Portugal, corría mansamente a mis pies : tendí por la última vez la vista sobre la Extremadura española ; mil recuerdos personales me asaltaron ; una sonrisa de indignación y de desprecio quiso desplegar mis labios, pero sentí oprimirse mi corazón y una lágrima se asomó a mis ojos. Un minuto después la patria quedaba atrás, y arrebatado con la velocidad del viento, como si hubiera temido que un resto de antiguo afecto mal pagado le detuviera, o le hiciera vacilar en su determinación, el expatriado corría los campos de Portugal.

While abroad he wrote little for the Madrid newspapers. At the end of ten months he returned—attracted, as he said in the first article written after his arrival, by the news that it was proposed at last to grant the Press its freedom.

¡ Yo, que de Calomarde acá rabio por escribir con libertad, no había de haber vuelto aunque no hubiera sido sino para echar del cuerpo lo mucho que en estos años se me quedó en él, sin contar con lo mucho con que se quedaron los censores !

But the hour of freedom for the Press was not yet ; all that actually happened was the very slightest loosening of its irksome fetters. To this event, however, we owe the three delightful political letters : "Fígaro de vuelta," "Buenas noches" and "Dios nos asista," which, like the three articles on the Carlist War, form a valuable whole, of historical as well as of literary interest, and will always be read with pleasure by all who know or study the Spanish language.

In these articles, nevertheless, the tone of Larra's writing begins to change considerably, and henceforward its transformation becomes more and more noticeable. There is hardly a trace left of the gay, bantering Larra of the *cuadros de costumbres ;* still less is there in the works which he wrote between this time and that of his death, now close at hand. In this year, 1836, as we have already said, the country suffered the gravest and most disastrous set-back. The authorities, obstinately intent upon resisting the advances of those who demanded further liberties, seemed to attribute no importance to various insurrectionary movements and to a widespread popular agitation.   On the heels of these beginnings of anarchy there followed indiscipline in the army— a fatal symptom, since the army, which had been struggling against the formidable Carlist faction with very unequal success and in the rest of the country was hardly sufficient to maintain order, was an indispensable support to the insecure constitutional throne.

Militarism, in its most repulsive form—with the armed forces of the Crown directing the course of politics and unscrupulous generals breaking their oaths and pressing violently for power—first made itself felt in Spain on August 12, 1836, and for forty years thereafter never ceased its nefarious operations.   On this day the troops garrisoned at La Granja, the summer seat of the Royal Family, sallied out, fully armed, into the street, and, with no other leaders than their own sergeants and corporals, made their way into the Palace and forced the Queen Mother to proclaim the Constitution of 1812 and to convoke a fresh parliament. Meanwhile the Government fell in Madrid, General Quesada was assassinated, and the ministers saved their lives only by fleeing from the capital or going into hiding.   Among these ministers was the Duque de Rivas, author of *Don Álvaro* and a personal friend of Larra.

This Constitution of 1812 had until now hardly been in operation ;  for, though it had been promulgated within the walls of Cádiz during the War of Independence, Ferdinand VII had promptly abolished it on obtaining possession of the throne.   To Larra's mind it was an object of antiquity, a heroic memory, worthy of respect only in the sense in which "Christ respected the old law when He founded the new." And, in point of fact, the deputies now elected according to its precepts at once resolved to draw up a new constitution ; but this Larra was never to see, for it came into force only some months after his death.

The mutiny of the garrison of La Granja, which divided the Queen's supporters permanently into two irreconcilably opposed parties, left Larra convinced of the total ruin of his hopes ;  he saw that it was madness to look for the regeneration of the country by means of freedom when militarism could trample so insolently upon freedom and yet triumph. In the highly original but lugubrious fantasy entitled "Día de difuntos de 1836," he represents the whole city of Madrid as a vast cemetery whose public buildings are tombs bearing such inscriptions as these :

Aquí yace el trono ; nació en el reinado de Isabel la Católica, murió en La Granja, de un aire colado.
Aquí yace el valor castellano, con todos sus pertrechos. R.I.P.
Aquí yace media España ; murió de la otra media.

He ends by describing his own heart, "not long since full of life, illusions and desires," as yet another tomb which reads : "Here lies hope."

The fantasy might almost be described as a poem ; or, at the least, like "La Nochebuena," "Las Exequias del Conde de Campo-Alanje," "Horas de Invierno," and a few others, as an excellent lyrical satire in prose. The Larra revealed in these essays is a man sunk in the profoundest depths of misanthropy and despair. In his sad tribute to the young Count of Campo-Alanje, on the occasion of his premature death on the battlefield, there is, as one realizes immediately, no fiction or declamation—only the genuine cry of a stricken heart, and a lament as much over his own fate as over that of his unhappy friend :

¿ Qué le esperaba en esta sociedad ?—Militar, no era insubordinado ; a haberlo sido, las balas lo hubieran respetado. Hombre de talento, no era intrigante. Liberal, no era vocinglero. Literato, no era pedante. Escritor, la razón y la imparcialidad presidían a sus escritos. ¿ Qué papel podía haber hecho en tal caos y degradación ?

The spirit of a man who could express himself sincerely in such terms at the age of twenty-eight is the spirit of a weary octogenarian already marked out as death's prey, on the very brink of the grave. It had been his lot to live at an unhappy period in his country's history, but he was also driven towards his tragic end by the nature of his character and the type of his genius.

His was a reserved and gloomy temperament, at times completely intractable, and, as the years went on, growing more and more so. Sharp and acrimonious in conversation, he readily made enemies and was too proud to ask pardon of

those whom he had offended.    Nor, it seems, was he happy
in his family life, no doubt because of his terrible ill-humour,
which he allowed free course in his own home and made no
attempt to dominate.    Once, writing of satirists, he made
this confession :

> Molière era el hombre más triste de su siglo ; entre nosotros
> difícilmente pudiéramos citar a Moratín como un modelo de
> alegría . . . y si nos fuera lícito nombrarnos siquiera al lado de
> tan altos modelos, confesaríamos ingenuamente que sólo en
> momentos de tristeza nos es dado aspirar a divertir a los demás.

The very success of his writings, which, though real
enough, was somewhat restricted, may very probably be
counted among the causes which aggravated his constant
temperamental restlessness.    He felt himself to be brimming
over with ideas and capable of great achievements.    He considered his success, therefore, to be less than he merited, and
chafed at finding himself reduced to improvising articles for
periodicals, which were talked of for twenty-four hours and
promptly forgotten, while other and more fortunate geniuses
outstripped him in the more brilliant and less ephemeral
writing in which he too would have indulged gladly.    All the
more honour do we owe to the nobility of the man when
we remember that, in spite of this, his impartiality and
generosity as a critic never failed him.    He never fell, for
example, like Sainte-Beuve, into the snare of feeling himself
humiliated by the superiority in poetry of Lamartine, Vigny,
Hugo and Musset, and for that reason of treating them somewhat less generously than they deserved, and giving preference to other and inferior writers.    Larra, as we have already
said, extended a warm and sympathetic welcome to dramas
which put his *Macías* quite into the shade, both by the
greater interest which they aroused and by the superiority
of their versification.    His generous critique of *Los Amantes
de Teruel* in *El Español*, for example, dated January 22, 1837,
is one of the last things that he published ; it was written
only a few days before his death.    In this last part of his life
he sought occasion to make eulogistic mention of rivals like
Ventura de la Vega and Bretón de los Herreros ; in
particular he praised Bretón's very happy translation of
Delavigne's *Enfants d'Édouard* and Ochoa's version of
*Hernani*.

For a short time he thought of expending his energy upon political conflict and of calming or stifling the restlessness of his spirit in the turmoil of the Cortes. He was, indeed, elected deputy for Ávila, but the unhappy mutiny of La Granja closed this avenue of usefulness to him, since the Cortes in which he would have figured never met. Everything seemed to conspire against him. He had surpassingly great qualities as an artist, a critical talent of the very highest order, and a penetrating vision which made him a consummate satirist. But his temperament was one of extreme and ardent sensibility—he was predisposed, as it were, to suffer unspeakably if he should be assailed by any great passion. And there came to him a terrible, overmastering passion, of the kind that he had described in justifying the fury of Diego Marsilla, the celebrated lover of Teruel,

> para la cual no hay obstáculo, no hay mundo, no hay hombres, no hay más Dios en fin que ella misma.

The woman who had inspired it strove to uproot it herself from the heart of the man who loved her so profoundly ; perhaps she had no conception of its depth, for, when she plucked at its roots, she destroyed not Larra's love but his life.

The news of his suicide caused an extraordinary sensation in the capital. During the course of that day (February 13, 1837), many people had seen him and spoken to him in various places without noticing any great difference in his behaviour. Mesonero Romanos, whose house he had visited, found him only "more sobered than was his custom." The Marqués de Molíns had a long talk with him about a play which they had begun to write in collaboration round the figure of the great Quevedo. On that very evening occurred the catastrophe.

The funeral ceremonies, the expenses of which were met by friends and admirers, have left an indelible mark upon Spanish literary history. For during the last rites, themselves deeply moving, when the grave was about to close upon the mortal remains of the talented young satirist, there arose a boy of nineteen—José Zorrilla—who, standing by the coffin, recited some now famous verses, in melodious and rhythmical tones which greatly enhanced the beauty of the reading.

It was a youthful composition that he read—unequal,
lacking in restraint, at times hardly making sense, but not so
greatly inferior to other lyrical efforts of its author in his
maturity, for as a purely lyric poet Zorrilla was never to
attain unusual brilliance. At a later date he spoke de-
preciatingly of these lines and of his dramatic entry into the
world of Spanish letters, but it will always be a memorable
coincidence that at the grave of one who may well be thought
of as the first great Spanish Romantic there should suddenly
and unexpectedly have appeared the most truly national of
the Spanish Romantic poets—the poet who, though neither
imitating Sir Walter Scott nor in the least resembling him,
was to write verse legends comparable with the narrative
poems of that great master.

# CHAPTER II

## ÁNGEL DE SAAVEDRA, DUQUE DE RIVAS

### I

On January 1, 1834, after an exile of more than ten years, there entered Spain, by way of the Perpignan frontier, a poet and former parliamentary deputy, Ángel de Saavedra, soon to become Duque de Rivas. He was forty-two years of age, and somewhere in his baggage was a new book of poems, which Salvá had just printed for him in Paris, together with the manuscript of *Don Álvaro*, a prose melodrama of the type that was being given at this time with great applause on the Parisian stage. This volume, and above all, in a revised verse and prose form, this manuscript, were shortly to complete that bold renovation of Spanish literary art (in particular, of dramatic art) which was being somewhat timidly attempted by Martínez de la Rosa and continued, with rather more assurance, by Larra.

Don Ángel de Saavedra, born at Córdoba on March 10, 1791, was by no means, of course, just beginning his career as a poet when in 1834 he returned to his own country. Not only was he already author of the *Moro Expósito*, of the first *Romances históricos*, printed with that poem in the Parisian edition referred to, and of the then unpublished prose version of *Don Álvaro*, but he had also written and published a large quantity of verse years previously. In 1814 he had printed his first volume of poetry, and during the following decade had composed half a dozen tragedies, some of which (*Aliatar*, for example, and *Blanca de Castilla*) had been given on the stage, and, according to one of his biographers,* well received. A second edition of the poems had been published in 1820. In 1823, the whole of Spain gave a vociferous welcome to another of his tragedies, *Lanuza*, as was to be expected in those days of revolutionary enthusiasm; for, in attacking Philip II, Saavedra was aiming at Ferdinand VII, and in the unfortunate Justice of Aragon

---

* Manuel Cañete : *El Duque de Rivas*, Madrid, 1884, pp. 27–8. Cf. also pp. 127–42.

was compassionating one more victim of the King's un-
bridled despotism.

The events of 1823 sent the dramatist to a stage more
perilous and insecure than that of the theatre. He was at
that time a deputy and secretary of the Cortes, and one of
those who boldly provoked war against the Holy Alliance—
that is to say, against the whole of Continental Europe—
feeling that Spain was quite capable of meeting the "hundred
thousand sons of Saint Louis" who were preparing to cross
the Pyrenees under the Duc d'Angoulême. Truth to tell, it
is difficult even to-day to see how they could have done
otherwise. Saavedra was one of the group of *exaltados* who
proposed the suspension of the King and prevailed upon a
majority to vote for it, subsequently taking him prisoner,
keeping the invading army at bay and finally shutting themselves up within the walls of Cádiz. Since they lacked the
power, prestige and national support to depose the monarch
and establish a new *régime*, they contented themselves with
humiliating and exasperating him, though they must have
known only too well, many of them from their own experience, that that revengeful heart had never harboured the
smallest or most fleeting sense of generosity. When at last
Cádiz surrendered, Saavedra, with the flower of the Spanish
nation, was forced to emigrate ; while the King, with that
peculiar combination of cynicism, inclemency and ferocity
which he had displayed so effectively in 1814, began a new
series of persecutions. Like all who voted for Ferdinand's
suspension, Saavedra was condemned to death and an order
was made for the confiscation of his property ; he could be
certain that the King, while he lived, would neither forget
nor forgive.

But this harsh sentence, from the effects of which only a
long and painful ostracism was to free him, became in the
end, by an unexpected disposition of fortune, a direct factor
in the development of his literary talent. It revealed to him
new and dazzling horizons. Nothing that he had written
before the *Moro Expósito* and *Don Álvaro* was of more than
moderate quality, nor is there any reason to suppose that by
continuing along his former road he would ever have
attained to great heights. With the slightest exceptions, the
whole of his early work can be disregarded in an estimate of
his place in Spanish literature, and no harm or injustice

will be done thereby to his reputation. His principal title
to glory is derived from the celebrated verse narrative inspired by the legend of the Infantes de Lara. Once this was
published his earlier work quickly began to pale, even to
fade into oblivion. His greatly applauded *Lanuza*, after all,
is of less merit than Quintana's *Pelayo*, or even than Martínez
de la Rosa's *Viuda de Padilla*. His other tragedies rank far
below Cienfuegos' *Zoraida* or *La Condesa de Castilla*, both
works of the same type and the same epoch. His two poems
in *octavas reales—El Paso Honroso* and *Florinda*—are certainly
no better than others now justly forgotten, such as Reinoso's
*La Inocencia perdida* or Torrepalma's *Deucalión ;* and none of
these, of course, is the equal of Nicolás Fernández de
Moratín's poem in sturdy *octavas* entitled *Las Naves de
Cortés*, itself no superhuman achievement. It is unnecessary
to extend the comparison to Saavedra's lyrics, for he was pre-
eminently a dramatist and a narrative poet and never shone
in the lyric art, either early or late ; no single lyric that he
ever wrote has the pathetic accent of emotion at once true
and deep.

Juan Valera, whose opinion in these matters is always
worthy of consideration, even where, as here, he is defending
an evident paradox, has maintained* that no such transformation as we have indicated was wrought in the poet's
talent during the emigration, as is the opinion of Rivas'
greatest admirers—of Pastor Díaz, of Cueto and even of
Cañete, who never misses a chance of eulogizing and
glorifying him. Valera explains the undeniable changes
observable in the nature of Rivas'-themes, in his choice of
metres and in the variety of his style, as the simple and
natural development of his faculties, or, in the critic's phrase,
"of his spirit." It is a fact, however, that the change became
suddenly manifest, to a public completely unprepared for it,
in a single year, for the *Moro Expósito*, some of the *Romances
Históricos* and *Don Álvaro* all appeared approximately within
that limit of time, when their author had passed some way
beyond the *mezzo del cammin di nostra vita*.

It is to be feared that the arguments with which Valera
supports his opinion can have convinced very few ; certainly
it is difficult to subscribe to the eulogies which he lavishes

* *El Ateneo*, Madrid, 1889. Cuadernos I–V. Cf. *Crítica literaria* (*Obras*,
Vol. XXVII, pp. 71–196).

on the love poems of Saavedra's youth, and even more so
to share the strange preference which moves him to describe
*El Paso Honroso* as "better than any of the Duke's other
legends, poems or narratives with the exception of the *Moro
Expósito* and the *Romances*." *El Paso Honroso*, a poem in four
cantos, each of about seventy *octavas reales*, is the imperfect
work of an able youth who meekly follows the path pointed
out to him by his earliest masters.    The casual reader will
put the book aside at once after glancing at so feeble, trite
and conventional an invocation as that of its second stanza :

> Dios de Amatunte, numen poderoso,
> Que en la diestra enojada del Tonante
> Logras helar el rayo riguroso
> Que dió castigo a Encélado arrogante :
> Pues inspiraste el hecho valeroso
> Que hoy el destino quiere que yo cante,
> Mi pecho inflama, dame aliento y brío,
> Y al tiempo venza el rudo canto mío.

The "Encélado arrogante" is a reminiscence of Herrera's ode
to Don Juan of Austria and the first line of the preceding
stanza,

> Canto el amor, la noble gentileza . . .,

recalls the beginning of *La Araucana*.    Other passages of the
same quality elsewhere in the poem give no support to
Valera's attempt to raise to so high a level what for the most
part is simply a mosaic of artificial versifying.

## II

On October 1, 1823—the very day when Ferdinand VII
regained absolute power—Saavedra travelled by sea from
Cádiz to Gibraltar ;  thence he went to England, at that
time the only place in Europe where victims of despotism
were allowed to live in tranquillity.    The English climate,
however, was unkind to him, and, as French territory just
then was forbidden ground to the Spanish exiles, he returned
to Gibraltar.    After some time, intending to settle in Rome,
he left Gibraltar, provided with a passport which his family
had obtained from the Papal Nuncio in Madrid and which
bore the words :  "Issued by the express order of His
Holiness."    On disembarking at Liorna he learned, to his

great chagrin, that the Pope had evidently changed his mind and refused him permission to reside in the Papal States. As the Grand Duke of Tuscany was equally opposed to the presence of Spanish liberals in his dominions, it was with the greatest difficulty that he obtained permission to stay at Liorna even for the few necessary days until a boat could be found to take him to the island of Malta. Thus did the tyranny of Ferdinand VII pursue and harry its victims over the whole Continent, and if all this could happen to one who, like Saavedra, had played only a secondary part in Spanish politics, it may be imagined what the Government would have done had it been able to lay hands on Alcalá Galiano, Istúriz, Argüelles or San Miguel.

To Malta, then, Saavedra made his way, guided, as we have seen, by a series of chances, almost as though he were in the charge of some invisible guardian. For he was to find in the island, not only the tranquillity which he so greatly desired, but also the friendship of an English gentleman who was to exert a beneficial influence upon his life and literary achievements.

John Hookham Frere—poet, critic, superb linguist and skilful translator of Aristophanes—had twice been Ambassador in Spain and had cultivated a closer acquaintance with Spanish literature than it was usual to find at this time, even in Spain itself. He had translated passages from the *Poema del Cid* and had developed a keen appreciation both of the forgotten Middle Ages and of the treasures of the seventeenth century. When Saavedra arrived at Malta in 1825, Frere was living in retirement there on account of his wife's health. He received the exiled poet with open arms, and Saavedra, attracted by the mildness of the climate as well as by the companionship of this English intellectual, decided to fix his residence there indefinitely.

Frere's influence soon began to wean him from the literary habits of his youth and from the metric, style, thought and general tendencies of Spanish literature of the eighteenth and early nineteenth centuries. The Marqués de Valmar, his brother-in-law, friend and constant admirer, tells us how great was the exiled poet's surprise on learning Frere's opinion that "the rude and spontaneous songs of the people, the tales and traditions which he had heard at Córdoba in their uncouth and uncultivated form, contained in essence sincerer and more fascinating poetry"* than all the literary models of the eighteenth century. Frere, who had picked up many rare and curious books in Spain, had a magnificent Spanish library, to which he gave Saavedra free access. In this way the exile was able for the first time to read and study many old Spanish plays of which he had never before heard, and he was led to seek new springs of poetry—not always, perhaps, the purest and richest, but tributaries, at least, of the great stream of national literature in the seventeenth century.

This change in Saavedra, as we have said, was produced slowly ; the neophyte was not in his first youth and the early impressions made upon him had been deep ones, extending over a very considerable period. Before setting to work on *El Moro Expósito*, which he began only in 1829, he wasted a great deal of time on the composition of an insignificant tragedy, *Arias Gonzalo* (1826), and a poor comedy, *Tanto vales cuanto tienes* (1827 : published in 1840). There are critics who profess to detect signs of the evolution of this pseudo-classical poet towards better things in the celebrated poem *Al Faro de Malta*, written in 1828, three years after his arrival in the island and the storm to which he refers in it. We confess that we have never been able to summon up much admiration for this poem, which has perhaps been overpraised by current opinion. The metre is that of the Classical ode *Á la Virgen de Lendinara*, but the poem lacks the sobriety and admirable precision of language characteristic of the younger Moratín. Its principal image occurs in the stanza :

> Tú, con lengua de fuego, *Aquí está*, dices,
> Sin voz hablando al mísero piloto,
> Que como a numen bienhechor te adora
>     Y en ti los ojos clava.

To say nothing of the artificiality of the expression "sin voz hablando," the simile can hardly be described as astonishingly original. It might, indeed, have occurred to anyone, for lighthouses pointing the way to safety are quite common. Again, to make the sailors of the *Maretino* cry "Malta ! Malta !" after a few days' rough weather, as Æneas' companions cried "Italia ! Italia !" or Xenophon's soldiers

---

* "Discurso necrológico literario en elogio del Duque de Rivas." In *Memorias de la Academia Española.* Año I, Tomo II, pp. 498–601.

"Thalassa ! Thalassa !" when they sighted the Black Sea, is to commit a totally unnecessary repetition of one of the best known and most frequently employed of current Classical devices.

The *Moro Expósito*, begun in Malta in September 1829, was not completed there. In March 1830 its author left the island for France. Even now he was not allowed to settle in Paris, but was detained in Marseilles and informed that he would not be permitted to go beyond Orleans. Fortunately for him, the fall of the Bourbons took place shortly afterwards and he was then able to proceed from Orleans to Paris, join his intimate friends Alcalá Galiano and Istúriz and await the fervently desired opportunity to return to his native country.

At this period the Romantic Revolt in France was at its height and could offer Saavedra precisely the elements that he needed to complete that evolution of his taste and literary tendencies which had begun so opportunely in Malta, and to lend brilliant colour to those newly acquired ideals which might otherwise have proved to be too strongly influenced by the north. Romanticism in Paris was enjoying a great triumph : among the idols of the new literature were Calderón, the anonymous bards of the *Romancero* and the poets of sixteenth-century France, while no little adoration was reserved for Shakespeare, Byron and Scott and for Goethe, Schiller and the Romantics of Germany. As long previously as 1822 Abel Hugo had published a collection of *Romances historiques,** and the dazzling *Orientales* of his brother Victor included one of the oldest and most interesting ballads belonging to the Infantes de Lara cycle, artistically paraphrased and disguised by the adjective "Moorish." In that notable manifesto of his campaign, the *Préface de Cromwell*, Victor Hugo quoted Lope de Vega and Guillén de Castro, and in 1828 Sainte-Beuve followed the brothers Schlegel in eulogizing the brilliant and fertile fancy of Calderón's dramas.† In reality neither the *Romancero* nor Calderón

---

* [French interest in the Spanish Romantic Revival was far earlier than this. No less noteworthy milestones were the ballads published in the "Bibliothèque Universelle des Romans" (1782–4), Creuzé de Lesser's *Amadis* (1813) and Cid-romances (1814) and Abel Hugo's articles on Spanish subjects in the *Conservateur littéraire* and his Spanish *Romancero e historia del rey de España Don Rodrigo* (1821).]

† *Portraits littéraires*, Paris, 1862, Vol. I, p. 45.

himself was ever thoroughly studied in France or properly understood ; but to hear their praises so loudly sung abroad was no doubt a powerful and welcome stimulus to Saavedra, prompting him to divest himself completely of the outworn precepts of another age and to continue his progress confidently along the path which he had already begun to tread.

At the beginning of this "leyenda en doce romances," as the *Moro Expósito* is termed in its first edition, is a dedicatory letter in English "To the Right Hon. John H. Frere," from which it may legitimately be deduced that it was this wise counsellor who suggested to Saavedra the idea of using the Infantes de Lara story. He could hardly have done him a greater service, for, with the exception of the life of the Cid as related in the *cantares de gesta*, the chronicles and the popular ballads, there is no mediæval story so interesting, so characteristic and so well adapted to literary development ; it can be made to present a complete picture of an entire century in the long and dramatic conflict between Mahommedans and Castilians.

It was unfortunate that Saavedra neither found in Frere's library nor sought elsewhere, during the continuation and completion of his work, any further sources for the details of the legend than two plays, both of poor quality, one by Hurtado Velarde, the other by Matos Fragoso, and a few ballads of the same period. No less unfortunate is it that, in order to justify his sub-title *Córdoba y Burgos en el Siglo X*, and to trace the historical background of his picture, he had recourse only to the histories of Ambrosio de Morales and P. Mariana on the one hand and to the now discredited Conde on the other. To this fact must be attributed what Sr. Menéndez Pidal calls "el gran desconocimiento de la antigua Edad Media que revela" and also the faults of the great scene where Gonzalo Gustios discovers the heads of his seven sons—a scene treated by Saavedra with undeniable ability, but a weak and crude one by comparison with the epic grandeur of the ballad *Pártese el moro Alicante*, discovered years later. No more flattering to Saavedra is the comparison of his poem with Sr. Menéndez Pidal's skilful reconstruction of the legend from the oldest texts of the *Crónica General*, a reconstruction involving only slight and entirely justifiable changes.

It would, however, be notoriously unfair to insist upon

these comparisons of the poem with works of which its author
was of necessity ignorant. It must be judged primarily on
its own merits, and in relation to the age in which it was
written. It is not a difficult or a complicated task to describe
its *genre* and to enumerate its sources, although many critics
are not completely in agreement on these matters. Cañete,
in particular, racks his brains to find a family name for
Saavedra's offspring, telling us that it has no connection
"either with the great Oriental epics or with those of Homer
or Virgil" and adding, with a curious *naïveté*, "neither can
its source be found in *Faust* or among the imitators of
Goethe." The panegyrist is not mistaken : neither Vyasa
nor Homer nor Goethe has any connexion with the *Moro
Expósito*. Saavedra conceived his plan in Malta, a British
colony, was helped in its execution by a former British
Ambassador, and was influenced by two British authors,
Byron and Scott, then in the splendour of their early fame,
whom he first studied there under Frere's able guidance.
For all these reasons, the *Moro Expósito*, wholly native as it
is in its argument and essentially Spanish in its form, belongs
to the same *genre* as the verse narratives of Byron and Scott,
so popular at this time—*The Corsair, The Siege of Corinth,
Marmion* and *The Lady of the Lake*. The interest of Saavedra's
plot, the general tone of the poem, the purely lyrical
passages scattered about the narrative, the diversity of the
style, which adapts itself equally well to tragic episodes and
to scenes of humble life, contribute, in Saavedra as in Byron
and Scott, to a poetic effect of singular beauty.

No legend could have lent itself better than the sombre,
dramatic story of the Infantes de Salas to the variety and the
rich colour of a verse narrative, a form susceptible of the
most attractive development, since, apart from the natural
interest of its story, it opens up possibilities of picturesque
digressions, lyric passages inspired by personal emotion or
reminiscence, and brilliant artistic touches which acquire
full power and depth of meaning only in verse, but in that
medium penetrate the reader's mind and reveal to him
fresh horizons of beauty. The principal and characteristic
element of Saavedra's talent, its *faculté maîtresse* (to use
Taine's expression), is the exuberant wealth of his imagination ; his language, style, versification and verbal harmony
may degenerate, as in fact they too often do, but his power

of invention is not easily exhausted. This explains how, with no more effective assistance in points of detail than that of two plays by third-rate dramatists, he sets out confidently upon his task, allows his fancy free play, adds new and original traits to his story, creates characters found in no version of the legend under treatment, and in doing all this gives full and complete proof of the power of his genius. The same may be said of the equally brilliant impression which he makes in *Don Álvaro* and elsewhere.

If he had but possessed the gift of poetical expression in the same degree as that of a powerful and fertile imagination, the Duque de Rivas would have been one of the greatest figures in the whole of Spanish literature. Unhappily the disastrous falls too often suffered by the reader after he has been caught up into the very clouds by the poet's fancy make him conscious of a most painful contrast ; from the heights of imaginative beauty he is plunged into the most uninspired and pedestrian prose. So astonishing is this inequality, so marked this contrast between good and bad in a single composition, even on a single page, that one cannot help wondering whether the poet himself was unconscious of it or was merely unable to avoid it.

Let us look for a moment at one example of this among many. In a section of the *Romances históricos* entitled "Recuerdos de un grande hombre" Rivas recounts certain episodes in the life of Columbus in Spain previous to his discovery of the New World. In one of these episodes he describes the scene in which (according to the poet) Queen Isabel parts with her jewels in order to raise money for the expenses of the enterprise. In doing so she speaks as follows :

> Vuela. En naves castellanas
> Mares nunca vistos rompe,
> Arrostra las tempestades,
> Tu estrella a los vientos dome.
>
> Lleva a ese ignorado mundo
> Los castellanos pendones,
> Con la santa fe de Cristo,
> Con la gloria de mi nombre.
>
> El cielo tu rumbo guíe :
> Y cuando glorioso tornes,
> Oh Almirante de las Indias,
> Duque y grande de mi corte,

4

> Tu hazaña bendiga el cielo,
> Tu arrojo al infierno asombre,
> Tu gloria deslumbre al mundo,
> Abarque tu fama el orbe.

Thus far the verses are good, there is something Calderonian about the style, and the sentiments are as well defined as they are nobly expressed. But from this point onward they begin to stumble; and we go from bad to worse until we come to a final line which is about the weakest in the poem :

> En tanto que así decía
> Reina tan ilustre, sobre
> Su cabeza colocaba
> Con altas aclamaciones
> Un ángel, corona eterna
> De luceros y de soles,
> Que mientras más siglos pasan
> Adquieren más resplandores.
> Con ella la admira el mundo
> Y adoran los españoles,
> Cuando absortos la recuerdan
> *En tan importante noche.*

The *Moro Expósito* is, as we said, a *leyenda novelesca*—a verse-novel, as it were, after the style of Scott's, but much longer : it must be twice the length, or even more, of *Marmion* or *The Lady of the Lake*. Its verse-line, too, is longer, and has neither the movement nor the lightness of the English rhymed octosyllable, so admirably suited to the quick, martial tone of *Marmion*, and making the impression on the reader, to use one of Scott's own similes, of a man journeying post-haste on a powerful charger. The rhymed hendecasyllabic chosen by Saavedra helps him very little : and his particular facility for versifying, his dislike of revising and polishing and the excessive plainness of his diction caused him again and again to fall into the inharmonious and the prosaic.

The foundling (*expósito*) who becomes Saavedra's hero is the Mudarra of the *gestas* and the ballads, stepbrother of the seven murdered Infantes, and son of Gonzalo Gustios and the compassionate sister of the *hagib* Almanzor who goes to comfort him in his prison. Mudarra's personality is entirely transformed by this modern author, who makes him the protagonist of his Romantic poem : he is no longer, as Menéndez Pidal observes, the sturdy, harebrained youth,

ready at any moment to split the skull of anyone who reproaches him with his bastardy.  The poem begins when
Mudarra is nearly twenty years of age, at the time when
his parentage is being revealed to him and he is being
charged with the terrible duty, laid on him by fate, of slaying
the villain Ruy Velázquez and so avenging the treasonous
ambush in which the seven Infantes were killed and the
iniquitous persecution of which Gonzalo Gustios is still a
victim.  Mudarra has become a melancholy youth, tender-
souled and virtuous :

> El cielo afable engrandeció su mente
> Con alto ingenio, concedió a su alma
> Virtudes y dulzura, y a su pecho
> El germen de las ínclitas hazañas.
> Si con ansia de gloria late altivo
> Su corazón, si ilustres esperanzas
> Se atreve a concebir, y noble gozo
> Su hermosa frente y sus mejillas baña,
> De pronto el azaroso pensamiento
> De que al crimen tal vez, o a la desgracia
> Debe el vivir, sus ilusiones borra,
> Nubla sus ojos y su faz espanta.

These traits and shades of his character are doubtless those
of a modern "Romantic hero" ; but, once he has determined
to set out for Castile to seek his powerful enemy, he neither
hesitates, like Hamlet, nor, like Hernani, pardons.  Only
once does he reveal a momentary weakness—in a single
phrase of the letter which before beginning his terrible
journey he sends to his Moorish love, Kerima, whose father
he has unwittingly slain.  In the letter he asks himself,
sadly :

> ¿ Por qué aún no ignoro
> La insigne sangre que en mi pecho abrigo ?

But, this said, he follows the call of duty without further ado.
   Giafar and Kerima, like Zaide, Nuño and others, are
characters created by Saavedra.  Nuño, the Muño Salido of
the *gesta*, "amo y padrino" of the Infantes, is not slain with
them (as in several of the other versions) but remains to the
end of the story as the companion of the blind and frail old
father.  Kerima, a beautiful and finely drawn figure,
sketched with real charm in the first two cantos of the poem,
which are perhaps the best written and the most original, is

present in disguise at the final duel when Ruy Velázquez is killed and Mudarra dangerously wounded. The poem then comes to an end with strange precipitancy ; after the baptism of Mudarra and Kerima and their subsequent nuptials have been arranged, Kerima averts her eyes from Mudarra at the crucial moment of the ceremony, refuses the hand which he extends to her and exclaims :

> No . . . ¡ jamás ! . . . Está manchada
> Con sangre de mi padre . . .
> Yo me consagro a Dios . . . Cristo es mi esposo.

To criticize this brusque conclusion is not to assert that Kerima's great renunciation is in disharmony with her character ; for the reader has long since realized her temperamental sincerity and ardour. But we fancy we can see in the final canto unmistakable signs of haste, as if it had been composed under pressure of time, possibly because for some reason the author had suddenly become anxious to bring his long work to a close. It is this feeling, perhaps, that has impelled many critics, from Enrique Gil to the present day, to describe the preparation for the *dénouement* as insufficient. And for ourselves we certainly think the final scene unexpected in its precipitancy, its brevity and its violence.

### III

Only two months after Saavedra's return to Spain in January 1834 his elder brother died without issue and he therefore succeeded to the title of Duque de Rivas, by which he is generally known. The two brothers had been close companions and had fought side by side in the Napoleonic Wars ; no doubt the keenness with which Ángel felt the bereavement was one reason why for a short time his literary work made no progress. It was not till the next year that he completed the revision of his drama *Don Álvaro o La Fuerza del Sino*, which was given its first performance in Madrid on March 22, 1835. It met with a very mixed reception and for a time its success appeared doubtful, but according to Hartzenbusch the vigorous opposition to it "died down after a time and in the end disappeared altogether."*

* Prologue to *Obras Escogidas de Don Antonio García Gutiérrez*, Madrid, 1866.

It has frequently been stated that while still in France Alcalá Galiano had translated the play into French with the idea that it might first be given in Paris.  This can hardly have been anything but a project, or, at the most, can have been only partially accomplished ; but it is quite certain that the Duke, on his return to Madrid, revised and altered the manuscript which he had brought with him from France, "making noteworthy changes in it and rewriting most of it in verse in the space of a fortnight," for, as we have already said, it was originally written in prose.  The testimony here comes from Pastor Díaz and is decisive, since the biography of Rivas which he wrote in 1842* is based upon data, notes and documents given him by the Duke himself, and Rivas' son, who prepared the third edition of his father's works, considered it as "a kind of autobiography."  Unfortunately no manuscript of the prose version is extant and nobody appears to have any knowledge of it.  Did it exist, it would tell us definitely whether or no Rivas used Mérimée's tale *Les Ames du Purgatoire* for two important scenes in the last act of *Don Álvaro*, which bring the play to its brilliant close and are essentially identical with Mérimée's *dénouement*.†

Cañete, forgetting the "noteworthy changes" which, according to Rivas' own testimony, were made during the final preparation of the play for the stage, proclaims triumphantly that, although *Don Álvaro* was produced a year after the publication of *Les Ames du Purgatoire*, Rivas could not have imitated it, having already written his play long previously.  This argument, however, in no way touches the difficult problem.  Rivas' brother-in-law, the Marqués de Valmar, in the address read at the session of the Spanish Academy held in honour of the poet's memory, declares his conviction that the novel did serve as a basis for the *dénouement* of the drama.  Mérimée, whose personal opinion he asked in 1866, informed him that the scene in which the friar challenges the brother of the seduced woman was taken from real life ; that event, he asserted, took place near a Carthusian monastery in Paris, which stood on the site of the present Luxembourg Gardens, and was reported in some old papers to which he had had access.  Finally, at a much later

* This is prefixed to Volume I of the current edition of Rivas' works (Madrid, 1894–1904) and also to the editions of 1854–5 and 1884–5.
† [This question is discussed in detail in E. Allison Peers : *Ángel de Saavedra, Duque de Rivas, a critical study*, pp. 448–58.]

date, Valera declared that Mérimée had seen the manuscript of the drama before writing his novel—an assertion which, unaccompanied as it is by proofs and contradicting Mérimée's own statement, is quite unconvincing.* The problem is, no doubt, insoluble, but all appearances suggest that the dramatist used the novel. It is not, of course, a matter of prime importance, the catastrophe of *Don Álvaro* being in accordance with both the logical and the poetical conclusions which follow from the premises of its argument ; and if, as is likely, Rivas based it upon this scene from Mérimée, he only did what another writer would have done in similar circumstances. Certainly, in that case, he made excellent use of it and adapted it with great effect.

There is a curious similarity between the first act of *Don Álvaro* and the starting-point of the argument in the *Moro Expósito*, in so far as it turns upon the love of Mudarra and Kerima. Mudarra unwittingly kills the father of Kerima, just as Don Álvaro, accidentally and to his great dismay, kills the father of Doña Leonor de Vargas ; in the one work this chance event prevents the hero's marriage, while in the other it ruins all his hopes. Kerima takes the veil and becomes the bride of Christ ; Leonor retires to the hermitage of the Convent of Los Ángeles. Both works were written about the same time, but these coincidences may quite well be purely casual.

A dominant influence in *Don Álvaro* is that of French forms and ideas ; from beginning to end it is Romantic, and, had it remained in its original prose, it would have seemed to be own brother to the plays of Ducange and those of other purveyors to the theatres situated in what the Parisians of that period called the "boulevard of crime." But the metrical variety of the play, its Calderonian savour and the lyricism of certain of its passages raise it to a much higher level and have, indeed, helped to save it from the discredit into which other plays, more popular in their day, have since fallen. This end was also furthered by the spirit and animation of the scenes depicting the life of the people

* The more so because Valera merely says that he had "repeatedly heard this" and elsewhere that "he believed he remembered" Rivas telling it to Alcalá Galiano. Valera also makes the strange assertion, which contradicts all our other evidence, that Rivas "rewrote the play in Seville, translated it into Spanish (*sic*) and partially versified it." It seems impossible to take Valera seriously here.

which serve as expositions to no less than four acts out of
its five.

Don Álvaro is a wealthy and valiant Indiano, as mysterious
as a Byronic hero, and residing in Seville, though none
knows whence he has come nor whither he is likely to go.
The author purposely keeps his title and origin hidden from
us ; an occasional veiled allusion takes us but a short way
towards solving the enigma ; and only in the last act do we
learn that he is the son of a "false viceroy" who, during the
War of the Succession in Spain, attempted to secure his
coronation as consort of the heiress of the Incas but was
deserted by fortune and condemned to languish in a Lima
dungeon.  Finally, therefore, the enigma is solved, but all
to no purpose, for, when the audience learns the solution,
the hero is within a few minutes of throwing himself from a
precipice, and no further interest attaches either to his
origin or to his antecedents, since these have played no part
in the development of the plot and have no historical value.
Don Álvaro's fantastic family tree, in fact, is the product of
Rivas' fertile imagination, and it would be a fruitless task to
search for his supposed father in the list of Peruvian viceroys
given in the *Diccionario Geográfico-histórico* of Colonel Alcedo.

The exposition of the play is as skilful as it is happy.  An
animated conversation among the *habitués* of an *aguaducho*
near the Triana bridge at Seville acquaints us with the love
affairs of Don Álvaro and Doña Leonor de Vargas, with
the opposition of her father, the Marqués de Calatrava, and
with the eminently sensible reasons which account for it.
As the conversation proceeds, Don Álvaro is seen crossing the
stage in the direction of the bridge, and the gossipers go on
to discuss his black servant, who has passed a little while
previously, with three horses ready harnessed, from which,
without any great mental effort, they deduce that he is
planning to elope with his sweetheart.  A canon in the
group, who is a friend of the Marquis, thereupon takes it on
himself to break the news to him.  So much of this exposition is necessary for an understanding of the action, which
now develops with great rapidity.

At the moment of the elopement, Don Álvaro is surprised
in the act.  He threatens the Marquis' servants with a pistol,
but, when the Marquis himself appears, defers submissively
to the father of his intended bride.  But as he casts away

the weapon in his hand it goes off accidentally, and the old man falls, mortally wounded. Upon that unfortunate event depends all the remainder of the drama.

In the turmoil and confusion which follow the Marquis' death, Don Álvaro and Doña Leonor become separated : each believes the other to be dead ; and when they meet again the play is only a few moments from its catastrophe. Leonor takes the habit of St. Francis and retires for life to a place "half grotto, half hermitage." Don Álvaro goes off to Italy to fight, under an assumed name, against the Germans ; here he is found by Leonor's eldest brother, who has been frenziedly seeking him everywhere ; a duel follows and the brother is killed. Don Álvaro, horror-stricken, flees to Spain, and is professed as a Franciscan, in the same convent of Los Ángeles near which is the hermitage that shelters Leonor.

Meanwhile the Marquis' second son, Don Alfonso de Vargas, has returned from Peru, where he has been hoping to find Don Álvaro, and, having tracked him to the convent, hastens to challenge him in his very cell, striking him, as in Mérimée's novel, in order to compel him to fight a duel. Don Álvaro, exasperated by the affront and by the young man's unquenchable hatred for him, accepts the challenge and deals him a mortal wound. To save the soul of the dying man, who begs for a confessor, Don Álvaro beats upon the door of the hermitage, entreating the holy penitent for help, and to his utter stupefaction finds himself faced by what he thinks to be the ghost of Leonor. Don Alfonso, however, recognizes his sister, supposes that she is living here with her seducer, and, with a superhuman effort, stabs her, crying that he dies avenged. Don Álvaro, in a frenzy, rushes to the top of a neighbouring precipice, and, exclaiming, "con sonrisa diabólica, todo convulso" :

> Infierno, abre tu boca y trágame. Húndase el cielo, perezca la raza humana. Exterminio, destrucción . . .

throws himself down from the heights, while the Guardian and the friars, awed by the terrible scene, utter the final words of the play :

> ¡ Misericordia, Señor, misericordia !

It is not surprising that "vigorous opposition" (to quote Hartzenbusch again) should at first have been offered by the public to so violent and convulsive a display of imagination. To write such a drama was to advance an immeasurable distance beyond *Macías* and the *Conjuración de Venecia* and the public needed a longer preparation before sitting down to a feast of such strongly seasoned victuals. Only after becoming accustomed to plays like *La Tour de Nesle* and *Catherine Howard*, and to others more horrible still, could Spanish audiences accept such a catastrophe as that of *Don Álvaro* without being appalled by its violence. It is not that the catastrophe was illogical, for it comes at the conclusion of a work which, despite its exaggerations, has all the dignity of a literary creation. It is rather that it took too advanced a place in the progress of the Romantic Revolt in Spain ; to witness it, as Larra would have said, was like finding one-self at the end of a day's journey without having started.

We ourselves think that the poet acted unwisely in leaving the final scene of the play in prose. The curses and ana-themas of Don Álvaro, driven to frenzy by the terror of his position, would have surprised and startled the audiences less had they been expressed in verse. The same is true of other parts of the play, such as the first scene between Don Álvaro and Leonor, which suddenly changes, halfway through, from verse to prose. The same happens at the end of this first act. The words of Don Álvaro, as he is about to kneel at the Marquis' feet and fling away his pistol, contain bold hyperboles, which nevertheless, with the help of rhyme, would have passed muster. Take, for example, the following lines :

> Vuestra hija es inocente. . . . Tan pura como el aliento de los ángeles que rodean el trono del Altísimo. La sospecha a que puede dar origen mi presencia aquí a tales horas concluya con mi muerte ; salga envolviendo mi cadáver como si fuera mi mortaja.

In prose this last figure is almost ridiculous ; only the music of verse could even conceivably have raised it to the level of the situation. It would have been better had Rivas left only the popular scenes in prose. These have the atmosphere of comedy, enhance the more dramatic scenes by the contrast with them which they display and form excellent *cuadros de costumbres*, full of the most delightful diversity of character. They are cast in just the right mould and finished off aptly and realistically with a few master touches.

The versification of the play is extremely unequal ; though often facile and harmonious, it declines only too frequently and at times descends to the level of dull prose. Yet both in brilliance and in variety it is superior to the succession of heavy, monotonous stanzas, all identical in structure, which we find in the *Moro Expósito*. It passes in turn from the *redondilla* to the *silva*, to the *décima* and to the octosyllabic *romance*. Its defects often arise merely from the poet's *insouciance*. He is satisfied with the weakest and most imperfect turns of phrase ; one sometimes thinks he must have committed to paper the first word that has come into his mind.

The only character in the play drawn with the slightest vigour is that of its hero. Leonor, her father and her two brothers are shadowy figures appearing one after another but leaving no deep impression on either reader or spectator. Don Álvaro, on the other hand, has a personality full of contradictions ; the profound melancholy of his two long monologues, for example, can hardly be reconciled with the boastful pugnacity which he displays elsewhere in the drama. He is the author of the ruin of the entire Vargas family and it cannot fairly be said that he causes the whole of this misery against his will. The first duel, that with Don Carlos, an affair of honour between two soldiers, may perhaps be considered to have been inevitable. But the second duel could certainly have been avoided, and with it the death of Leonor.

The sub-title of the drama, *La Fuerza del Sino*, an unnecessary addition not entirely justified by the nature of the plot, seems to have had a considerable influence upon a subsequent discussion, to which several notable critics contributed, as to whether or no the drama is informed by a "Greek fatalism" and whether Don Álvaro can or cannot be called a "Christian Œdipus." Into this discussion, sustained principally by Rivas' personal friends and admirers, were dragged familiar stories from Greek mythology and the celebrated tragedy of Sophocles. But it no longer has any interest. For, whatever may be the merits and defects of the play, it is now recognized as having nothing whatever to do with myths of Hellenic religion, still less with the masterpiece of a great poet of antiquity.

IV

Hardly was Rivas settled in Madrid when his old political
interests were aroused again and he founded a periodical
called *El Mensajero de las Cortes*.    The ideas to which this
periodical gave expression were those which had been the
cause of his protracted exile ;  but he did not long continue
his championship of them.    When he inherited the ducal
coronet and, in his own right, entered the Upper Chamber,
then known as the Estamento de Próceres, he gradually
began to modify his opinions and soon allied himself with the
party that had been reorganized by his old friends Istúriz
and Alcalá Galiano.    In May 1835, having joined the ranks
of those whom Espronceda was later to term "rabiosos
moderados," he became Minister of the Interior (*Gobernación*) under Istúriz.

If at this point politics had not begun to harass and
embitter his existence, Rivas might well have been considered the happiest of mortals living.    His great affability
and proverbial Andalusian good-humour, his fortune, his
talents, his attractive family and his love of literature would
have been amply sufficient to bring him happiness.    But his
immersion in politics caused him periods of great trouble.
In 1854 he once more became a minister.    His first term of
office had lasted some three months ;  his second was of less
than three days.    On both occasions he had to leave his post
in undignified haste and take refuge, once in the British
Embassy and once in the French, from the possible excesses
of the people.

Few narratives of the time are more diverting than George
Borrow's account (in *The Bible in Spain*) of the interviews in
which he asked leave of the literary Minister of the Interior
to print a Spanish edition of the New Testament.    Well
recommended by the British Ambassador, and a personal
friend of Rivas' Cabinet colleague Alcalá Galiano, he was
naturally received with great friendliness, but without being
allowed to explain what he wanted to do.    Rivas, "with a
most captivating bow and a genuine Andalusian grimace,"
merely handed him over to his secretary, who, he added,
"will have great pleasure in serving you."    This secretary
was Oliván, an obstinate Aragonese reactionary, who had a
good deal less pleasure in serving the importunate Borrow

than his chief pretended. Nor did Borrow ever obtain anything from Rivas himself, who, after one further interview
similar to the first, successfully avoided all contact with his
unwelcome visitor, even going so far as to "disappear by a
side door" in order to escape from him.*

The ministry was dissolved by royal decree, and, after
spending several days in hiding in the house of the British
Ambassador, the Hon. George Villiers (afterwards Earl of
Clarendon), Rivas succeeded, with many precautions, in
leaving Madrid in disguise and reaching the Portuguese
frontier. From Lisbon he at once proceeded to Gibraltar.
His second exile was shorter than his first, lasting only a little
over twelve months. He swore fidelity to the latest Constitution (that of 1837) before the Spanish Consul at Gibraltar
and was then allowed to return home and re-enter politics
as an elected senator. But a new gap was made in his public
life by the abdication of the Queen Regent, María Cristina,
the triumph of the Liberals and the regency of Espartero.
For three or four years he lived in retirement in Andalusia,
devoting himself mainly to literature. Though he had
resigned his activities, however, he was by no means
resigned in spirit. In his lyrics of this period—in *Lamenta-
ción*, for example, and *La Asonada*—his inborn courtliness
could not prevent him from hurling abusive epithets at the
party in power ; he considered all as lost, because General
Espartero and not General Narváez headed the procession
in Madrid.

In 1841 Rivas collected the *romances* which had appeared
at the same time as the *Moro Expósito*, together with a number
of others which he had written subsequently, in a volume
bearing the title *Romances históricos de Don Ángel de Saavedra,
Duque de Rivas*. These poems recount events, traditions and
anecdotes taken from the history of Spain over a long period
ranging from the reign of Peter the Cruel (1350–1369) to
the battle of Bailén (1808). It was a happy idea to publish
a series of verse narratives describing characteristic events
during five centuries of national history, and, as would be
expected, the collection was well received by a people proud
of their country's glories. The metre which Rivas used in
this collection was the octosyllabic *romance*, familiar to
Spaniards as enshrining poems known in Spain from time

* *Op. cit.*, London, 1893, pp. 133–45.

immemorial and handed down from one generation to another. During the eighteenth century, the national taste has been side-tracked to such an extent that, like certain other metrical forms, the octosyllabic *romance* was very little used by poets who prided themselves on their erudition, and never in the sense in which it had been used, cultivated and popularized by Sepúlveda, Timoneda and so many others. Hermosilla, too, a preceptist who had died in 1837, but had not completely lost his prestige even as late as 1840, had attacked the *romance*, saying that even though Apollo himself should write it, it would always have "el corte, el aire y el sonsonete de jácara." Rivas, therefore, thought it necessary to preface his volume with a brief dissertation in defence of the metrical form in which he presented his historical sketches to the public. In this dissertation, without troubling to achieve greater clearness by distinguishing between the simple assonanced octosyllabic metre and the poetical composition styled *romance*, he endeavours to prove that all kinds of subjects can be treated in this medium by quoting not only such poets as Góngora, Quevedo and Meléndez Valdés, but also dramatists like Lope, Calderón and Guevara, and then, delving slightly farther into history, by reproducing a few passages from the purely artistic *romances* of the sixteenth century. He seems all the time to be disregarding the essential distinction between the erudite modern *romances* and the older ones which are genuinely popular. And he completely forgets—if, indeed, he was ever aware of it—that the true title to nobility of the assonanced octosyllable consists in the glory of its earlier career as a hemistich of the long heroic sixteen-syllabled line, that metre of the lost *cantares*, re-established by the celebrated philologist Jakob Grimm in his *Silva de Romances Viejos* (Vienna, 1815, 1831), which he might have seen during his travels.

Rivas is less convincing as a preceptist than in the illustrations of his precepts embodied in the brilliant series of compositions, lyric in character rather than epic, which compose this volume. They lack, of course, the vigour and sobriety of the ancient *romances*, which spring directly from the old *cantares*, and it would be too much to expect to find in them the natural simplicity of early times, although the preface to the collection announces that its author has endeavoured to lead this kind of composition "back to its original object, and to its early vigour and energetic simplicity." But neither Rivas nor anyone else could possibly accomplish such an ideal ; and these new *Romances históricos*, overloaded with descriptions, philosophical and moral ideas and personal reminiscences, cannot conceal the modernity of their construction and markedly Romantic flavour. Still, taken as a whole, they form a work truly national in character, which appealed to the heart of the people, as it deserved to do, by its brilliant evocation of shades of the past and of glorious national memories. As the reader recalled these memories, he would find some consolation in them for present miseries of civil war and military anarchy ; and he would see in the hope with which they inspired him the silver lining to the dark and lowering clouds which during these critical years had overshadowed the nation's future.

About this time, besides completing and publishing the *Romances*, Rivas wrote four full-length plays : *Solaces de un Prisionero* (1841), *La Morisca de Alajuar* (1841), *El Crisol de la Lealtad* (1842) and *El Desengaño en un Sueño* (1844). None of these is as good a play as *Don Álvaro*. Far removed from the foreign influences which had worked so beneficially upon him in Malta and in France, Rivas was now set upon following and imitating his predecessors of the seventeenth century. *El Crisol de la Lealtad* and *Solaces de un Prisionero*, with their three acts and their inevitable but by no means always amusing *gracioso*, might have been written by a contemporary of Calderón's ; like all such artificial productions, they hardly once rise above the level of mediocrity.

But in *El Desengaño en un Sueño* Rivas gives rein to his imagination, developing a theme identical with that on which Calderón based his masterpiece *La Vida es Sueño*. As far as style and versification are concerned, the Duke was so thoroughly familiar with his model that he occasionally managed to rival it in brilliance ; but as regards conception of the plot there is a vast difference between Calderón and Rivas and the difference is all in favour of the former.

In *La Vida es Sueño*, Segismundo, the protagonist, has been brought up in the bondage of a prison at the foot of a tower in the mountains, because at the time of his birth his royal father was apprehensive of certain prophecies and a certain

fateful horoscope.   He is suddenly set at liberty and taken to
the Court to fill his proper place there.   But, following his
first animal impulses (for he has been brought up and treated
like an animal), he behaves so badly that the King has him
drugged and taken back to his earlier environment.   So
sudden and so violent is the transformation that the melancholy prince believes all the past to have been a dream ;
the spectator, however, knows that these things have actually
happened and sincerely sympathizes with Segismundo in
his great misfortune.   Here is an interesting dramatic situation, vigorously conceived and executed, and involving all
the principal characters of the play—the king, the prince,
the noble gaoler, his daughter, and so forth.   The audience
is genuinely moved and it is with real emotional tension that
it awaits the *dénouement*.

*El Desengaño en un Sueño*, though its title is suggestive of a
fantastic drama, has in reality little plot.   From the very
first, the spectator grasps the aim and realizes the limitations
of its double allegory, and, as a result, finds it of but little
interest.   Its fundamental improbability exceeds what can
reasonably be overlooked and acquiesced in by the imagination.

Marcolán, an old magician, and his son, Lisardo, live in a
desert island in the Mediterranean.   Lisardo, like Segismundo, comes on the stage "dressed in skins and with a wild
aspect" ; his stars, like those of his prototype, have foretold
a troubled and stormy existence, which his cautious father
seeks to avert from him by keeping him in confinement.
Like Segismundo, Lisardo uses *décimas* to expound his
unhappy situation to the audience, though these, if less
artistic, are less affected and Gongoristic than the famous
"Apurar, cielos, pretendo . . ." of Calderón.   So great is
his despair that he determines to cast himself into the sea.
The father, divining his feelings, sends him into a magic
sleep, during which he reveals to him all the unspeakable
horrors, crimes, remorse and misery which the stars have in
store for him, that he may take warning from them.   So
impressed is the youth by this lengthy nightmare that, when
at the end of the fifth act he awakens and Marcolán inquires
if he still wishes to leave the island, he disclaims all such
intention, embracing his father "con la mayor expresión de
terror."

Such, in brief, is the synopsis of this philosophical drama. Cañete prefers it to any of its author's other works and Cueto thinks it "not unworthy of a place among the finest productions of Goethe and Lord Byron." Valera, on the other hand, condemns it as "fundamentally unreal and devoid of interest."

On concluding the play, Rivas apparently believed it to be quite suitable for stage production. It was not given, however, till some years after his death, and, as might have been expected, its success was but small. The performance was a combination of semi-official function and conventional tribute of respect. *Faust* and *Manfred*, despite their complicated character and their profound symbolism, are susceptible of representation because they contain true drama, a conflict of passions and the clash of feelings deeply experienced and sincerely expressed. In *El Desengaño en un Sueño* the spectator is very conscious of the artificiality of the play, since, notwithstanding its frequent and necessary changes of scenery, "the grotto of Marcolán in which Marcolán sits studying" has to remain, "unchanged" and continuously visible in a corner of the stage, during the entire performance. The characters are not living beings but move and speak like dressed-up puppets. Their stage, in fact, is that of a marionette-show, except that Maese Pedro, instead of being in his usual place "within," is sitting in view of the spectators in his grotto. How, in these circumstances, can we take any interest whatever in the plot or cherish the very slightest illusion of reality? Everything is cold, empty and allegorical : no Margaret is here to suffer in real earnest and fall on the dungeon floor in an agony of grief ; no Manfred, puffed up with pride, devoured by remorse, unmoved in the hour of death and defying alike the powers of heaven and of hell.

The style of *El Desengaño en un Sueño* is no doubt better than that of *Don Álvaro ;* its versification is more artistic and comes nearer to attaining perfection. Yet its language has not the same power of attractiveness and charm, for it lacks *Don Álvaro's* youthful colouring and freshness. At its best, *Don Álvaro* is full of warmth and life and throbs with inspiration. In the *Desengaño* there are signs of effort throughout, and the play is dominated by one most serious defect, an almost complete lack of communicable emotion, which inevitably deprives it of sincerity of expression.

V

Whenever the moderate party in Spanish politics regained a temporary ascendancy, the Duque de Rivas accompanied it in its return to office.   In this way he twice held diplomatic posts : first in Naples, where he spent several years as Ambassador ; then in Paris, where, however, he remained only for twelve months.   Later still, he became President of the Council of State.

His long residence in the capital of the Kingdom of the Two Sicilies inspired his one important prose work : an historical study entitled *Sublevación de Nápoles capitaneada por Masanielo, con sus antecedentes y consecuencias* (1848), in the composition of which he utilized all the data and documents that it was possible to collect there.   The result is a highly meritorious piece of work, not only interesting but admirably impartial, for Rivas attributes a due proportion of blame for that popular movement, as well as for earlier and later movements, to the "unfortunate administration of the successors of Charles V and Philip II."   In prose, as in verse, he wrote with great facility ; and, as the results of excessive spontaneity and failure to discriminate in the use of words are less serious in prose than in verse, he contrived to preserve the tone of historical narrative throughout his work, despite his frequent descent to familiar and colloquial expression.   Without having (or pretending to have) gifts that would enable him to aspire to the achievements of historians like Mendoza, Solís and Melo, he succeeded in producing a creditable piece of historical work by no means devoid of literary charm.

Rivas gained the warm affection of the Neapolitan royal family, and in his official despatches he continually speaks with great admiration of Ferdinand II ("Il Rey Bomba," as he was called in Italy), praising "his humane feelings, loyalty and kindness of heart"—traits of that monarch's character which were perhaps not too obvious.   Such enthusiastic eulogies came strangely from one who had fought so energetically against the tyranny of Ferdinand VII.   He did all in his power to support the King of Naples and maintain him on his throne, which at one time seemed to be tottering,

5

and also to hasten the preparations for the expedition sent by Spain in support of Pius IX. Nevertheless, his ambassador-ship came to an untimely end. In 1850 he discovered that the King had made a secret arrangement for his sister to marry the eldest son of Don Carlos, the vanquished Pre-tender of the Carlist War. When this was known in Madrid, the Ambassador received instructions to break off diplo-matic relations immediately and to return to Spain.

Removed as he was, while in Naples, from the intrigues and fluctuations of Spanish party politics, he found time, not only to write his book on Masaniello, but also to take up once more his favourite pastime of painting, which had occupied him in Malta and helped him to gain a livelihood during his exile in France. He finished a number of pictures, which were sent to Academy exhibitions in Madrid and, according to his biographer, obtained some success. But few people can excel, or even approach distinction, in occupations as dissimilar as oil-painting, history, poetry, politics and diplomacy. Perhaps this dispersal of his talents accounts for the amateurish air of many of the verses that he wrote during this period : there is but little in them of the work of the artist intent upon perfection.

In Naples, however, he wrote the last of his important works : *La Azucena Milagrosa*, a verse *leyenda* displaying all the rich abundance of imagination characteristic of the *Moro Expósito* and the *Romances*, though an abundance now less ably directed and controlled. Two later *leyendas*, *Maldonado* and *El Aniversario*, are shorter ; were these two poems written wholly and not partly in assonanced octosyllables, they would conform exactly to the type of the *Romances históricos*, to which they are very similar in character.

The *Azucena Milagrosa* differs from all Rivas' other writings in the predominance of the religious element, which, especially in the second part of the *leyenda*, transcends the dramatic interest entirely. The first part is on the whole the better of the two and written with the greater care. The end of the story describes a human skull, complete with eyes and tongue, waiting twenty years in a field near Seville for the hero to return from America and stumble upon it. When he does so, it calls him by name and reveals the solution of the problem which forms the starting-point of the story. All this, no doubt, was meant to be impressive, but unfortunately an excursion so completely transcending the bounds of possibility produces none of the effect of terror which its author intended.

It is easy enough to see how Rivas was moved to the display of religiosity which we find in this narrative. Zorrilla had dedicated to him his *Azucena Silvestre* (described as a "religious *leyenda* of the ninth century") and Rivas was anxious to return the compliment.

> El don le ofrece de sabroso cuento
> A quien da otra azucena el argumento.

He makes no attempt in his poem, as he explicitly states, to rival Zorrilla, but he executes the *tour de force* of creating all the elements of a *leyenda* built on a religious theme without making use either of tradition or of any earlier fable. The *Azucena Milagrosa* has the vaster and finer argument, embracing the taking of Granada and the conquest of New Spain, and drawing great military pictures and historical sketches. On the other hand, it has none of the music to be found in Zorrilla's verses.

Rivas next went as Ambassador to France, returning to Spain at the beginning of 1858. At this juncture both his literary and his political career may be said to have ended. His health broke down, but he lived in retirement till 1865, honoured and respected by all.

From whatever aspect we regard him, Rivas is a striking literary figure. If his merits and defects be considered as a whole, he emerges as an eminent poet, endowed with the power and inspiration of a great writer. In none of the *genres* which he attempted can it be said with strict truth that he came to the foremost rank, yet in all of them he left work worthy of note and in none of them was he entirely a failure. Had he come nearer to perfection in the technical mastery of his art, very few perhaps would have surpassed him ; but the instrument upon which at times he managed to play with such skill by no means always responded to his efforts, and too often our ears are offended by its discords. Occasionally his language and style seem quite incapable of clothing his thought and imagination in an artistic manner. But his wonderfully brilliant fancy always attracts, even when it fails to move us. The permanent position assigned him by posterity may well prove to be no great distance below that to which he was raised by his contemporaries.

# CHAPTER III

## ANTONIO GARCÍA GUTIÉRREZ

García Gutiérrez differs principally from the other great Spanish Romantics in having adhered all but exclusively to the dramatic *genre* which first gave him his reputation. True, he published two small collections of verse—*Poesías* (1840) and *Luz y Tinieblas* (1842)—and in 1850 a weekly periodical reprinted a *leyenda* written by him and published four years earlier in America, entitled *El Duende de Valladolid*. All this, however, is of such inferior quality that there is nothing to be gained by recalling it. As to non-dramatic prose, beyond two feeble sketches in the symposium entitled *Los Españoles pintados por sí mismos*, we are acquainted only with the address delivered at his reception into the Academy, which again is of very slender literary value.* Our sole concern with García Gutiérrez here, therefore, is as a dramatist.

He was born in the extreme south of the Peninsula, near Cádiz, in 1813. In order to please his family he began to study for the profession of medicine, but at the age of twenty left home, gave up his studies and went to Madrid to seek his fortune as a writer. This is never a very easy enterprise in Spain, but at that time the obstacles were perhaps fewer than usual, for the political *régime* of the nation was about to undergo great changes, and with these changes came new hopes for literature. Like many of his contemporaries, García Gutiérrez began by translating foreign plays, principally those of Scribe, and later of Alexandre Dumas ; the latter was a master and guide of the Spanish dramatists of the age and his influence on the young playwright is evident and easily traceable throughout the first part of his

---

* [We may add to this list a *Noticia histórica-descriptiva del Museo Arqueológico Nacional* (Madrid, 1876) and an ode to Amadeo I (Madrid, 1871). These additions, however, though made for the sake of exactness, only emphasize the poverty of García Gutiérrez' non-dramatic output.]

career, from *El Trovador* to *Simón Bocanegra*. It would have
been difficult, indeed, to handle and to translate into Spanish
such characteristic plays of Dumas as *Caligula, Don Juan de
Marana* and *La Tour de Nesle* * without catching much of
their spirit in the process.

After several fruitless attempts at writing original
comedies, which gave him little chance of exercising his
talents and had no success with the managers, he suddenly
had a happy inspiration. Attracted by the success of
*Macías* and *Don Álvaro* and carried away by the revolutionary
impetus which these two plays had given to drama, he conceived the idea of a play to be described as "chivalric" and
entitled *El Trovador*. This he offered to a well-known
manager named Grimaldi, who quite realized its originality,
boldness and brilliance, but returned it to the author with
the remark that it displayed all Rivas' audacity "without
having the shelter of Rivas' well-established fame."† After
making other unsuccessful attempts to find a manager, the
young author lost all hope and enlisted as one of the hundred
thousand soldiers with whom Mendizábal proposed to ex-
terminate the Carlists. But his friends, among whom was
Espronceda, prevailed upon an actor in the company at
the Teatro del Príncipe, in Madrid, to choose García
Gutiérrez' play for his benefit performance, despite the fact
that there was no *gracioso* or similar comic part in it such as
he himself habitually played. This was the history of the
first production of *El Trovador* in Madrid on March 1, 1836.
Its success was as boisterous and as complete as it was unexpected, and in connection with it occurred a number of
incidents which have since become famous. At the end of
the performance the author was called before the curtain to
respond to the plaudits of the audience. But unfortunately
the author had absented himself without leave from the
barracks where he was in training, and was so shabbily or so
insufficiently dressed that he had to borrow a coat from his
friend Ventura de la Vega to make himself presentable for
this his first public appearance. His triumph, however, soon
smoothed his path, and in a few days the Ministry of War
sent him a pardon for breaking barracks and permission to
leave the army.

* The Spanish version of *La Tour de Nesle* was known as *Margarita de Borgoña*.
† Ferrer del Río : *Galería de la literatura española* (Madrid, 1846), p. 256.

*El Trovador* was no flower that withered in a day, nor did its popularity last but for a single season. No other Romantic drama, save Zorrilla's *Don Juan Tenorio*, the popularity of which had less to do with literary merit, left so immediate and deep an impression upon the country in general. And even to-day its reputation is almost intact, and stands higher than that of *Don Álvaro* or of *Los Amantes de Teruel*, which alone could ever have been preferred to it. Besides being García Gutiérrez' masterpiece, it is the most popular of all Spanish Romantic dramas. It may not be quite the best of them ; but it resembles Schiller's *Räuber* and Victor Hugo's *Hernani* in that its appearance betokened the triumph of something fresh and new, destined to symbolize the brilliant climax of a rapidly growing movement, of a revolution in dramatic taste and of an entire literary period.

There are two distinct actions in the play, not perhaps as well combined as Larra would have us believe, but at least not seriously transgressing poetical verisimilitude and certainly giving the argument a breadth which goes well with its outstanding characteristics—the soaring of the poet's muse and the freedom proper to every type of romanticism. One of its two actions alone would have sufficed for the building up of an interesting drama after the manner of Lope de Vega or Calderón. But the poet seeks to do more than this, and so he creates the tragic figure of the gipsy, Azucena, who, year after year, has been preparing a terrible vengeance. In this way he enlarges the scope of his work and turns it into a vast canvas of violent passion, a drama of love and hate, giving it a far-flung horizon and characters that stand out clearly against a background of history : the city of Zaragoza and the kingdom of Aragon during the first years of the fifteenth century, in the days of the rebellion of the once famous Count of Urgel.

The not inconsiderable defects of the play nearly all arise from its author's inexperience ; some of them he corrected at a later date, but all his corrections combined did little to improve his work, while they took from it something of the perfume of freshness and youth of which, as we read the earliest version, we are still conscious. This revised draft of the *Trovador*, which is entirely in verse, is to-day completely forgotten, and only the original text appears in the collection of *Obras Escogidas* which the author's admirers published in his honour in 1866.

The exposition, which, as in *Don Álvaro*, is in prose, has neither the clarity nor the animation that distinguishes Rivas' drama. But the chief defect of the play is inherent in the very nature of its argument, which is somewhat confused, and, as Larra said, more suitable for a novel than for a drama. The two chief springs of its action, Leonor's love and Azucena's vengeance, are very loosely held together and the arguments which depend upon them ramble about uncertainly, and are devoid of that artistic unity which, with rather more effort and attention, would not have been difficult of achievement. In reality, therefore, there are two expositions, corresponding to the double development of the argument.

When the curtain rises, the servants of the house of Artal, before telling us of the passionate love of Don Nuño and his jealousy at Doña Leonor's preference for the Troubadour, Manrique, recapitulate past history for the purpose of acquainting us with the existence of an elder brother of Don Nuño, stolen, when only two years old, by a gipsy-woman whose mother Don Lope de Artal had previously caused to be burned as a witch. This brother, though nobody knows it, is the hero of the play, Manrique. Azucena, the gipsy-woman who abstracted him, has led him to believe that he is her own son, while everyone else has always believed the kidnapped child to have died. The scene between mother and son introducing the third act serves as a subsidiary exposition to the drama. In this Azucena recounts her mother's horrible death in the flames, the kidnapping of the heir of the house of Artal and the terrible error which she herself committed in her frenzy, that of casting into the flames, in expiation, not the stolen child but her own son.

"Your son ! " cries Manrique. "Then who . . . who am I ?"

The strange mother hastens to retract the confession, but from this point onward the spectator is aware that Don Nuño and the Troubadour are brothers, and, when he sees them so fiercely engaged on opposite sides of the combat and each in love with Leonor, he foresees the final catastrophe, divines Azucena's terrible vengeance and anxiously awaits its consummation.

This unlooked-for detail, by no means easy of explanation —this son thrown into the flames by a dreadful mistake or in a horrible refinement of cruelty—is a surprising and indeed a repellent addition to the play, adding little to its true plot-interest. We have known persons who, after frequently hearing Verdi's opera *Il Trovatore*, and never having read or seen the Spanish play upon which it was founded, have been quite unable to explain the drift of this scene which Verdi set to such vigorous music.

It might almost be imagined that García Gutiérrez wrote his play with the idea of its being set to music and did all he could to facilitate the task of the composer. There is probably no other drama of the period in which music plays a part of such importance. In the play, as in the opera, Manrique announces his arrival by singing a *trova* behind the scenes. Azucena's first words in the play are preceded by a song, which also occurs in the opera and occupies the same position. In both play and opera, when Leonor takes the veil, a responsory is sung "within," and until the end of the act choir and organ are heard continuously. The magnificent *Miserere* scene, the plan and construction of which only a musically minded author could have conceived in this way, owes nothing, from the dramatic point of view, to Verdi or the Italian librettist : the chorus of muffled and funereal voices, the tenor's lament, the impassioned outburst of the unhappy woman—all this was thought out by García Gutiérrez with the aim of producing the same effect of pathos, and Verdi did no more than transpose García Gutiérrez' inspiration into music. This task, as everyone knows, he accomplished with the greatest skill, as a result of which *Il Trovatore* can be reckoned among the three or four greatest works of his full maturity. Poetry and music, however, are such dissimilar arts, and their technique and resources are of so different a character, that the play and the opera have in no way injured each other.

García Gutiérrez' supreme gift, which from his very first play appears in all its brilliance, is that of facile, attractive and melodious versification. Through the entire course of his long life this quality hardly suffered decline, even when the art of his contemporaries was plumbing the depths of decadence. It is as noteworthy in his last play, *Juan Lorenzo*, as in *El Trovador*. Combining as it did with the naturally melancholy tinge of his character and the instinctive disenchantment of his poetry, this gift is responsible for some of the deepest and most penetrating pathos which we find in Spanish dramatic poetry of the nineteenth century. The instantaneous and extraordinary vogue of the *Trovador* weighed heavily upon its author's later dramas. It marked the decisive victory and the brief triumph of romanticism, bringing to a sudden climax of popularity the movement initiated with such doubtfully successful plays as *Macías* and *Don Álvaro*. Never again, however, did García Gutiérrez receive such a warm and sincere ovation from the public—or not, at least, until nearly thirty years later, on the appearance of his *Venganza Catalana*. The *Trovador*, without the slightest doubt, had more originality and brilliance than any of the plays that had immediately preceded it. Romantic in form, combining verse and prose, bright with varied and dazzling colour and dominated by an all-pervading tone of concentrated sadness and impassioned grief, it also recalled the dramas of the Golden Age in the energy of its action, the briskness and vitality of its individual scenes and the stamp of chivalric ardour and poetic beauty so appropriate to its subject and so markedly impressed upon it.

*El Paje*, given a year later, seems also to have been well received, though, save for its equally brilliant versification, it is of considerably less merit than *El Trovador*. Its plot is disagreeable, even repulsive. A son who kills, or is about to kill, his mother, as in *Lucrèce Borgia* and *La Tour de Nesle*, can only be of interest against an historical background very different from that of *El Paje*, and the characterization must be loftier out of all proportion than in this play. As we read *El Paje* to-day, we can hardly believe that it could ever have had a good reception anywhere ; it is only too evidently influenced by the least recommendable characteristics of Alexandre Dumas and of other dramatists resembling him.

*El Rey Monje* (1839) is not so much a drama as a dramatic chronicle, picturing successive scenes in the life of Ramiro the Monk, King of Aragon, from his youth until his death. It is written, like its two predecessors, in verse and prose and its versification is of an even higher quality ; in it García Gutiérrez reaches the climax of his career as a writer of purity and elegance. He was capable of attaining, and did in fact ultimately attain, a greater degree of sobriety and precision of language ; but he never surpassed the fluidity and spontaneity of form which give the dramas of this period an enduring charm and make them a joy for ever. The drama is no longer played in Spain, but the confession scene in the last act and above all the delightful *quintillas* beginning "Enlutada misteriosa . . ." are still familiar to lovers of Spanish literature.

From this point onward García Gutiérrez' dramas were written almost entirely in verse. *El Encubierto de Valencia* (1840), despite the sumptuousness of its poetry, was a comparative failure. The public principally disliked its unexpected *dénouement*, which was not only contradictory but also dramatically ineffective ; Juan Martínez Villergas tells us that at the *estreno* it was received with hisses,* though Ferrer del Río (a close friend, however, of the author) will have it that it was not unsuccessful.

Undeterred by this set-back, García Gutiérrez, to his great credit, made a successful return to the stage in *Simón Bocanegra*, a drama with a prologue and four acts which was excellently received early in 1843. Its novel-like plot is lengthier and more complicated than the plot of the *Trovador*. Indeed, it is not easy to give a satisfactory description of the various scenes leading to the *dénouement*, which are by no means always well combined. The prologue is in itself an interesting little drama. The famous Genoese mariner, Simón Bocanegra, returns to his country, covered with glory, in the hope of finding a certain Mariana, daughter of the noble Jacobo Fiesco, whom he has seduced years previously. He discovers that she has died, broken-hearted with grief and shame at his abandonment of her ; meanwhile the people, full of enthusiasm at his heroic deeds, proclaim him Dux of the Republic.

A daughter of Bocanegra and Mariana, who has disappeared in infancy from a place where her father has left her, and now reappears in the most unlooked-for way before his eyes, is, as it were, the central figure towards which the different episodes of the drama gradually converge. It would be difficult to relate all these episodes, and in such a brief survey as this it is hardly necessary. In the final scene Simón Bocanegra dies magnificently, poisoned by one of his friends and favourites who aspires to the hand of the lost

* *Juicio crítico de los poetas españoles contemporáneos*, Paris, 1854, p. 95.

daughter, María. He transmits the ducal coronet to
Gabriel Adorno, a former implacable adversary reconciled
with him through María's influence. In the course of the
drama Simón conducts himself like a tyrant whose hard
heart can be softened only by the love of his daughter. But,
as the play approaches its conclusion, he rises to greater
heights, and, like Macbeth, is inspired by the nearness of his
impending doom with phrases full of the profoundest disillusion. Such are the lines spoken from his balcony as he
looks toward the Mediterranean :

> ¡ Ay ! esas puras
> Ráfagas de la mar que el aire bañan,
> Consuelo son de mi mortal angustia.
>
> ¡ La mar ! ¡ La mar ! Cuando en su claro seno
> Gallarda y altanera se columpia
> La armada nave, que a cruzar se apresta
> La inmensidad del piélago profunda,
>
> ¡ Ah ! mil recuerdos de placer, de glorias,
> En mi mente fantásticos se agrupan
> Con incansable afán que me devora,
> Con brillo seductor que me deslumbra.
>
> ¡ La mar ! ¡ La mar ! ¿ Por qué, desventurada,
> En ella no encontré mi sepultura,
> Sin la ciega ambición que me sujeta
> De esta prisión dorada a la coyunda ?

At the beginning of his career García Gutiérrez had all the
makings of a supremely great dramatist. He had a potent
instinct for dramatic technique and construction ; a delicate
ear for verse-melody ; great fertility of production ; and a
gift for creating the most admirable of women. Examples
of these are Leonor in *El Trovador*, Isabel in *El Rey Monje*, the
three exquisite Marías in *El Encubierto de Valencia*, *Simón
Bocanegra* and *Venganza Catalana* and the perfect Bernarda in
*Juan Lorenzo*. The pity is that he failed to devote his early
years, which he could never live again, to that assiduous and
diversified study indispensable to the true artist. He had
thus no great store of education to draw upon when he
needed it, and furthermore he was handicapped by his own
character, for, according to all his contemporaries, he was

unusually indolent and entirely unmoved by applause and glory. His friend Ferrer del Río speaks quite frankly of his "negligence and indifference." The two best known and very similar portraits of him, one in the *Obras escogidas* referred to above, and the other made by Maura when he was much older,* both give an excellent impression of his temperamental pleasantness and good nature.

These, however, were not the traits which best fitted him for wrestling to good purpose in such a turbulent arena of politics and personalities as Madrid, where the chief topic of interest was the continual rise and fall of ministries, which followed one another with extraordinary rapidity. He lacked the energy, confidence and self-possession necessary for scoring victories in the struggle for office and reward, and, as not even the most popular authors in Spain could maintain themselves in comfort on their dramatic profits, and journalism, for a man of so little aggressiveness, was the most precarious of occupations, he became a prey to profound depression and resolved to emigrate to Spanish America in search of a less hazardous livelihood. Accordingly he embarked for Cuba, and for a short time vegetated in Havana, where he had a post on the *Gaceta Oficial*, the least literary periodical in a country where no periodical was distinguished for its literary qualities. At Havana he produced an excellent translation of a celebrated French melodrama by Lemoine under the title *La Gracia de Dios*. He then went to Mexico, residing chiefly at Mérida de Yucatán and meeting with no greater success. After five years' fruitless wanderings, he returned to Spain, as depressed and poverty-stricken as when he had left it.

Until this date he had written or translated nothing for the stage but comedies and dramas. After his return, however, he discovered a new vein to exploit and began to produce librettos for *zarzuelas*, which, if a less literary occupation, was an infinitely more profitable one than any he had discovered previously. In June 1853 he staged *El Grumete*, the first and perhaps the most popular of his *zarzuelas*, and between this date and February 1864, that of the *estreno* of *Venganza Catalana*, he produced (according to the catalogue drawn up by Hartzenbusch for the *Obras escogidas*) no less

* See *Autores dramáticos contemporáneos y Joyas del Teatro español del siglo XIX* (Madrid, 1881).

than twelve "letras" for as many *zarzuelas*, or, in the sum total, some thirty acts.

Only one play of merit stands out in this list of third-rate productions—*Un Duelo a Muerte* (1860), an imitation of Lessing's *Emilia Galotti*, written for his own enjoyment, in the most concentrated and dramatic style of his mature years, though with little of the brilliant and impassioned melody of his early dramas. The theme is that of Virginia, the victim of the Roman decemvir, who is slain by her own father in order that she may be saved from dishonour. The story is transported by Lessing to one of the minor courts of Italy, treated in accordance with modern ideas and developed with clear signs of effort, for Lessing found it difficult to confine such a narrative within the five acts of his tragedy. García Gutiérrez begins by reducing the story to as few as three acts, and thereby gravely prejudices the verisimilitude of his conclusion. He then completely disfigures it by making Emilia's murderer not her father but her husband, the motive being to free her from the lust of the great Duke of Tuscany, into whose power she falls, as the result of an ambush, a few moments after her marriage, when the bride and bridegroom are fleeing in a carriage to Modena, to escape the clutches of the Florentine tyrant. This disastrous change involves the suppression of one of Lessing's essential characters, Emilia's father, Odoardo Galotti, a figure delineated with great skill as a gloomy and fanatical soldier, who from the very beginning of the play must be made to appear capable of the terrible resolution the fulfilment of which brings it to its close. Together with Galotti there vanish other important traits : the mysterious words, to take but one example, in which Emilia describes her misgivings as to her own powers of resistance if left alone and exposed to the Duke's blandishments ; this suggests the idea that she may possibly love him and is a further reason impelling her father to grasp the fatal dagger and commit the irrevocable deed. By such means García Gutiérrez softens anything in Lessing's material that seems to him harsh and severe and over it all he throws the charm of his melodious poetry.

Though an Andalusian by birth and education, García Gutiérrez spent the greater part of his life in Madrid ; the regions of Spain, however, whose history he most frequently chose as a background to his plays were the Mediterranean provinces and Aragon. These are the scenes of *El Trovador*, *El Rey Monje* and *El Encubierto de Valencia*, and the history of these regions inspires the two fine dramas of his later career, *Venganza Catalana* (1864)\* and *Juan Lorenzo* (1865). The former of these he wrote after a careful study of such sources as Muntaner and Moncada, as becomes clear from the erudite explanatory notes accompanying the play, which constitute a departure from his usual practice.

The hero and heroine of *Venganza Catalana*, Roger de Flor and María, Princess of Bulgaria, are not Spaniards. Roger is the famous Italian adventurer, the "son of the devil," who offered his services to the tottering Byzantine Empire at the head of an expedition organized in Italy and composed principally of Catalonian and Aragonese mercenaries who found themselves idle after the Peace of Calatabellota. María, his wife, is cousin of the Emperor Michael Palæologus. Both live in the Imperial palace, and Roger, in recognition of the great services which he has already rendered, is loaded with honours. But Michael, fearful of his glory and of the powerful force which renders him blind obedience, causes him to be treacherously assassinated at a banquet. This murder occurs in the fourth act, but is not represented upon the stage.

The fifth and last act, the events of which take place at a rather later date, describes the expiation of the crime—the memorable vengeance taken by Roger's soldiers, who are "tired" of killing Greeks and Alanese and Genoese auxiliaries in a pitched battle, the various vicissitudes of which are anxiously followed by Roger's widow from the walls of the city in which the Emperor has taken refuge.

> ¡ En sangre puede nadar
> El ataúd que lo encierra !

exclaims the Catalonian Berenguer, who takes Roger's place at the head of the expedition. "Bien habéis cumplido," answers María, the moving spirit of the action,

> ¡ Bien habéis cumplido, hermanos
> De aquel varón noble y fuerte !
> ¡ Habéis cansado a la muerte !

\* [This is the date of the *estreno* and in this year appeared no less than six editions of the play in Madrid. The first edition, however, is dated 1863.]

The dramatist very skilfully extracted an excellent plot from the interesting and reliable Catalan chronicle in which Ramon Muntaner, one of the members of the expedition, recounts the episodes of this "strange, romantic, heroic, barbarous and sanguinary odyssey."* It was hardly possible to pack the whole of its episodes into the drama, so García Gutiérrez omitted the entire sequel to this extraordinary history—namely, how the adventurers eventually reached Attica, founded a new state on territory of Classical fame, and appointed one of their number Duke of Athens.

The author makes no secret of his anxiety to sound the patriotic note and in particular to arouse feelings of national pride and enthusiasm. We may suppose that to a large extent these elements contributed to the great success of the drama ; if so, this is in one way to be regretted, for while patriotism has in the past lent a superficial reputation to dramas as poor as Gil y Zárate's *Guzmán el Bueno* and Rodríguez Rubí's *Isabel la Católica*, *Venganza Catalana* needs no addition to its own merits to enhance its literary fame. Nor is its appeal to patriotic sentiments altogether justified by history. Its characters invoke the name of Spain and its power and glory, in a sense which has only been true of Spain since the Reconquest. At the beginning of the fourteenth century the position was very different. Spain was then no more than a geographical expression, as applicable to Catalonians and Aragonese as to Navarrans, Portuguese and Castilians, who in those days were so frequently at war with one another.

The literary and historical value of the drama is diminished rather than enhanced by this confusion of sentiments belonging to different epochs. When, after the death of Roger, María sounds the bell summoning his soldiers, the Emperor asks her what is the meaning of the ominous sound. "¡ Pregunta necia !" she answers,

¡ Pregunta necia !
¡ Anuncia el fin de la Grecia !
¡ Anuncia el rencor de España !

The audience may burst into frantic applause and be entirely

* G. Schlumberger : *Expédition des "Almugavares" ou routiers catalans en Orient de l'an 1302 à 1311* (Paris, 1924). [On this subject, see principally L. Nicolau d'Olwer : *L'Expansió de Catalunya en la Mediterrània Oriental* (Barcelona, 1926), which contains a useful bibliography.]

carried away by the conclusion of the act, but an impartial spectator and a believer in precision will probably remark that María is a Byzantine Greek, and the dead man a *condottiere* born in Italy of a German father : Spain has therefore very little to do with the situation. In various other places the author seeks to convey the same effects and uses similar means to attain them.

As far as María is concerned, García Gutiérrez appears to have foreseen this objection, which he makes María herself answer in the act following. The answer is by no means convincing, but it is expressed in lines which deserve to be remembered. "Mas tú, en fin, ¿dónde has nacido?" inquires Michael. This is her reply :

> En los brazos de Roger.
> La patria de la mujer
> Es el amor del marido,
> Y más la que consiguió
> En él tantas dichas juntas.
> ¿ Tú, Miguel, tú, me preguntas
> Dónde mi vida empezó ?
> —En la gloria de sus hechos,
> En su cariño aquí fijo :
> ¡ En su grandeza !　¡ En el hijo
> Que he alimentado a mis pechos !

This contradiction, though not after all of the greatest moment, perhaps explains why García Gutiérrez denied *Venganza Catalana* the place of honour among his dramas, which he reserved for *Juan Lorenzo*, a four-act drama first performed in December 1865. This is in fact the superior of the two in style—perhaps, indeed, in this respect, it is the best of all his plays—but it has, of course, none of the historical importance of *El Trovador*, nor, whether in loftiness, in breadth or in vigour of inspiration, does it rival the vast canvas of *Venganza Catalana*.

In *Juan Lorenzo*, as in almost all García Gutiérrez' dramas, there is one admirable woman. Bernarda is adorned with the author's most striking poetic charm. Very effective, too, is the final contrast, in which the bride-to-be, in her nuptial finery, searches for Lorenzo, her promised husband, to find him apparently asleep in a chair, but in reality dead, his heart, already weak, having succumbed to a cruel blow dealt by the bitterest disillusion. But the hero is an indecisive creature, drawn with an uncertain hand, as though the dramatist were doubtful what to do with him. Of the political domain, which García Gutiérrez enters in this drama, he was entirely without experience, for he stood out among his principal literary contemporaries as never having been actively concerned with militant politics. He sets the scene of his play in Valencia during the famous Germanías, which brought the country so much unrest and bloodshed during the first quarter of the sixteenth century, and gives us a character and a situation to which parallels might easily be found in the political and social reform movements of later days. But it soon becomes clear that his Muse is not a sufficiently virile divinity to penetrate these controversial thickets and negotiate them successfully.

Timid and conciliatory by temperament, and both morally and physically weak, Juan Lorenzo has been chosen, despite his character, to lead the popular revolution which is brewing in Valencia. When he finds that his hand lacks the strength to direct the helm in such tempestuous weather, that in the hour of battle the seething masses pay no heed to the timid voice of an irresolute leader, and that other and less honourable leaders, by dint of their greater sagacity, unscrupulousness and violence, readily attract them and divert their course—then his heart fails him and he likens himself to the disillusioned Phaeton of mythology, exclaiming :

> ¡ Noble y santa libertad,
> Mi consoladora idea ! . . .
> Vuelve a Dios, no te desea
> La mísera humanidad.

If this spiritual crisis had occurred in the midst of an interesting and a closely-knit action, the hero's candour and vacillation would be of little moment. But it was never the dramatist's intention to describe a spirit like Hamlet's, unable to cope with the demands of circumstances. Again, if the Count of * * * *, the Marchioness and the false tribune, Guillén Sorolla, were anything more than shadows, if the plot were more skilfully woven and the death of Lorenzo did not appear to be a mere accident, the drama, enhanced by the elegance of its versification, would have triumphed ; and it would be unnecessary for the critic to

6

follow Blanco García* in attributing its lack of success to "party intolerance" and "factional fanaticism." It could not have failed, in such a case, to make an impression upon its audiences, and members of all parties would have been found to applaud it and give it their support.

After the production of *Juan Lorenzo*, García Gutiérrez still continued writing, and published more *zarzuelas*, comedies and dramas ; but never again did he reach the height of his earlier productions. The Government, which in 1854 had found him an administrative post in London, later gave him a consulate, first in Bayonne and afterwards in Genoa ; and in 1872 he was made Director of the National Museum of Archæology. At this post he remained, amid general esteem, till his death in 1884.

* *La Literatura Española en el Siglo XIX* (Madrid, 1891), Vol. I, p. 234.

# CHAPTER IV

## JUAN EUGENIO HARTZENBUSCH

After *El Trovador*, and during the short period in which Spanish romanticism still held the stage, there was no play more consistently applauded, more frequently represented and more characteristic of its epoch than Hartzenbusch's *Amantes de Teruel*. Like several dramas approximately contemporary with it—notably *Macías* and *Don Álvaro*—it was not only Romantic in the general sense of the word, but also essentially Spanish. The nature of its plot, the diversity of its metres and many of its individual reminiscences unite it closely with the works of some of Spain's greatest playwrights who endowed the Golden Age with so brilliant and original a body of national drama.

Spain was peculiarly fortunate in that, when her literary leaders broke with the traditions and threw off the shackles of the eighteenth century, she had only to go back a little more than a hundred years to find herself in an admirably fertile field of literature perfectly adequate for all her needs. Her exhausted talent could draw new power from the rich and energizing currents that flowed so abundantly in Spain from the earliest years of Lope de Vega to the latest years of Calderón. In France, on the other hand, the Romantic movement was compelled to divorce itself, not only from the dominant ideals of the eighteenth century, but also from the period of France's own chief glory—from the Golden Age of her principal dramatists, Corneille, Molière and Racine, and of Boileau, that literary legislator who was treated with such widespread veneration. Romantic drama in France might appear, at first sight, to have been cast in the same mould as earlier French drama, especially since the metre of each was the superficially identical alexandrine couplet. But, in reality, the arguments, structure, versification and general character of the new drama were all very different from those of the old ; they had had no antecedents in French literature for two centuries and were far nearer to Shakespeare, Schiller or Goethe than to Corneille or to

Racine. Spanish drama, like French, went back for a renewal of its inspiration beyond the eighteenth century, which in Spain had been but an imperfect reflection of the same age in France. But it needed to go back no farther than the literature of the Philips of Habsburg. On this congenial ground was cast the new seed brought from nineteenth-century France ; when this sprang up and bore fruit it did so on the Romantic soil, under the Romantic skies and in the Romantic atmosphere of Spain.

If we except Larra, who died after he had written *Macías*, his one drama of merit, it is Hartzenbusch, of all the Spanish Romantics, who most aptly illustrates this truth. His combination of the Spanish and the French elements of romanticism is one of his most striking characteristics. Another is his erudition ; for, unlike Rivas, García Gutiérrez, Espronceda, Zorrilla and all their contemporaries, he was at once poet and scholar, and it is difficult to decide whether poetry or scholarship predominated the more markedly in him.

Hartzenbusch was born in Madrid, in 1806, of a Spanish mother and a German father who was an artisan from the district of Cologne and had settled in the Spanish capital as a cabinet-maker. Until after he was twenty, the youth, who had lost both his parents in childhood, followed the occupation which had been his father's. He managed to secure an adequate education in one of the best schools of the city, and from a very early age showed a taste for literature, especially for drama. When he gave up cabinet-making he learned shorthand and joined the staff of the *Gaceta*, where he began to practise writing and cultivate drama in earnest. He haunted the theatre, which until then lack of means had prevented him from attending, except very occasionally. He began to write by translating French plays and recasting old Spanish plays, and, after some fruitless attempts at the writing of original drama, he set himself to study the legend of the lovers of Teruel and plan a dramatic treatment of it. He had just concluded a first draft of *Los Amantes de Teruel* when there came into his hands a copy of Larra's *Macías*, one of the plays which he had never seen on the stage. He read it and was astounded by the extraordinary resemblance it bore, both in theme and in construction, to his own drama still in manuscript. It was a strange coincidence, but it made the production of his play, as it stood, impossible. So, unperturbed and undiscouraged, with a patience and an industry inherited from his German forbears, he set to work to recast his drama throughout.

Soon, no doubt, this misfortune came to the ears of Larra, and it may well have prejudiced him in favour of his fellow-dramatist. At any rate, when it fell to him to describe the *estreno* of the *Amantes de Teruel*, at the Príncipe, on January 19, 1837, his critique of the play, published immediately afterwards, was singularly noteworthy for its tone of enthusiastic friendliness, surprising in so acute and exacting a critic, the more so as Hartzenbusch, though three years older than Larra, was entirely unknown. Less than a month later Larra was dead, while Hartzenbusch, encouraged by his influential aid, was starting upon his career.

> Pasar cinco o seis lustros obscuro y desconocido, y convocar a un pueblo, hacer tributaria su curiosidad, alzar una cortina, conmover el corazón, subyugar el juicio, hacerse aplaudir y aclamar . . . es nacer, es devolver al autor de nuestros días por un apellido obscuro un nombre claro, es dar alcurnia a sus ascendientes en vez de recibirla de ellos . . . Y tener mañana un nombre, una posición, una carrera hecha en la sociedad, el que quizá no tenía ayer donde reclinar su cabeza, es algo, y prueba mucho en favor del talento.

In this unmistakably sympathetic manner, the young-old critic, at the height of his reputation, wrote of his less fortunate contemporary. He examines his play in great detail and finally, writing now not as a judge but as an admirer,* encourages him to new efforts. His eulogies, we repeat, are by no means unduly exaggerated, and their writer would certainly not have repented of them had he lived to witness Hartzenbusch's maturity ; the worst he might have said would have been that his contemporary never went farther than in the *Amantes de Teruel*, which may well be held to represent the sum total of his abilities and the culminating point of his endeavours. In all Hartzenbusch's writings one is conscious of study, profound knowledge, continual application and solid good taste attained by the constant companionship of great authors. But we do not always find, as in this earliest of his plays, the brilliance of a

* "No ya como jueces de su obra, sino como émulos de su mérito, como necesitados de sus producciones."

free and spontaneous inspiration. He wrote the *Amantes* at
the one great moment in his life when for the time being will
and talent worked in closest harmony, and he produced one
of those masterpieces which a reader always feels that its
author thoroughly enjoyed writing.

The legend of the *Amantes de Teruel*, which many Spaniards
still consider authentic, supposes that at the beginning of the
fourteenth century there lived at Teruel two lovers, Diego
Marsilla and Isabel de Segura.  Isabel's parents objected to
their union, since they were ill-matched as to means, pre-
ferring that she should wed a well-to-do gentleman, named
Azagra, of the same city.  They allowed Marsilla, however,
a certain time in which to go and seek his fortune and, if he
should be successful, to return and claim his lady's hand.
He succeeds, and returns wealthy, eager and full of hope,
but too late, for the day of his return is the very day on which
the allotted period comes to an end and the hour is that of
Isabel's marriage to Azagra.  In the very church, according
to some versions, or, as others have it, shortly afterwards, the
lovers meet, and Marsilla dies of grief, while Isabel falls
dead upon his body.  With regard to details, there are
naturally many different versions which need not all be
enumerated.  As early as the seventeenth century the
historian Blasco de Lanuza argued that the legend was
purely fictitious and the proofs alleged by writers who insist
upon its historicity are far from being convincing.*

Mediæval traditions closely related to this have come down
to us in other parts of Europe ;  this legend of lovers dying of
love is the subject of a familiar story in Boccaccio's *De-
cameron ;* the details are different but the catastrophe is the
same.  Aureliano Fernández-Guerra, intent upon vindicat-
ing the Spanish origin of the tradition, thinks that a *trova* on
the subject must have come to Boccaccio's ears through some
Aragonese writer, for the Aragonese were the rulers of Sicily
at this time and had commercial relations all over Italy.
This, however, is a purely hypothetical theory which leaves
the question in exactly the same state as before.  All we
know is that no credible document has been found of date
earlier than the fifteenth century and the skeletons preserved
at Teruel may perfectly well belong to other persons.

* Cf. on this point Hartzenbusch : *Obras completas* (Madrid, 1887), Vol. I,
p. 43.

Various writers dramatized the legend before Hartzenbusch—Rey de Artieda, Tirso de Molina, Montalván—all with but small success. It is difficult to shape a story of this kind to the requirements of the stage ; the sudden catastrophe needs a long and careful preparation if it is to have the slightest appearance of probability and make any impression, especially upon spectators who are acquainted with its nature and know what to expect, as is the case with the majority of Spanish spectators. The story is inferior to that underlying other famous works on a similar theme, in that it lacks a certain element of tragedy and emotion which we find in *Francesca da Rimini*, *Romeo and Juliet* and *Tristan und Isolde*. This element precipitates the catastrophe, accounts for the deaths of hero and heroine and makes a deep impression both on reader and on spectator. In the first story it is the assassin's sword of the outraged brother ; in the second, the double suicide in the Verona churchyard ; in the third, the poisoned wound inflicted upon Tristan, which only Isolde can cure.

Hartzenbusch found an excellent explanation for the lover's delay ; he represents him as being forced to languish as a prisoner of the Moors in Valencia while Isabel is awaiting him at Teruel. He also skilfully reconciles us to Isabel's acceptance of Azagra in spite of her longing for Marsilla. But the death of Marsilla occurs as in the legend : he dies of unrequited love—first, because he finds Isabel married, and secondly because, in a moment of despair, fearing that if he fights with Azagra he may render useless the sacrifice she has made in giving her hand to save her mother's honour, she says to him : "Ya te aborrezco."

Hartzenbusch wrote two versions of the *Amantes de Teruel*, as well as the original draft which he laid aside because of its resemblance to *Macías* and as to which, as far as we know, there is no authentic information. There are, however, not counting this original draft, three distinct texts of the play. The first is the original edition of 1837 (dated 1836) ; the second is the Baudry edition of 1849, "expressly recast" by the author ; the third, which is definitive, appears in Volume I of the *Teatro* (Madrid, 1888).* The differences between the editions of 1837 and 1849 are of the greatest

* [The second volume of the five-volume edition of *Obras* mentioned in the Bibliography, p. 240, below.]

importance : while some are purely formal, others imply essential modifications of the argument. These last greatly improve the play ; the rest are sometimes commendable and sometimes not. It was a wise decision, for example, to reduce the five acts to four, which entirely suffice for the requirements of the plot, and also to put a number of the prose scenes into verse. Other changes made by the author are less happy : he is over-scrupulous in correcting small oversights and insignificant faults of style and versification, at the cost of the freshness and spontaneity of his original version, which to a great extent is lost in the revision. Any judgment delivered on the play to-day must, of course, be based upon its definitive edition, but it is impossible to forget certain merits which belonged to the earlier version.

The first act, which is entirely in verse and full of poetry, takes place in the kingdom of Valencia. Marsilla, returning happily to Teruel with his newly gained wealth, has been taken captive on the journey and is now a prisoner of the Amir. In six days the period of grace apportioned him at Teruel will come to its conclusion. Zulima, the Sultana, captivated both by his physical charms and by the daring with which on various occasions he has attempted to break his bonds and escape, offers him his freedom provided that he will take her with him. Gently but firmly he repels her, his heart belonging to the loved one awaiting him in his native city ; but she considers herself slighted, and, as she is in any case about to leave Valencia for fear of the wrath of the treacherous Sultan, she swears in her fury to avenge herself on Marsilla and Isabel. At this moment a violent conspiracy breaks out in the palace ; Marsilla puts his strength and valour at the Amir's service, helps him to triumph and, as a reward, obtains his freedom and the return of the wealth which has been taken from him.

Unfortunately Hartzenbusch was not content with a skilful and tactful alteration and rearrangement of these scenes and certain details of the argument. In several places he spoils the fine dialogue between Marsilla and the Sultana, quite unnecessarily cutting out some of his *redondillas* and altering others without in any way improving them. When, for example, Marsilla relates the adventures of his six years of wars and wanderings and mentions the battle of Las Navas de Tolosa, Zulima exclaims :

¡Lugar maldito del cielo,
Donde la negra fortuna
Postró de la Media Luna
La pujanza por el suelo !

The interruption, though not, of course, essential to the
dialogue, is perfectly in keeping with the character of a
Mohammedan woman, and its omission from the definitive
version is difficult to account for.   Again, there is a charming
and melodious *redondilla* :

Mi nombre es Diego Marsilla
Y cuna Teruel me dió,
Ciudad que ayer se fundó
Del Turia en la fresca orilla.

Having once embarked upon his corrections, Hartzenbusch
remembered that, politically speaking, Teruel is not a
*ciudad* but a *villa*, and that the river which passes near
it is not called the Turia until after it has left Teruel,
down to which point it is known as the Guadalaviar.   So
the lines are struck out and two inferior ones substituted for
them :

Pueblo que ayer se fundó
Y es hoy poderosa villa.

Other examples of the same kind of thing might easily be
cited, but these will probably be sufficient to give an idea of
the talented author's meticulous and even excessive scrupu-
losity in his artistic revisions.

The most vivid and brilliant creation in *Los Amantes de
Teruel* is the figure of Isabel de Segura.   She is no child of
fourteen, like Shakespeare's Juliet, allowing herself to be led
blindly away by passion, nor is she an innocent without a will
of her own like the Bride of Lammermoor.   Rather she is a
woman of heroic temper, who for six years, with exemplary
determination and patience, has awaited the return of her
beloved, and who yields only when confronted with obstacles
and misfortunes that are really insurmountable.   Azagra
has letters which tarnish and compromise the reputation of
her mother, Margarita—letters that have come into his
possession in a curious way though quite a credible one.
Isabel involuntarily overhears a conversation between
Azagra and her mother, and, having thus learned the terrible

secret, resolves to sacrifice herself as an expiatory victim.
She will accept the union which is so repellent to her if,
upon the expiry of the time-limit, Marsilla fails to appear ;
in that bitter hour she supposes him to be lost to her—dead,
no doubt—since for a long time there has been no news of
him whatever. The spectator, knowing that, on his return
from Palestine, Marsilla has been captured by pirates and
has since escaped unharmed from Valencia, expects him to
return at any moment. The situation is, therefore, full
of dramatic interest and the emotion which it arouses
is not only logical and natural but also of a gripping
intensity.

Zulima, less poetically conceived than Isabel, is the melodramatic personage of the play, and stamps it indelibly, as
Azucena stamps *El Trovador*, as belonging to the Romantic
movement of the early nineteenth century. Her interven-
tion precipitates the events of the drama and prepares the
catastrophe. The violently revengeful spirit which she
displays is, up to a certain point, improbable, for it is hardly
justified by the motives of her resentment. She brings
Isabel the false news of her lover's death, and plots with
highwaymen to capture Marsilla and keep him prisoner
during the performance of the religious ceremony. Then,
still dissatisfied with the results of her own wickedness, she
conceals a poisoned dagger in order to kill both Marsilla and
Isabel. But, as fortune decrees, she dies before this can be
accomplished, at the hands of the emissary whom her consort,
the King of Valencia, has sent after her.

The scene immediately preceding the catastrophe of the
play is a particularly fine one. It is, of course, of the utmost
importance to the plot ; a high degree of passion and lofty
poetry are necessary to it if it is to produce its full effect and
stir the spectator's emotions to such a point that he accepts it.
It was greatly improved by the careful revision and partial
reconstruction which it underwent before it appeared in its
definitive form ; a number of its blemishes were expunged,
as well as a good many feeble and prosaic turns of expression.*

* *E.g.* Isabel's reply :
              Respeta los secretos de una dama
to Marsilla's anxious inquiry as to the reason
              Del prodigio infeliz de su mudanza.

This scene is in hendecasyllables throughout, assonancing in *a-a ;* never again did Hartzenbusch quite equal it in rotundity and vigour. As a rule he was unable to handle heroic verse as readily and as effectively as octosyllabic metre. The latter, in all its forms—whether *redondilla, quintilla* or *romance*—he treated with a consummate skill and mastery as effective as that of the facile, warm, melodious verse of García Gutiérrez, though the poetry of these two dramatists is of a very diffcrent character. The lyrics of Hartzenbusch, none of which are of notable merit, only rise above mediocrity when they are written in short lines : such are *Al Busto de mi Esposa, La Cama de Matrimonio* and *La Despedida.* Even in the *silva* he reaches no very great heights ; the translations from Schiller—*La Campana, La Infanticida*—are elegantly written, but are almost devoid of the lyrical movement and the high seriousness of their originals.

But the author of the first and the last act of *Los Amantes de Teruel* has certainly no need to envy even the best work of any of his contemporaries ; none of the Romantic dramatists rose higher than did Hartzenbusch here. For the first time that immortal pair of lovers whom we meet in the legend become real to us. The breath of Hartzenbusch's poetic inspiration endows them with life, and the material in which they are carved is therefore more vital and more enduring than bronze or stone ; they can never fade from the memory.

> No le mató la vengativa mora,

cries Isabel, ere she falls upon the body of her lover,

> Donde estuviera yo, ¿ quién le tocara ?
> Mi desgraciado amor, que fué su vida . . .
> Su desgraciado amor es quien le mata.
> Delirante le dije : "Te aborrezco."
> El creyó la sacrílega palabra
> Y expiró de dolor.
>          . . . Mi bien, perdona
> Mi despecho fatal. Yo te adoraba.
> Tuya fuí, tuya soy : en pos del tuyo
> Mi enamorado espíritu se lanza.*

* This is the passage as given in the definitive version, which is so unlike the once so popular original that the two have hardly more than a few phrases in

Nearly two years after this dramatic triumph, Hartzenbusch produced his second notable work : *Doña Mencía o La Boda en la Inquisición*, a three-act drama in verse, the success of which was somewhat less pronounced than that of *Los Amantes de Teruel*, though nevertheless considerable. The play is a striking study of Spanish life at the beginning of the seventeenth century, with no historical or legendary basis. The action, which takes place in Madrid, is overhung with the dark shadow of the Inquisition. Without any reactionary exaggeration, and in a thoroughly artistic form, it traces, in a way never previously achieved, a vigorous picture of the incessant terrors and disastrous events which in those days troubled and vexed the lives of so many Spaniards. Human bloodhounds known as familiars of the Holy Office would seek victims everywhere, tracking them down without scruple and causing them to be mangled and tortured by the implacable tribunal until they lost life or reason, as happens to the characters in this drama.

Without making use of violent apostrophes or futile imprecations like those of Gil y Zárate's *Carlos II el Hechizado*, which had been performed a short time previously, Hartzenbusch, with all the skill and perspicacity of the true poet, communicates a vivid impression of truth and sets before our eyes an exact picture of happenings and sufferings, not (as would have been an easier and a more conventional proceeding) within the walls of the Holy Office, but in private life, in the home, among helpless and unprotected people. A description and portrayal of these martyrs in body and spirit in a picture of reduced proportions, wrought with delicate lines, flawless language and exquisite versification—this had not yet been achieved in the new type of drama, and we do not know that it has been attempted

common. It is interesting to set the lines down here in their original form, though this is inferior in beauty to that given in the text above :

> . . . Yo le maté : quise alejarle . . .
> Que le odiaba le dije . . . El sentimiento,
> El espanto . . . ¡ Y mentí ! . . .
> Pero también de mí se apiada el cielo.
> Ya de la eternidad me abre la puerta
> Y de mis ojos huye el mundo entero,
> Y una tumba diviso solamente
> Con un cadáver, y a su lado un hueco.
> ¡ Marsilla ! yo te amé, siempre te amaba . . .
> Tú me lloraste ajena . . . tuya muero.

since. Such, at any rate, was Hartzenbusch's admirable accomplishment in *Doña Mencía*.

It is now many years since the play was last given in a Spanish theatre. The passage of a century has blurred the terrible reality of the Inquisition, long since abolished for ever and relegated to the background of history. But Ferdinand VII, who had only been dead five years when the play was first produced, would gladly have restored it in all its primitive vigour, and this fact gave the drama an actuality which it can never regain, especially since a great part of the cultured Spanish public hardly thinks it seemly to revive such unpleasant memories. Further, *Doña Mencía* has one serious defect : its argument is complicated, obscure and full of situations difficult to grasp at first sight, so that the final impression left upon the spectator is distinctly lacking in clearness.

Don Gonzalo de Mejía, a Peruvian, betrothed to Doña Mencía, has served his mother-country in the wars as captain in a Flanders regiment. Denounced to the Holy Office for having in his house a vernacular Bible and a portrait of Luther, he is haled off to prison by a familiar of the Inquisition who is also Doña Mencía's guardian. Doña Mencía is advised by her guardian to attend the tribunal in order to set forth the scruples which oppress her for having been in love with one of its suspects. She obeys, and as a result is herself arrested, suffers a month's imprisonment and is subjected to torture. Thinking to save herself, she confesses all that is asked of her, is forced to marry Don Gonzalo and finally leaves prison beside herself with grief and shame, but relying on a promise that her husband shall soon be set free. He is, however, condemned to a long period of incarceration in a Toledo convent, whence he escapes in the disguise of a friar. Reaching Mencía's house, he is discovered, after various coincidences and surprises, to be in reality the father of the girl whom he has married. He is about to kill himself, when Mencía snatches the dagger from him and stabs herself to the heart, while Gonzalo is carried off again by the *alguaciles* and condemned to life imprisonment.

This brief summary of the main action is by no means exhaustive. Mencía, for example, has a bastard sister, who at the beginning of the play is the object of Don Gonzalo's love and at the end enters the life of religion ; a poetic figure this, crossing the stage as an innocent, flower-crowned victim, full of the grace and charm of youth, but condemned to bury herself for ever in the cloister. Other events complicate the story still more, but fortunately without unduly weakening its dramatic effect, which reaches a climax in the final scenes of the second act and again at the play's heart-rending conclusion.

For a long time Hartzenbusch continued to write for the stage, but never again did he display the abundance of inspiration which gave birth to these two harmonious and symmetrical dramas and showed posterity what his talent was capable of achieving. By these he must be judged. In his later works defects, both in his choice of argument and in the development of his plan, became more and more pronounced as his poetic talent gradually diminished. The dramatic vigour of his imagination grew less, though he contrived to maintain his purely formal excellence. Always a skilful workman, he became progressively more proficient in the handling of his tools and in the chiselling of that fine metal which was the material of his greatest creations.

*Alfonso el Casto*, which appeared nearly three years after *Doña Mencía*, has little interest other than stylistic ; the King's supposed passion for his sister leaves both reader and spectator completely cold. Such unnatural amours, if they are to acquire tragic force, need to be hinted at rather than fully developed, and to be enshrouded in such an atmosphere as that of the incurable melancholy of Chateaubriand's *René* or the terrible misanthropy of Byron's *Manfred*. Of anything like this Hartzenbusch was temperamentally quite incapable ; his play is weak, and contains only a few vigorous speeches, which have something of the fire of those declaimed by Marsilla, in the *Amantes de Teruel*, or by Inés, in *Doña Mencía*. Such are :

> ¡ Qué poco, serrana bella,
> Te ennegrecieron los soles !
> ¡ Qué poco se ha ejercitado
> La mano con que avergüenzas
> El blanco vellón que coges !

Or again, in the same scene :

> Con ese desdén, zagala,
> Con que tus elogios oyes,
> Me pagó también un día
> La ingrata de mis amores.

Era una tarde de otoño,
Trasponía el horizonte
El sol, dorando la cima
De los árboles mayores
Que daban sombra a una casa
Coronada de una torre :
Cantaban allá a lo lejos
Alegres trabajadores,
Que cerraban los portillos
De unos rotos paredones :
Percibíase a otro lado
El eco de una harpa, dócil
A una mano que en la tuya
Hizo el Señor que se copie . . .

After writing a play called *Primero yo* (1842), which, with but little success, dramatizes an episode from a German philosophical novel, Hartzenbusch obtained a better reception, in 1844, with *La Jura en Santa Gadea*. The protagonist of this play is the Cid, who is always well received by a Spanish public, but the author gives us not so much the hero of Guillén de Castro and Corneille as the Cid of the *gestas* and the chronicles. He is the tenacious and intrepid Rodrigo, who extracts from the King the famous oath of humiliation by which he denies his complicity in the treason of Vellido Dolfos. At times the action of the play languishes and the plot is overweighted with useless detail which we owe to the author's meticulous anxiety to follow tradition. Yet in one or two places dramatic effect is happily combined with poetical expression to produce scenes of real beauty.

None of Hartzenbusch's later compositions reached this level. The chief of them are *La Madre de Pelayo* (1846), a gloomy play clothing in Spanish dress a story somewhat similar to that of Mérope, which provided Voltaire with the argument of what was perhaps his finest play, and *La Ley de Raza* (1852), an obscurer and more artificial drama than any of its predecessors. But as before, and as always, the form of both plays is noteworthy ; and at times the industry with which it has been chiselled and polished ceases to be perceptible and we have the charm of apparent naturalness and facility.

Little by little, the erudition of Hartzenbusch began to transcend his merits as a poet. For a great part of his life he worked in the National Library of Madrid : after spending nearly twenty years as an assistant there, he was promoted, in 1862, to be its Director. He published various editions of classical Spanish authors (principally of dramatists), studying texts that had never previously been examined or collated. The important part which he played in the publications of the Spanish Academy fully occupied the remainder of his time and kept him from creative production.

To all these tasks he applied himself with exemplary constancy and punctiliousness, though he had not all the scrupulous accuracy demanded by modern scholarship. He was sometimes led astray by his poetical imagination, which in crucial questions would lead him to propose illogical solutions or over-audacious changes. His edition of *Don Quijote* so far disfigures Cervantes' prose that he himself afterwards repented of having published it. In many volumes of Rivadeneyra's "Biblioteca de Autores Españoles" the student comes across words and phrases which, to quote Cuervo, he believes to have been written by authors of the Golden Age, but which in reality belong solely and exclusively to their collector.

Hartzenbusch never entered politics. He remained true to the same liberal ideas that he had embraced in his youth and accepted only such public offices as were congenial to his tastes and relevant to his studies. He died in his native Madrid, in August 1880, a month before his seventy-fourth birthday. He was an excellent poet, a cultured, scholarly and industrious worker and at the same time a pleasant and modest man in private life. Few men in his own country have possessed all these qualities in equal measure.

# CHAPTER V

## JOSÉ DE ESPRONCEDA

### I

Espronceda, in Emerson's well-known phrase, is the "representative man" of Spanish romanticism. And this not only by virtue of his writings, intensely personal and intensely revolutionary as they are, but also in his physical appearance, his character, his excesses and the entire story of his conflict-ridden life. Had he, like Byron, been a man of means, and had the hostility of public opinion forced him to leave his country and seek outlets abroad for his abundant energy, he would very probably have crowned his career, as Byron did, by embracing some great enterprise involving fierce military strife and giving him the opportunity for outstanding heroism.

So frequently has Espronceda been called the "Spanish Byron" that it is difficult to avoid repeating that phrase in referring to his life and writings. Not only are the two poets alike in the general tone of their works, and in many of the details of them, but, quite apart from this relationship, there is a marked personal similarity between them as regards both the best and the worst of their qualities.

It is only as a lyric poet that Espronceda reaches distinction ; in no other *genre* does he even approach the same level. His one novel, *Sancho Saldaña*, and the fragments of his drama *Blanca de Borbón* make it clear that his incursions into these fields have only done harm to his reputation. The satirical part of the *Diablo Mundo* is weak ; unlike the satires of Byron, it lacks both depth and range. The lyrical part of that poem, on the other hand, contains some magnificent passages : such are the brilliant arpeggios of its introduction and the impassioned octaves of the *Canto a Teresa*. The same is true of the *Estudiante de Salamanca* : its finest passages are the descriptions of the delirium and the death of Elvira and the lyrical fantasia which brings it to a close. On the other hand, the meeting of Don Félix and the brother of the victim in the gambling-house lacks the dramatic force essential to the situation.

No other lyrical poet in Spain of the same calibre can be found till the very end of the century. Neither García y Tassara, nor Zorrilla, nor Campoamor, three poets all of approximately the same age and all younger than Espronceda, nor any of their successors, with the possible exception of Bécquer, can fairly be said to have surpassed him. Earlier in the century and in the century preceding no lyric poet can approach him save Quintana in the finest of his compositions, and Quintana and Espronceda, after all, were attempting two entirely different things. Quintana, in such odes as *Al Combate de Trafalgar*, *A España* and *Al Armamento de las Provincias*, reached as high a point as was possible to one shackled with eighteenth-century formulas ; Espronceda broke away from the bonds of tradition, found new sources of inspiration and soared aloft into new worlds of which his predecessors were ignorant.

The vicissitudes of his troubled existence are in the closest harmony with the character and form of his writings : his life and his works are a mutual commentary on one another. Before attempting a judgment of his writings, therefore, we shall examine his life story.

II

Espronceda was born in 1808 in the little Extremaduran town of Almendralejo ; his father, a colonel in the army, happened to be engaged in some operations in that district and his wife was accompanying him. At that time the Napoleonic wars were in progress, and the very foundations of the country, so soon to be rudely shaken, were already beginning to tremble.

The boy spent his childhood and early youth in Madrid. After a short course of military instruction in the Artillery College at Segovia, the discipline of which he was unable to tolerate, he studied literature with some success at a newly founded clerical school, the Colegio de San Mateo, one of the masters in which was the erudite Sevilian poet Alberto Lista. He remained here until 1823, when, under Ferdinand VII's resuscitated *régime* of tyranny, the college, with many other centres of learning and culture, was closed.

Espronceda, like many of his companions, could not endure the oppression which the country was now suffering. A natural leader, a temperamental revolutionary and a boy of unusual pugnacity and courage, he was anxious to do what he could to prevent Spain's further decadence. Hardly had he left college in 1823 when Madrid was stirred by one horrible act of cruelty after another, in particular by the unnecessarily barbarous execution of Riego. Young as he was, Espronceda began to dabble in conspiracy. Youths of fifteen not being admitted to membership of secret societies, he founded one of his own, composed entirely of boys, and called the Society of the Numantinos. Before long its existence was discovered, its members were brought to trial and Espronceda was condemned to five years' reclusion in a Franciscan friary at Guadalajara. He was set free long before the five years were over, for the Superior preferred taking the risk of letting him go to having so intelligent and excitable a youth among his novices. Soon after, whether (as Escosura tells us) because of his complicity in a military *pronunciamiento* or whether (as he himself says) because he wanted to see the world, he left his country for Gibraltar, whence he sailed in a short time for Lisbon.*

His brief and animated description of this short voyage concludes with a frequently quoted and most characteristic passage :

> The quarantine officer came on board and demanded some small payment. I took out a five-peseta piece, the only money I had, and they gave me two pesetas' change, which I flung into the Tagus, for I had no desire to enter so great a capital with so little money.

By the time he wrote this, Espronceda, for all his youthfulness, had evidently donned the disguise of a nineteenth-century Romantic and acquired the habit of those Byronic *boutades*, which were not always as innocuous as on this occasion, and in which he indulged to the end. Already, when in Madrid, he had shown signs of future poetic talent, conceiving and, at Lista's advice and under his direction, partially composing the epic poem of *Pelayo*, fragments of

---

* *Tres poetas contemporáneos.* Discurso leído por Don Patricio de la Escosura en la sesión inaugural de la Academia Española (Madrid, 1870). "De Gibraltar a Lisboa. Viaje histórico," published in *El Pensamiento* and reproduced by Rodríguez Solís in *Espronceda : su tiempo, su vida y sus obras* (Madrid, 1883), p. 77.

which appear at the beginning of his collected writings. The form in which we now have them, however, represents, not the original work of the boy of eighteen, but a revision made for inclusion in the first collection of the author's poetry, published in 1840.

Lista not only arranged the plan of the poem for his pupil but also helped him in its development. According to Escosura's testimony in his edition of Espronceda's works (published, long after his death, in 1884) two of the stanzas were written entirely by Lista ; they are perhaps more correct but are certainly no better than Espronceda's own. Furthermore, Lista prepared many other stanzas, which Escosura disinterred and published in an appendix to the same edition ; but Espronceda's sudden departure from Madrid left the work half finished and it was never resumed. If we consider the early date of the fragments and assume the corrections subsequently made in them to have been chiefly verbal, we shall allow that they were a notable achievement and a sure presage of future greatness.

The argument of *Pelayo* is not so much that of an epic poem as of a long semi-classical *leyenda* in twelve cantos, containing erudite reminiscences of famous precursors, from Virgil to Tasso and Voltaire. One is reminded somewhat of Rivas' *Florinda* : neither in the *genre* nor in its conception does the poem bear the slightest resemblance to any of its author's later work, from the *Pirata* to the *Diablo Mundo*.

Despite the importance in Spanish history of the semi-legendary Pelayo, his story has never inspired a Spanish work worthy of high eulogy. Neither in the times of the *gestas* and the popular ballads nor in any later epoch is there a single noteworthy epic or semi-epic poem built around the hero of Covadonga, nor, if we except Quintana's *Pelayo* (a piece of eloquence rather than of poetry, the execution of which is superior to its conception), is there any drama that achieves more than mediocrity. Spanish writers might well see in Pelayo a symbol of the inspiring principle of the Reconquest and the heroic spirit of a conflict which extended over many centuries. Yet in the literature and pictorial art of Spain Pelayo occupies a position of far less importance than either Count Fernán González, the fabulous Bernardo del Carpio or the Cid Campeador. It is hardly likely that if

Espronceda had taken up his epic again at a later date he would have done it greater justice than his predecessors.

He remained only a short time in Lisbon, for Portugal offered scant hospitality to the victims of Ferdinand VII's despotism : Don Miguel de Braganza lost little time, as a rule, in either imprisoning or expelling them. So Espronceda soon set sail again, this time for England.

Among the many Spaniards in England who met his boat —which was known to be bringing Spanish exiles—was a girl of singular beauty whom Espronceda had met in Lisbon and with whom he had fallen deeply in love. When he had first made her acquaintance she was unmarried, but since that time she had become the wife of a Spanish business man living in England. This girl was Teresa, whose love was for a long time to fetter Espronceda's steps, and who was to die in despair and abandonment after both lovers had brought upon themselves the sum total of misfortunes that can result from the indulgence of ardent passion accompanied by a disregard for the laws and customs of society. But she was also to inspire her former lover, who survived her but a short time, with the most beautiful, sincere and eloquent of all his poems, if also the least noble and generous. The ill-fated union which the two began in London was to be an inexhaustible source of pain and misery, but the artist's talent was to become fruitful and multiply there, through his contact with a new fount of poetry—that of Byron, Scott, Shelley, Keats and all the other great poets and prose-writers of that time who were bringing new glory to English literature.

The youthful studies of Espronceda, both at school and under the private tuition of Lista, had thoroughly prepared him to receive and retain impressions of this new literature. He had already some theoretical knowledge of English and with his increased opportunities of practice quickly improved in it ; he was thus able to read all these writers with ease and to assimilate their genius. Later, in Paris, when he came into touch with the distinctively French type of romanticism, which was in closer harmony with his character, he read Béranger and Victor Hugo with no less enthusiasm ; he may also have enjoyed the first works of Alfred de Musset, so full of an audacity and irony well befitting the *début* of this Byron of France. But nothing that

Espronceda wrote before his return to Spain can convey an adequate idea of the depth of the revolution that was taking place in his literary ideas. The elegy *A la Patria*, the poem inspired by the death in battle of Colonel De Pablo, the sonnet to Torrijos and his fifty-two companions shot in Málaga were merely the natural outcome of Lista's instruction and Quintana's example. We cannot detect in them the accent of the enthusiast for Byron and Victor Hugo, the vibrations of which will soon be heard in the *Pirata* and the *Reo de Muerte*.

With the fall of the French Bourbons and the ascent of the Duke of Orleans to the throne, Espronceda entered upon a period of active politics and convulsive agitation which lasted for three years, until the death of Ferdinand VII and the complete amnesty that followed it. During these years he naturally had neither time nor opportunity for the employment of his poetical talents. Hardly had the numerous exiles learned that the King of Spain had decided not to recognize Louis-Philippe than they flocked from all sides to the departments nearest the Spanish frontier, and, ready armed, awaited the opportune moment to enter their oppressed country and provoke guerrilla warfare till they should succeed in arousing a general rebellion against their oppressor. Like most political exiles, they were victims of their illusions and knew little of what was going on in their own country, so that they hoped easily to obtain at least the tacit approval of the French government and imagined that the Spanish people, tired of their unworthy and ungrateful king, would at once respond by enlisting with them against the regular Spanish army.

Espronceda was among the first of the exiles to descend the slopes of the Pyrenees into Navarre. He was one of a company of nearly two hundred men, of various nationalities, under the command of Colonel De Pablo. Hardly had they left Valcarlos, the frontier village of the Pass of Roncesvalles (Roncevaux), when they met a small army of more than a thousand Royalists awaiting them with the cry : "¡ Viva el Rey absoluto !" The centre of this army was formed by a company of Navarrans, belonging to the regiment formerly commanded by De Pablo, who had believed that his presence and the sound of his voice would suffice to awaken in his former subordinates the old sentiments of love

and respect. Vain hope! At the first volley a number of
the rebels fell, mortally wounded, among them De Pablo
himself. The remainder returned to France as best they
could, and with them Espronceda, who had fought courage-
ously beside his unfortunate leader. The other groups of
rebels all suffered a similar fate : Mina, Valdés and Méndez
Vigo in the north, from Catalonia to Galicia, and in the
following year Torrijos in Andalusia.

When Ferdinand saw that enemies were gathering on the
French frontier, he hastened to give Louis-Philippe his
official recognition. From that time the difficulties of
organizing expeditions in France against Spain increased
greatly, and even the die-hards among the rebels had
perforce to acknowledge the uselessness of the proceeding,
since the masses in Spain lent their willing support to the
King, whether from lack of initiative or from a recollection
of all the sacrifices they had made to defend the throne
against Napoleon.

Eager for activity and combat, Espronceda now turned
his eyes towards unhappy Poland, for, as the Czar of Russia
was also slow to recognize Louis-Philippe, it had been
thought possible to gain the latter's moral support for a
great movement of all friends of liberty towards the Vistula
and that region where blood and fire were mingling in one
last effort for independence. But this hope, too, came to
naught. Czar Nicolas at once put aside his haughty attitude
and yielded to the point of conforming to the international
protocol and welcoming his new colleague ; while Casimir
Périer became president of the Government with the special
aim of disillusioning all the revolutionaries. Once again
Poland succumbed and Spain dragged on in the same state
of lethargy as before.

Some two years had still to elapse before the exiles could
return to their own country. Still living with Teresa,
Espronceda spent the greater part of this time in Paris,
finding interest and attraction in witnessing the spectacle of
an active literary renaissance in the French capital and
possibly schooling his temperament somewhat to learn the
lessons of adversity ; this, however, to no great extent, since
his own line never ceased entirely to be true of him :

Siempre juguete fuí de mis pasiones.

Fortunately he was not, like some of his compatriots, entirely devoid of the means of livelihood, nor was he forced into the humiliating position of accepting financial assistance from the French government.  His family had not forsaken him, and from time to time sent him help, despite the suspicious attitude of the authorities at Madrid, who dealt vigorously with persons supposed to be communicating with agitators abroad, especially with such as were conspiring so openly against the throne.

At length, however, Ferdinand died, and the frontiers were thrown open to those who had been in exile.  A mere list of the men who returned to Spain and began immediately to take part in its literary and political life would have sufficed to establish the certainty of its early regeneration.  Martínez de la Rosa, Saavedra, Alcalá Galiano, Argüelles and many more were well known : hardly known at all to the majority of Spaniards was this poet of twenty-four years of age, whom a literary education received abroad and the spontaneous activity of a soaring fancy predestined, as a matter of course and with no great effort on his own part, to be one of the leaders of the new literature.  Indeed, he might well have been the outstanding figure in Spanish literature of the entire century had he been content with the future greatness which was opening before him instead of plunging so deeply into politics that it absorbed the best part of his energy.  But his natural grace, his elegant figure, his relative financial independence, his prodigality, talent, energy and frankly vicious life, helped, in the continually disturbed state of internal Spanish politics, to make him at once an arbiter of fashion, a leader of youth and a popular agitator, sceptical, ambitious and ready at any time, like another Alcibiades, to descend at the risk of his own life into the arena.

At first he favoured the idea of imitating his former school-fellows, Pezuela and Escosura, and of following his father's example, by becoming a soldier ; his father, who lived till the year after his son's return, had by now been given a brigade.  The young man therefore entered the select military body known as the Guardias de Corps, but remained there for a short time only.  He was imprudent enough to write a few *décimas*, now lost, which were recited at a banquet, and which, under pretence of extolling freedom, abused the Government. As a result he was arrested, expelled from his regiment and exiled to the village of Cuéllar, near Segovia, where he found the inspiration for his novel *Sancho Saldaña o El Castellano de Cuéllar*, published shortly afterwards. As we have already said, the novel is of little value : it consists of a series of tableaux with the vaguest claims to be considered historical and presenting only the slightest interest.

When Martínez de la Rosa came into power, Espronceda returned from Cuéllar to Madrid without permission. It was publicly asserted that the author-statesman was aware of this disobedience of a brother author and had overlooked it, a suggestion which Espronceda hastened to deny in the Press with his usual outspokenness. "I came to Madrid," he wrote, "as I go everywhere, relying upon myself entirely ; I never go about under the patronage of any minister or ruler."

These events caused Espronceda to change the direction of his career. Early in 1834, with Ros de Olano, Ventura de la Vega and others, he founded a journal called *El Siglo*. Though its politics were in opposition to those of the Government, it was quite reasonable in its tone and won the approval and collaboration of many older writers of recognized judgment, such as Quintana, Lista and the Duque de Frías. There was nothing in Madrid at this time even faintly approaching liberty of the Press, and *El Siglo*, harassed by the censorship, found its contributions incessantly abridged and mutilated, so that in the end it died a violent death, after living seven weeks and making only fourteen appearances. The last issue was composed of blank pages, together with the titles of the articles which should have appeared in it and which the censor had forbidden. "Nos deja en el siglo XIV," was Larra's apt remark, "es decir, en la Edad Media." It has always been said that the idea of this original kind of adieu to the public came from Espronceda.

Though still but twenty-six, he now found himself something of a political personage. It soon became clear, at all events, that there were those who so considered him. Early on one July morning of this same year, his house was suddenly invaded by the police, his papers were seized and he was haled off to the public prison. Here for several days

he remained, being at first allowed no communication with
the outside world.    Finally, without any form of trial, he was
commanded by a royal decree to settle his affairs within a
week and leave for Badajoz, with the express prohibition to
return to the capital.

It was with difficulty that he was able to get this decree
countermanded, but in the end it was rescinded while
Martínez de la Rosa was still in office.    In the next year,
under another man of letters—not a poet, but a historian,
the Conde de Toreno—freedom of the individual was no
more secure : the idea prevailed that one could always
fight Carlist "obscurantism" and at the same time minimize
the interference of the people in politics.    In August 1835,
the national militia in Madrid rose against the ministry ;
among the insurgents was Espronceda, a captain in the
third battalion, who thus found occasion to teach his fellow-
countrymen something of what he had seen in Paris of the
art of barricading.    Toreno fell, but in the next year there
was a more serious rising, a repercussion of the movement
of La Granja which had forced Queen Cristina to revive
the defunct Constitution of 1812 and proclaim it ;  this
movement overthrew Toreno's successor Istúriz.

We shall make no attempt to detail the vicissitudes of
political life in Spain during those years of tumult.    Espronceda continued to be a conspirator—occupying himself
either in proclaiming advanced ideas with increased vigour
or in exciting the people against Queen Cristina, once the
idol of the Liberals but now the object of implacable hatred.
In September 1840, when a periodical called *El Huracán*
was prosecuted for maintaining Cristina's legal incapacity
for the guardianship of her daughter the Queen by reason
of her secret marriage with Don Fernando Múñoz, Espronceda appeared for the defence and made an impassioned
speech in which he boldly predicted the future victory of the
Republican ideal, prophesying that the day would come
when, if they wished to uproot it, they would have to "shoot
the entire human race."

The Prime Minister at this time was the vanquisher of
Carlism, General Espartero, in whom the Liberal opposition
had found a leader of great military prestige.    Cristina now
abdicated the regency.    In this same year Espronceda lost
his mother—a sore and irreparable bereavement for him,

for it was she who had stood by him through thick and thin and sent him money whenever he was in need of it, despite his incorrigible recklessness and extravagance. His own life, therefore, underwent a radical change just at the time when the political situation of the country was changing also.

The Cortes met again in the summer of 1841, when Espartero assumed the regency and Argüelles was appointed guardian of the Queen, who already had Quintana as her *ayo instructor*. At the end of this year, whether from weariness of a life of conflict, or whether because the loss of his mother had temporarily diminished his resources, Espronceda accepted the post of secretary to the Spanish Legation in the Low Countries—quite a minor appointment, which hardly seems to have been in keeping with his age and literary reputation.

He remained at this post but for a few months. Elected a parliamentary deputy, for Almería, he returned to his country at the beginning of 1842, took his seat in the Chamber and set about his new duties with all seriousness. He addressed the House frequently, and his contributions to its discussions, though not brilliant (for he had no great gifts of oratory), showed marked application and a real anxiety to master whatever subject he might be treating. Here we appear to be seeing Espronceda under a new aspect. Unfortunately, however, we also begin to see a change in him physically. His impetuous entry into party politics, his excesses of every kind, his by no means affected weariness and depression—all these things predisposed him to fall victim to the first illness that might attack him. Such an attack, as it chanced, came quickly. He spoke in the Cortes for the last time on May 16, 1842, was present at the next day's session, and, six days later, on May 23, was dead. His age was but thirty-four ; and in him the country lost its most skilful craftsman in lyric poetry at the very time when that poetry was reaching a period of renaissance and new fertility.

### III

Espronceda's verse compositions were first collected and published in book form in May 1840. The volume would seem to have been completed and prepared for publication some time previously, since its prologue, written by García de Villalta, is dated June 1839. It contains all Espronceda's best work with the exceptions of *El Diablo Mundo* and the short poem *Al Dos de Mayo*. This latter was written in 1840 and published in various periodicals of that year.

Any edition that omits *El Diablo Mundo* undoubtedly lacks some of Espronceda's most original and brilliant writing. Yet such varied productions as *El Pirata* and *El Mendigo*, the gloomy fantasy *El Reo de Muerte*, the *leyenda* entitled *El Estudiante de Salamanca* and the lines *A Jarifa* are sufficient to convey a clear and precise impression of the range and vigour of his genius.

The *Pirata*, in its own way, comes very near to perfection ; it is one of those rare and finished productions in which the artist accomplishes precisely what he has set out to achieve and contrives to satisfy both his least cultured reader and his most exacting literary critic. The idea or design of writing it was probably suggested to the poet by the song of Conrad's companions which forms the opening of Byron's *Corsair*. Although the two poems are by no means identical, they convey a similar effect : without directly imitating Byron, Espronceda has surrounded his poem with a Byronic atmosphere. There is, however, a very marked difference between them. The majestic tone of Byron's magnificent verse—he writes in that "good old and now neglected heroic couplet," as he calls his measure—certainly suggests that he is intending to compose a poem of epic character. Espronceda's variety of metre and diversity of rhythm, even apart from the musical refrain which ends each of his *coplas*, announce that he is not engaged upon a narration, but is outlining one single figure, at full length and in heroic proportions, against the background of a luminous seascape, and that the exquisite music of his versification and the symmetry and harmony of the entire piece are introducing a fresh art, a new kind of poetry. Other poets—Luis de León, for example, and Quintana—had written master-pieces of lyric verse, expressing thoughts of vaster import than Espronceda's and creating images unforgettably precise. But never before had a Spanish poet displayed such great variety and drawn pictures so full of poetic truth and plastic vigour, in verses more robust, more harmonious and of more brilliant colouring.

*El Mendigo*, cast in a similar mould, is more of a satire and

the general effect it produces is one of excessive artificiality
and remoteness from real life. But in Spain, where the
practice of mendicity is recognized and the beggar is a
familiar figure at the church door, Espronceda's lines ring
quite true :

> Que mis rezos
> Si desean,
> Dar limosna
> Es un deber . . .
> Y doquiera
> Vayan leyes,
> Quiten reyes,
> Reyes den,
> Al mendigo
> Por el miedo
> Del castigo,
> Todos hacen
> Siempre bien.

Next to these two *canciones*, the best known of Espronceda's
short poems is that entitled *A Jarifa, en una orgía*, especially
noteworthy for the accent of personal emotion which persists
throughout the piece and makes itself heard beneath the tone
of pompous affectation characterizing such declarations as :

> ¡ Sólo en la paz de los sepulcros creo !

The variety of rhythm in the poem is admirable. Compare,
for example, these two stanzas constructionally identical but
in their music quite unlike :

> Yo me arrojé, cual rápido cometa,
> En alas de mi ardiente fantasía,
> Doquier mi arrebatada mente inquieta
> Dichas y triunfos encontrar creía.
>
> Pasad, pasad en óptica ilusoria
> Y otras jóvencs almas engañad :
> Nacaradas imágenes de gloria,
> Coronas de oro y de laurel, pasad.

But the pearl of the collection of 1840 is *El Estudiante de
Salamanca*, a fantastic piece clothing a popular tradition with
the splendid finery of Romantic poetry. Of all Espronceda's
works it is this that shows the most direct influence of Byron.
Don Félix de Montemar, a Salamancan student and a

libertine ("segundo Don Juan Tenorio"), woos, seduces and
abandons Doña Elvira de Pastrana, and so becomes the cause
of her death. This crowning deed of villainy completes the
measure of his crimes in the eyes of divine justice. Don
Diego challenges him to a duel and is slain.

After the duel, however, Don Félix encounters a
mysteriously veiled woman, clad in white, whom he pursues
on a journey picturesquely and fantastically described, until
he meets a cortège which proves to be that of his own funeral.
He, too, has died, and his victims come to meet him : Don
Diego, "traspasado el pecho de fiera estocada" and Elvira
in the form of a "cariado, lívido esqueleto."

This concluding part of the story belongs to the fourth
and last section of the poem, which is longer than the other
three put together. Nowadays, it seems to us very anti-
quated. Even in the days when the most violent form of
romanticism was in favour, its accumulation of garish
colours was thought to be exaggerated and excessive—the
red of blood, the yellow of fire, the black of death,

> Todo en furiosa armonía,
> Todo en frenético estruendo,
> Todo en confuso trastorno,
> Todo mezclado y diverso.

But so vast is the verbal wealth of the descriptive part of the
poem, so extraordinary and harmonious its poetic style, so
skilful the gradation of its metres, passing from two-syllabled
lines to *versos de arte mayor*, and utilizing all the resources of
Spanish metric, that it will always be remembered and
quoted as a striking example of its particular class of
poetry.

The first two parts of the poem still retain their interest
and value. Espronceda's portrait of Don Félix, in octosyllabic stanzas, is perfect ; that of Elvira, in *octavas reales*,
is somewhat vaguer but none the less beautiful. The figure
of the unhappy girl, outlined with a delicate brush against a
background of exquisite poetry, is in perfect harmony with
the beautiful descriptions of her love, delirium and death.
Elvira very closely recalls Byron's Haidée, and, but for the
letter which she writes to Don Félix shortly before her death,
she would be as pure and as divinely tragic a type as that
Greek girl, the victim of another Don Juan, who, after her

lover is taken from her, remains as in a trance—"not speechless, though she spoke not"—until, after twelve days, "without a groan, or sigh, or glance to show a parting pang," she dies.

> And they who watch'd her nearest could not know
> The very instant, till the change that cast
> Her sweet face into shadow, dull and slow,
> Glazed o'er her eyes.*

As an epigraph to the second part of his poem, Espronceda prints the last lines of the stanza in *Don Juan* describing Haidée's tomb in the desert island :

> . . . no dirge, except the hollow sea's,
> Mourns o'er the beauty of the Cyclades.†

Espronceda's own painting of Elvira's sepulchre is not unworthy of a place beside this description of Byron's :

> . . . Tristes flores
> Brota la tierra en torno de su losa,
> El céfiro lamenta sus amores.
>     Sobre ella un sauce su ramaje inclina,
> Sombra le presta en lánguido desmayo,
> Y allá en la tarde, cuando el sol declina,
> Baña su tumba en paz su último rayo.

It is very strange, and indeed almost inexplicable, that for Elvira's farewell letter the Spanish poet should have imitated, and in parts should have literally copied, the very farewell which in an earlier canto of Byron's poem Julia, the married woman who was captivated by Don Juan and seduced him, writes to him as she enters the convent where her husband confines her on account of her own fault.‡ Undeniably the letter has eloquence, but the two situations and the characters are profoundly different. Espronceda, with typical brilliance, makes what he translates his own ; but nevertheless to anyone who recognizes the source of the letter it will always strike a discordant note.

---

* *Don Juan*, Canto IV, Stanza lxix.
† *Op. cit.*, Canto IV, Stanza lxxii. It is strange that in the Spanish editions of Espronceda this epigraph is invariably printed without the first two words and thus is completely devoid of meaning.
‡ *Don Juan*, Canto I, Stanzas cxcii–cxcvii.

IV

The close and direct imitation of Byron which we find in the *Estudiante de Salamanca* is very different from the use that Espronceda makes of him in *El Diablo Mundo*. With greater command of his own talent, the Spanish poet is no longer seeking a support to lean upon ; and thus this poem, in which both the constant mingling of lyric, satire and narrative, and the zigzag course of its plot, so frequently interrupted by its author's whimsical humour, recall the heroic-satirical *Don Juan* type of poem, is nevertheless a highly original work, which Espronceda fills with an abundance of poetry entirely his own.

It is essential, above everything else, to distinguish two elements in *El Diablo Mundo* : the unfinished poem in five cantos, developing the theme indicated by its title, and the so-called *Canto a Teresa*. This last is an elegiac poem of an almost unique type, comprising forty-four excellent *octavas*, so diversified in form, so skilfully constructed and so full of power and energy that it is hard to recall anything of the same kind in Spanish comparable with them.

Teresa and Espronceda, who, as we have said, had lived together since the arrival of the boy-poet in England, separated definitely and finally, at Madrid, in 1836, after an endless series of disagreements. Teresa died in 1839 ; the *Diablo Mundo* began to appear in serial form at the end of 1840 ; and the *Canto a Teresa* came out in its second instalment.

Love affairs of this kind, so publicly conducted, so violently ended, and over which death has so quickly and compassionately cast a veil of oblivion, would demand of the surviving partner, it might be supposed, the most rigorous silence. It might be hoped, at the very least, that they would not be retailed to the world with the violence and crude frankness which Espronceda displays in this Canto. When Musset published his famous *Nuit d'Octobre*, it was during the lifetime of George Sand, the woman whom he apostrophizes and curses with such fierce eloquence ; further, she was, like himself, a great literary figure, quite capable of taking her own revenge and of fighting him with his own weapons, as indeed she did, telling the world, when it suited her, what there was to be said on her own side.

The unfortunate Teresa, on the other hand, had died after this shipwreck of her love, and left children, and it was both unjust and unworthy of Espronceda to go into detail about the disorders which characterized his life between the time of the separation and Teresa's death.

It is right, then, to enter a vigorous condemnation of the poet's conduct ; yet at the same time it must not be overlooked that this very conduct is a testimony to the sincerity which inspired him. He described his own true feelings, as it were, with the very blood from his veins ; as he himself said, he unbosomed himself completely. For this reason, and despite the futility and impertinence of its final piece of sarcasm, the *Canto a Teresa* is equalled by few elegies for pathos and heart-rending appeal. It shows barely a trace of effort, of literary preparation or of revision. In the full maturity of his talent, impelled and inspired by the greatest crisis in his life, Espronceda wrestled boldly with the experience that, while he was still writing, oppressed him grievously and translated it into imperishable verse.

The beginning of the *Diablo Mundo* is not unlike that of Goethe's *Faust*, but the resemblance is very superficial and soon comes to an end. The idea of the rejuvenation of an old man and of his beginning life anew has been familiar in various spheres of art from time immemorial ; there is no certainty that Espronceda gave any special attention at all to the work of Goethe. In any case the German Faust is not "un hombre ya caduco," who, at a single stroke and by means insufficiently explained, obtains youth and immortality ; nor is there any point of contact between the development of *Faust* and that of the fragmentary poem of Espronceda. He seems, in this work also, rather to be following the example of Byron, who chooses for his hero "our ancient friend Don Juan," in the same way that Espronceda calls upon another "ancient friend" to help him write a poem

> Con lances raros y revuelto asunto
> De nuestro mundo y sociedad emblema.

Byron's *Don Juan*, written with the same intent, is no less full of

> Batallas, tempestades, amoríos,
> Por mar y tierra lances, descripciones

8

De campos y ciudades, desafíos
Y el desastre y furor de las pasiones ;
Goces, dichas, aciertos, desvaríos,
Con algunas morales reflexiones
Acerca de la vida y de la muerte
De mi propia cosecha, que es mi fuerte.

Nor could a philosophical work like Goethe's be built upon such foundations as those laid by Espronceda. The hero of the *Diablo Mundo*, Adán, is not a rejuvenated old man but a being newly born, for nothing remains to him of his primitive form, nor has he any consciousness of it. A lusty and vigorous youth, he enters life as Kaspar Hauser entered the streets of Nuremberg in 1828, totally devoid of knowledge, having lived down to that time in complete confinement and isolation, far removed from all human society. One could hardly travel farther from the legend of the sage who has drained all human learning and sells his soul to the devil in exchange for one instant of a complete felicity which he seeks in every source of pleasure and along every path of human activity. Espronceda makes no pretensions to portray all this—he merely asks for free room to play, laugh, scoff and give full rein to his fancy.

The only probable reminiscence of *Faust* in the *Diablo Mundo* is to be found in the first octave of the *Canto a Teresa*, where the passage beginning

¿ Por qué volvéis a la memoria mía . . .

recalls certain lines of the dedication (also written in octaves) of *Faust :*

Ihr naht euch wieder, schwankende Gestalten,
Die früh sich einst dem trüben Blick gezeigt . . .

These Espronceda might well have read in some translation which would recur to his memory when he began to write this elegy. But even such verbal similarity may be due to simple coincidence ; perhaps, indeed, this is its most likely explanation.

If the *Diablo Mundo* is not, as it professes and announces itself to be, a

traslado fiel
De la vida del hombre y la quimera
Tras de que va la humanidad entera,

it is certainly an exact reflection of the soul and the life of its author, and of all his yearnings and dreams in the course of an existence which, however brief, was a singularly full and troubled one. It reflects his errors, his passions, his griefs, his illusions, his disappointed ambitions and all the bitterness of his manifold experiences. Over all this, even over the inmost secrets of his heart, he spread a flimsy veil of sarcasm and irony and considered himself justified in concealing nothing, in making his confessions before the world and in scoffing at others as freely as he laughed at himself.

The introduction to the poem is a passage written for full orchestra, like the overture to an opera, an exquisite symphony in which almost every metrical form in the language plays its part and makes its own particular contribution to the general harmony. The whole of Romantic poetry is here in its full splendour ; no other poet has had a greater genius for that harmonious phrasing which of itself, by means of the delicate succession of its sounds, inspires a sentiment or moulds an image, never—or hardly ever—falling into triviality or vacuity.

The first Canto is also of a high order : irony, satire, quip and lofty poetry combine, sometimes on one and the same page, or even in one and the same stanza, with a strange enchantment. Its inspiration never halts, but proceeds surely, without hesitation, until it reaches the *octava* announcing the next Canto,

> El cual sin falta seguirá, se entiende
> Si éste te gusta y la edición se vende.

It is better than the first Canto of *Don Juan*, for it has more grace and variety, although Byron's Canto does not fail to convey that impression of strength and power which always characterizes him. Unhappily the inspiration of the latter part of the *Diablo Mundo* falls off greatly ; the sixth Canto and the fragments included in the posthumous edition are very weak. In the months preceding his fatal illness, Espronceda's talent seems to have become impoverished in proportion to his physical decline.

Such premature decadence and so pitiful a conclusion to so promising a life recalls the career of Espronceda's French contemporary, Alfred de Musset. Though Musset lived rather longer, until 1857, everything that he wrote after the age of thirty shows that his great faculties were rapidly diminishing and becoming exhausted. Had he died at the age of Espronceda, posterity would have lost nothing. Both poets tried to live at too rapid a pace, and so wore themselves out and reached the end of their achievements at an age when others who had grown up with them were starting to make fresh conquests and to score new triumphs.

# CHAPTER VI

## JOSÉ ZORRILLA

### I

In his *Recuerdos del tiempo viejo*, an untrustworthy authority as regards facts and dates but a pleasant narrative clearly inspired by a wish to set down a faithful account of the past, Zorrilla describes how, soon after the day when he read those verses at the grave of Larra which were to place him in the front rank of his contemporaries before he was twenty, he was taken by José García de Villalta to pay a visit to Espronceda. The two poets quickly developed the closest friendship. "Yo creía, yo idolatraba en Espronceda," writes Zorrilla in the *Recuerdos* :

> Si aquel oráculo divino desaprobaba mis versos, desdeñaba el homenaje, no tenía más remedio que suplicar contrito a mi padre que me matriculase en la universidad de Vergara.

The idolized poet, who was recovering at the time from a serious illness, gave the warmest of receptions to his hero-worshipper ; the two would often remain together into the small hours of the morning, long after Espronceda's other visitors—political friends, for the most part—had left the house. In this way Zorrilla came to know more of Espronceda's poems than were published in the periodicals. The elder poet read and discussed with the younger others which he was engaged in writing or had only planned : such were the lines *A Jarifa*, the *Estudiante de Salamanca* and perhaps the first draft of the *Diablo Mundo*.

At this time Zorrilla was on the staff of *El Español*, a journal edited by García de Villalta. He published his poems in its special Sunday edition, and for these, apart from his salary as a staff contributor, he received a fee. The paper was widely read and had an excellent reputation ; Larra, among others, had written for it and Espronceda was one of its principal collaborators. Zorrilla was thus well established on the way to success from a very early point in his career and found himself in a position to give rein to his talent and write with complete independence.

García de Villalta, who did so much to lighten and shorten the trying period of Zorrilla's apprenticeship to the literary art, receives a striking eulogy in the *Recuerdos*. He was already known as author of *El Golpe en Vago*, a fairly successful novel attacking the Society of Jesus as it had existed in Spain during the eighteenth century, in much the same spirit as *Doña Mencía* exposed the social troubles caused in the seventeenth century by the cruelty, intolerance and vigilance of the Holy Office. To posterity he is better known as the author of a verse translation of Shakespeare's *Macbeth*, which was greatly praised by Enrique Gil in the *Correo Nacional* (December 1838), but on the stage, notwithstanding the vogue of Romantic drama, was greeted only with hisses and laughter. This failure, famous in the annals of the Teatro del Príncipe, cannot be wholly attributed to the translator, whose work is deserving of appreciation, and, in parts, of great praise. It is probably due rather to the lack of interest that Spain has always shown in the plays of Shakespeare, the more striking when contrasted with the popularity of Byron and Scott. Even a critic as well read in various literatures as Juan Valera could write at a later date : "I should place Shakespeare below the level of Cervantes, and about on that of Calderón ; he is almost the equal of Lope." To at least one Spanish-speaking critic this amounts to literary heresy, if not, indeed, to blasphemy.

In another part of the *Recuerdos* Zorrilla describes the English as "the most disagreeable individuals in the human race." Certainly what he took from Espronceda's writings —in particular from the *Estudiante de Salamanca*—was not the exotic and Byronic elements, but only the essentially Spanish. It was probably owing to Espronceda's influence, however, that he very soon left behind his early attachment to purely lyric verse of the type of *El Reló* or *El Día sin sol*, a *genre* in which he was incapable of rising above a definitely low level, and that he discontinued his feeble imitations of Victor Hugo's *Orientales*. His future lay along quite a different road, that of patriotic legend and picturesque, animated narration. In this type of poetry he achieved brilliance at a very early date, with *El Cristo de la Vega*, and above all with *El Capitán Montoya*, the hero of which, like Don Félix de Montemar, is a new incarnation of that imperishable national type Don Juan Tenorio, and, when presented in another legend, and also in a most successful drama, was destined to lay the firm foundation of his creator's amazing popularity.

## II

Zorrilla paid even less attention to his country's politics than did García Gutiérrez and Hartzenbusch, and as there is no extraordinary event in his life to be related, the essential part of it can be described very briefly.

He was born at Valladolid on February 21, 1817.

> Valladolid, hoy triste y silenciosa,
> En otro tiempo alegre y bulliciosa
> Y de la corte de Castilla asiento.

His education was begun in Madrid and continued in the universities of Toledo and Valladolid, where, at the wish of his father, a former magistrate, he began studying for the same career. One day he suddenly threw up his studies and returned to Madrid. Helped by the fame which had attached to his earliest verses, he remained in the capital and settled down to write others for so long as there was a publisher or a journal that would pay for them or a theatrical manager who would purchase and stage his dramas. When he realized that his verses were becoming less warmly received and his popularity was declining, he went to live for some time in France ; there he wrote his long-announced poem *Granada* (1852), publishing it at his own expense in Paris. This enterprise was something of a failure. One of his booksellers went bankrupt ; others failed to pay him their debts ; and in Belgium, as well as in certain parts of America, the work was reprinted without the author's permission. At this time both his parents had recently died in Spain, leaving him no inheritance : on the contrary, to use his own words, "por salvar su honor vendí mi hacienda." So far removed was he from officialdom that he had not even taken possession of the seat which had been offered him in the Spanish Academy—that of Lista. There was nothing in Spain, apparently, to keep him there ; so, at the end of

1854, he determined to emigrate to America and settle in Mexico.

In America he spent more than eleven years : for part of this time he was in Havana, but for other and longer periods in Mexico City, publishing his poems in journals or issuing them privately to subscribers.  Compatriots who had made their fortune in industry or commerce were delighted to entertain him, and ministered to their own vanity by patronizing literature in the diminutive and congenial person of the author of works as popular both in Spain and in America as *Don Juan Tenorio* and *El Zapatero y el Rey*. Like some mediæval jongleur or troubadour, he went from *liceo* to *liceo*, and from town to town, giving public readings, in a solemn voice and with rather a monotonous and sing-song intonation, like Espronceda's, of verses decidedly inferior to his own *juvenilia*.  But this poet who, according to his own confession, "never sought after fortune" was only too unsuccessful in finding it.  Certainly, for one brief and exceptional period during the ill-fated reign of the Emperor Maximilian, it seemed as though he were likely to enter politics.  But he did so only in appearance.  The Emperor appointed him, first of all, director of his private theatre, and then his Reader, "on condition that he did no reading" ; each appointment carried a salary which, after meeting his expenses, left only the smallest surplus.

"An event for which God alone was responsible completely changed my social position," he says, without any further explanation, in the *Recuerdos*, and he decided, by agreement with Maximilian, to return for a short time to Spain ; the Emperor commissioned him to write part of his history, with the aid of data and documents that he would give him, and to have it published in Europe.  But events made this impossible and the defeat and execution of the Emperor, in 1867, upset all his plans.  He could not make up his mind to return to Mexico.  "I was plunged into affliction," he wrote, "and burdened with debt, but at least I was free to say what I liked and to choose a corner of the world to die in."

But he was a long way, as events proved, from dying.  He was fifty years old when the second monarchical *régime* came to so untimely an end with the shooting of Maximilian at Querétaro, and more than twenty-five years of abundant productivity were to elapse before he finally laid down his pen. He wrote, according to his own somewhat gloomy account of himself, because poverty had forced him into "the insecure and hazardous profession of literature, quite devoid of a future in Spain." No collection has yet been made of the whole of his productions during this quarter-century, nor is it likely that any such collection will be attempted. His original inspiration seldom revisited him and little that he now wrote is worthy even of mention. The Academy again elected him to membership, and this time he did not scorn to accept the invitation and write his *discurso de ingreso ;* he composed it, however, in verse, and remained about the least academic of Spanish poets either of his own day or of any other. The usual *salón* of the Academy used for such ceremonies as the admission of new members was thought to be too small for so notable an occasion as his solemn reception and the great hall of the University of Madrid was requisitioned, the King presiding.

Few of his latest works found purchasers, and still fewer, it would seem, readers ; but some of his dramas, especially *Don Juan Tenorio*, continued to be given on the stage, and to all Spaniards he became and remained the glorious monument of a past age, of a romanticism long since extinguished. He was known everywhere as "our national poet." As such Granada honoured him, some four years before his death, by an impressive "coronation," in Charles V's palace, the crown used in the ceremony being made of gold from the river Darro. Till the end of his life, despite chronic ill-health, he remained agile and erect in bearing and never lost his native good-humour. No sooner had he died, in a Madrid attic, on January 23, 1893, shortly before his seventy-sixth birthday, than the mania for ceremonial broke out again and preparations were made for giving him a great funeral. One newspaper demanded that the coffin should be draped with the national flag, and great was the indignation when it became known that the Government, acting on lack of precedent, had refused to sanction the official participation of the army. Yet Zorrilla had never been in love with such pomp as, both in life and in death, was showered upon him so freely.

As the legendary hero *par excellence* of national tradition, he won many posthumous victories. One of the first of these may here be recounted. The last year of his life was that of the quatercentenary of the discovery of America, and a prize of one thousand pesetas was offered for the best sonnet eulogizing Isabel the Catholic.  Zorrilla's sonnet gained the prize, which was duly handed over to his widow.  Anyone who reads the sonnet, however, will find it difficult to believe that worse efforts can possibly have been submitted ; the prize was awarded not so much to Zorrilla as to his reputation.*

### III

No doubt the great age to which Zorrilla had attained, together with the recollection of his constant poverty and of the disinterestedness of his character, contributed to the outburst of enthusiasm for his talent called forth by his death.  Though he had been in receipt of an official pension from the Government, it was the people who had made him, as it were, their poet laureate.  He was probably best known, however, as a dramatist rather than as the author of those numerous verse legends, based on national traditions, which were the finest of his productions.

We have said that Zorrilla had no particular love for such pomp and circumstance as that attending his "coronation" at Granada.  The reputation, on the other hand, of being the uncrowned laureate of the people—the "national poet" of Spain—he both coveted and, from the very beginning, deliberately courted.  In the dedication of the second volume of his verses to his earliest literary patrons, Donoso Cortés and Pastor Díaz, he declares somewhat pompously that, being above all things "cristiano y español," he will not "sing hymns to Hercules, Leonidas, Horatius Cocles and Julius Cæsar and leave the Cid and Don Pedro Ansúrez in the dust of oblivion."  It would have been well if he had remained faithful to this programme, and reserved his oblivion for the Greek heroes ; he would then never have marred one of his most popular lyrics, *Gloria y Orgullo*, by lines so sonorous and so ridiculous as

> Por ti una noche con aliento extinto
> Tumba Leonidas demandó a Platea.

* There is an interesting picture of Zorrilla late in life in Boris de Tannenberg : *La Poésie castillane contemporaine* (Paris, 1889).  For the details of his death and funeral and the posthumous prize, see Emilia Pardo Bazán's *Nuevo Teatro Crítico*, Año III, nos. 25 and 26.  [The standard authority on Zorrilla's life is the three-volume biography of Narciso Alonso Cortés : see Bibliography, p. 241, below.]

Little by little this position of Zorrilla's became converted into an affectation and a pose, of a much less artistic and transcendental kind than the Byronic dandyism of Espronceda and his group, until he reached an extreme as absurd as that of the imprecation which he calls down upon himself in a feeble *redondilla* in *Las Vigilias del Estío* :

> ¡ Fálteme la luz del sol
> Si algo impío ni extranjero
> Que haya en mis versos quiero !
> Que al cabo nací español.

It is curious that the writer of these lines should have been the man who, long before, had begun his career by translating Hugo's *Orientales* and who had taken from Alexandre Dumas a large part of *Don Juan Tenorio* which is not to be found in the original sources of that drama. Presumably this was merely a weakness of Zorrilla ; it is not, of course, for that reason to be any the less condemned, but it was certainly over-emphasized by an applauding public which always tended to look approvingly upon its favourite author's pronounced *españolismo*. This may possibly have been because both author and public were unconsciously seeking some element to counterbalance the predominance of the extraordinary and the exotic in an art that had become enriched and rejuvenated by contact with other elements, which had arrived from abroad complete with their dazzling halo. It was indisputable, nevertheless, that Espronceda, with all his eagerness to follow in the steps of Byron and become byronized, had written in a language of great magnificence and vastly increased the wealth and beauty of Castilian versification ; and further, that dramatic art, which had fallen so low in Spain during the eighteenth century and at the beginning of the nineteenth, had taken new life and was being cultivated with no less brilliance than in the days of Moreto and Calderón, by García Gutiérrez, Hartzenbusch and Rivas. Spain's literary language and literary traditions made it unnecessary for an author to affect patriotic exclusiveness in order to give to anything he might fashion in conformity with the new ideas and the canons of good taste a characteristic national flavour.

Before publishing his *Granada*, Zorrilla wrote some thirty verse tales, embodying traditional or legendary material, and there is hardly one of these in which both the scene and the characters are not Spanish. Almost the same may be said of his dramas, also about thirty in number ; all of them are set in Spanish territory except *Sofronia* and *La Copa de Marfil*, two plays which, though abounding in fine lines, are but unhappy attempts at tragedy.

*El Capitán Montoya* and *Margarita la Tornera*, though not the best of Zorrilla's *leyendas*, are the best known of them, and, on the whole, the most widely esteemed. The former suffers from its similarity to the *Estudiante de Salamanca* ; the narrative is distinguished by those great gifts of facility and sonority which from this time forward characterize its author, but the poem has neither the lyrical ardour nor the massive eloquence of Espronceda.

*Margarita la Tornera*, which, like *El Capitán Montoya*, is a new version of a popular tale, is greatly superior to it. In plan it is less incoherent and scene succeeds scene more logically, though, like most of Zorrilla's works, it betrays a lack of thought and study. The public demanded verses of him and he supplied them, without devoting sufficient time to their preparation and revision. In this he resembles Lope de Vega and others both of his precursors and of his successors ; but Zorrilla's chief gifts were the superficial and musical ones of an artist and a *virtuoso*, and, as he lacks a powerfully creative imagination and a feeling for the sublime, the effect of this negligence was frequently disastrous and could not well be otherwise.

Some of Zorrilla's other *leyendas* are superior to these two and raise him to the level of Scott ; such are *La Princesa Doña Luz*, *La Azucena Silvestre* and the poem *Granada*, which closes its author's great period of fertility and brilliance. There are admirable passages in them all : *redondillas*, *quintillas*, *romances*, *versos cortos*, *octavas reales*—indeed, there is scarcely any metrical form that he does not occasionally use in his superb performances on an instrument of which he was so completely master. Of not one of his *leyendas* can it be said that it contains no single stanza, no single passage worthy of remembrance.

His influence in Spain and Spanish America was tremendous, though perhaps, in the last resort, harmful. His numerous faults—verbosity, monotony, abuse of epithets, the noisy bombast with which he endeavoured to conceal the unworthiness of an image or poverty of ideas—were all too easy to imitate, while his excellent qualities, derived not from study, perseverance and application but simply from nature, were peculiarly his own, and as such unique and inimitable. But there were naturally a few prudent and experienced writers who could appreciate and profit by all the good that was in his fertile inspiration, as we see in the later works of Andrés Bello. This may be deduced, to take but one example, from that lovely image which Bello added to his translation of Victor Hugo's *Prière pour tous* and which is not found in his original :

> ... Que cual del ara santa
> Sube el humo a la cúpula eminente,
> Sube del pecho cándido, inocente,
> Al trono del Eterno la oración :

It can hardly be doubted that this is a happy reminiscence of a passage in *La Azucena Silvestre* :

> Como al pie del altar, del vaso de oro
> De perfume oriental se exhala y sube
> Pura, ligera y transparente nube
> Que embalsama la regia catedral,
> Así a los cielos la oración del justo
> Sobre sus alas místicas se eleva.

### IV

The arguments of various of Zorrilla's best dramas—*El Zapatero y el Rey*, *Sancho García*, *El Alcalde Ronquillo* and part of *Don Juan Tenorio*—are also the themes of *leyendas* from his pen. In this as in other matters, Zorrilla followed the example of Dumas and other of the French Romantics who liked to turn their novels into dramas.

If we exclude *Juan Dandolo*, a weak play written in collaboration with García Gutiérrez, Zorrilla's first drama to be applauded on the stage was *Cada cual con su razón* (1839). Were its language a little more archaic this piece might nowadays easily pass for a cloak-and-sword play ; one would suppose it to be the work of Moreto or Rojas Zorrilla, or even of Calderón. This comparison will indicate the extent to which, at the beginning of his career, Zorrilla was immersed in Golden Age drama. But he soon became convinced that this was not the road to dramatic triumphs. The public could only endure plays of the Golden Age when they were recast to suit their liking. What in a *leyenda* might be allowed to keep its own character had on the stage to be adapted to more modern taste and to the literary conventions which came in with *La Conjuración de Venecia* and *Macías*, and were being repeated in Madrid each season in a large number of newly staged plays, some original and others translated.

The first of Zorrilla's dramas which has any significance for posterity is *El Zapatero y el Rey*, written in two parts (1840–41). Many readers consider this to be his best play, which the second part probably is, though we have also to read the first part if we are to understand the character of the captain, Blas Pérez, and if his loyalty and blind obedience to the King are not to appear to us as "fantastic and exaggerated" as the "Castilian honour" of Victor Hugo's *Hernani* appeared to Larra.

Peter the Cruel, than whom no King of Castile has endowed Spanish literature with greater picturesqueness and popularity, had from very early times supplied themes for an infinity of romances, tales and legends before Zorrilla utilized his personality in two of his dramas. For the second of these he also made very direct use of a seventeenth-century play by Hoz y Mota, *El Montañés Juan Pascual y Primer Asistente de Sevilla*, which, according to Menéndez y Pelayo,* is perhaps an adaptation of another and an older one, possibly by Lope de Vega.

The anecdote of the young shoemaker who avenges his father by killing the noble Don Juan de Colmenares, the father's murderer, was used by Zorrilla for the *leyenda* entitled *Justicias del rey Don Pedro* as well as for this drama. Blas Pérez justifies himself as follows :

> Mató a mi padre, señor,
> Y el tribunal por su oro
> Privóle un año del coro,
> Que en vez de pena es favor.

And the King, in his turn, declares :

> No han de decir, vive Dios,
> Que a ninguno de los dos
> En mi justicia prefiero,

* *Obras de Lope de Vega* (Madrid, 1899), Vol. IX.

and sentences the avenger—to make no more shoes for a year!
In both works the poet employs the same phraseology.

There is "the germ of a drama," as Zorrilla modestly
expressed it, in this part of *El Zapatero y el Rey*, but his youthful audacity and his still greatly restricted experience of the
theatre caused him to invent scenes and incidents without
troubling to lead up to them or to give them even the
slightest semblance of probability. Peter the Cruel was
already a popular figure, and his boastful sallies and parade
of judicial equity, expressed with brilliant and ready eloquence, delighted the public and made the success of the
play a certainty.

With the second part it is different. The catastrophe,
described without any excessive disfigurement of history ;
the siege of Montiel ; the iniquitous conduct of Bertrand
Duguesclin, the fierce struggle between the two brothers and
finally the shameful death of King Peter—all these incidents,
as in Ayala's chronicle, Prosper Mérimée's history or Rivas'
*Romances*, impede the progress of the spectator who may be
interested in a situation full of tragedy and violence. To
this page of history, in itself so rich in poetry and drama,
Zorrilla adds the splendid figure of Blas Pérez, the shoe-
maker-captain, grateful and loyal to his master even to the
point of sacrificing his love and his life to avenge him. The
King and his vassal are a magnificent pair of figures, as
inseparably united in the memory as Don Quijote and his
squire. The comparison is not an inapt one, if we make
allowance for the immeasurably more majestic proportions
of the characters of Cervantes.

Stylistically, again, the second part of *El Zapatero y el Rey*
is superior to the first ; it is somewhat more temperate and
much more poetical, though, as ever, the action is full of
inequalities and incoherences. Almost all the speeches of
Blas Pérez are characterized by an admirable disenchantment and nobility of feeling. One thinks, for example, of
his soliloquy when Inés has vainly implored her liberty of
him and withdraws after reminding him that in a short time
he will have to give an account of his actions to God.*

* Act III, Scene 1 :

> INÉS : Sí, Capitán, yo os perdono
> mi bárbaro sacrificio
> pero os aguardo en su juicio,
> y os emplazo ante su trono.

> Emplaza, emplázame, sí :
> Breve ha de ser este plazo,
> Pues tu muerte de rechazo
> Me dará la muerte a mí.
> ¡ Oh ! si asomarte pudieras
> A mirar mi corazón,
> Moviérate a compasión
> El ver cuál me lo laceras . . .
> Mas ¡ ay ! con cuánta verdad
> Me culpas mi villanía ! (*Pausa*)
> Y atrás no me volvería
> Por toda una eternidad.*

Then there is the magnificent ending of Act III, where the King sets off for the French camp and Blas Pérez reflects :

> Ahora, o trono para él,
> O tumba para los dos.

The last scene, which successfully overcomes the difficulty of maintaining the spectator's interest after the death of the protagonist of the play, concludes no less skilfully with these words of the Captain to Don Enrique :

> Vos por tan fiera traición
> Su corona os ceñiréis,
> Mas de espinas llevaréis
> Coronado el corazón.

For it is at this moment that Don Enrique discovers that this Doña Inés who has been sacrificed in reprisal for the death of the King is his own daughter.

No less popular than *El Zapatero y el Rey* have been the two one-act dramas *El Puñal del Godo* (1842) and *La Calentura* (1847), the first of which, according to the *Recuerdos*, was written in twenty-four hours.† The two are similar in construction and have similar general characteristics. The action in each is continuous, and the first scenes are written in octosyllables, while the others are in hendecasyllables, all stately in their sonorous eloquence. It was a real *tour de*

---

* Act III, Scene 2.
† In the dedication to Rodríguez Rubí, however, whose evidence is invoked in support of this statement, it is merely described as having been composed in a "determinado número de horas."

*force* to write over seven hundred lines of as high a standard
as these in so short a space of time, and the more incredible
a feat since Zorrilla appears to have based them upon
nothing more than four lines which he quotes from Mariana's
well-known *History*. This may not, however, have been his
only source, for Menéndez y Pelayo has made it quite clear
that, although ignorant of English, Zorrilla knew Southey's
poem *Roderic, the last of the Goths*, and both the greater part of
the story of the *Puñal del Godo* and the whole of that of *La
Calentura* may belong to him.\* From Southey, at any rate,
he must have taken the name of Romano, which he attributes to the monk in whose cabin or hermitage Don
Rodrigo lives after the rout of the Guadalete, uneasily
awaiting the Count, Don Julián, who, according to a
prophecy, is destined to seek him out and to assassinate him
with his own dagger. In *La Calentura* Rodrigo is represented
as returning to the cabin after having fought under an
assumed name at Covadonga, and Florinda as coming from
Africa in a fantastic way—"de ola en ola"—in order to seek
him, forgive him and die in his arms. Rodrigo flees from
the cabin in terror without permitting even the faithful
Theudia to accompany him. "Solo en la culpa," he
exclaims,

> Solo en la culpa, solo en el castigo,
> La maldición del cielo me acompaña.

Such brief and forceful sentences, brilliantly summing up
the situation at the end of an act or a scene, are of frequent
occurrence in Zorrilla.

Rather more than two years after the composition of *El
Puñal del Godo* came the first performance of a drama which
was to surpass all Zorrilla's other plays in popularity : *Don
Juan Tenorio* (1844). The widespread and persistent vogue
which it acquired, and which it still boasts to-day, would, if
a purely literary reason had to be found for it, be one of the
insoluble enigmas of literature. There is something really
mysterious about the established custom of representing it
every year during the week in November in which occurs
All Souls' Day. Possibly, or even probably, the custom is

---

\* [On this point, and on the theme of these two plays in general, see
R. Menéndez Pidal : *El Rey Rodrigo en la literatura* (Madrid, 1925).]

9

due to a caprice which, at some time when one least expects it, may come to an end even more suddenly than it began. At present, however, as Ernest Mérimée puts it, the thing is still "a national institution, like the bullfight."

Manuel de la Revilla, an excellent critic who died in 1881 at the early age of thirty-five, remarked in a long essay on the different manifestations of the Don Juan type in literature, that "in both his good and his bad points Tenorio is the complete personification of the Spanish character, and especially of the Andalusian character." He sums him up as "an indefinable admixture of Roman haughtiness, Gothic ferocity and Arabic generosity, an admixture which at best produces Cids and Guzmáns, and at worst Tenorios and Corrientes."* Possibly it is along these lines that we must look for an explanation of the problem of the constant popularity of the drama ; perhaps, too, it is because of this reason for that popularity that the poet is invested with a permanent laureateship and the title of "national poet" *par excellence*.

Zorrilla, however, seems to have taken but little notice of all this metaphysical criticism. He was acquainted with Tirso's *Burlador de Sevilla*, its adaptation by Zamora, Molière's *Don Juan*, the libretto of Mozart's *Don Giovanni*, and, most important of all, Dumas' *Don Juan de Marana*, both in its original French and in García Gutiérrez' translation. He was attracted by the tremendous notoriety and popular appeal of this personage—by precisely, in fact, what he had sought in Peter the Cruel. He set to work, drawing upon more or less unconnected reminiscences of all these earlier productions, and forcing himself, pen in hand, to improvise with all the vigour of youth. He was barely twenty-seven when he completed that drama composed with such gay facility and destined to win a success so extraordinary that it surprised its own author as much as it surprises us to-day.

Its similarity to Dumas' drama is very noticeable. Ernest

---

* *Obras de Don Manuel de la Revilla*, con prólogo del Excmo. Señor Don Antonio Cánovas del Castillo (Madrid, 1883), p. 433. The article is entitled "El tipo legendario de Don Juan Tenorio y sus manifestaciones en las modernas literaturas." The author mentions only Byron's poem, Dumas' play and Guerra Junqueiro's *A morte de Dom João*. He cites neither Hoffmann nor Pushkin nor Musset, nor any other foreign author.

Mérimée once truly said that "instead of rejuvenating and modernizing earlier models, he is content to copy *Don Juan de Marana*, to whom almost exclusively belong the most notable modifications which he introduced into the traditional *leyenda*."* Strange to say, Zorrilla in his *Recuerdos* omits to mention a predecessor who played so important a part in his own drama, just as he says nothing at the appropriate place of Southey and his poem, which was so useful to him in the winning of a wager, the composition of *El Puñal del Godo* and the completion of it later with *La Calentura*.

To the original tradition, which, it would seem, was first effectively dramatized by Tirso, something was added by Zamora, Molière and Lorenzo da Ponte, who adapted the story better to the exigencies of the theatre, depriving the servant of some of the excessive importance of Tirso's *gracioso*, Catalinón, and concentrating the tradition in a plot at once more compact and more firmly outlined. Zorrilla, on the other hand, completely destroys its nature. In this he was led astray by Dumas' melodrama, which is very far from being one of his better plays and the principal scenes of which we owe less to himself than to Mérimée's *Ames du Purgatoire*. The terrible and tragic catastrophe of all earlier versions becomes a vulgar scene from some *comedia de magia ;* the dramatist's principal aim seems to be to offer the producer an opportunity of presenting a grand finale "amid flowers and perfumes, to the sound of sweet music in the distance, the stage being illumined by the light of dawn while the souls of Don Juan and Doña Inés, in the form of two brilliant flames, are lost in space." Meanwhile the imposing statue of the Comendador, which has come to life —one of the most original and vigorous creations of modern poetic art—has vainly pronounced the terrible "Ya es tarde" and returns to its pedestal in sorrowful silence. Don Juan obtains pardon for all his crimes because at the last moment he has repented. The assassin's soul, in the form of a flame, soars upward towards bliss ; his victims will lie among the reprobate. This is indeed an incomprehensible piece of theology, for when Don Juan displays contrition he is already dead ; like Don Félix de Montemar and the

* *Bulletin Hispanique*, Vol. III, p. 73.

Capitán Montoya, he has attended his own funeral. This
we learn from the Comendador :

| JUAN. | ¿ Conque por mí doblan ? |
| ESTATUA. | Sí. |
| JUAN. | ¿ Y esos cantos funerales ? |
| ESTATUA. | Los salmos penitenciales |
| | Que están cantando por ti. |
| JUAN. | ¿ Y aquel entierro que pasa ? |
| ESTATUA. | Es el tuyo. |
| JUAN. | ¡ Muerto yo ! |
| ESTATUA. | El capitán te mató |
| | A la puerta de tu casa. |

Greater incoherence than this is hardly possible. But it is
shrouded with the gorgeous purple mantle of its splendid
versification, the brilliance of which dazzles every eye.
There is not an audience in Spain, once under the spell of
this exquisite melody, that can resist its influence. As a
piece of writing, it is no more praiseworthy than other
dramas by the same author ; indeed, it bears more signs of
carelessness and haste than most of them. But the traditional thrill which its hero produces upon the audience
cancels all its defects and weaknesses, and the insolent trifler
with womankind is allowed to continue seducing his victims
and flouting his enemies with impunity.

If we were asked which we consider to be the best of
Zorrilla's dramas, we should probably hesitate for a moment
and then name *El Zapatero y el Rey*. When the same question
was put to Zorrilla he hesitated not at all and declared
himself for *Traidor, Inconfeso y Mártir* (1849), a play composed
expressly for the benefit performance of a certain actress
and the last that he wrote which can be considered worthy
of mention. This is only one more example of a father
whose youngest child is his favourite. Having written each
of his other plays with such rapidity that none of them
completely satisfied him, he may have thought that, if he
wrote one more slowly and took more pains over its details,
it would turn out to be more satisfactory. It is true that
*Traidor, Inconfeso y Mártir* seems to be more highly polished
and more carefully written than the rest of Zorrilla's
plays. Its weak point is its plot, which offers but little
interest.

It is based upon the famous imposture-story of the pastry-cook of Madrigal, used also by Escosura for his novel *Ni Rey ni Roque*. The protagonist of the drama is not the Gabriel Espinosa who tries to pass as King Sebastian of Portugal, but the King himself, in flesh and blood, who, after living fourteen years in Madrigal as a pastry-cook, is surprised in Valladolid on a journey, by the "alcalde de casa y corte," Don Rodrigo de Santillana, and taken back to Madrigal, where he is tried, tortured and condemned to death as an impostor. The plot is complicated by the introduction of another character, Doña Aurora, a beautiful young woman who accompanies Gabriel and worships him as if he were a god, and who in the end turns out to be the daughter of the terrible *alcalde* Santillana. Aurora swoons when the condemned prisoner is led out to the gallows, and afterwards, in a delirium, watches from a window the punishment of a man whom she has blindly worshipped. She learns the identity of her father, and, half beside herself, turns upon him in fury, to curse him. This scene was composed to suit the particular gifts of the actress for whom the play was written, and who was especially brilliant in such situations ; it fails for want of harmony and through excessive violence, being inspired by motives foreign both to poetry and to the logical progression of the argument.

As the poet wished to present the false Gabriel as King Sebastian himself, he had to find a plausible explanation of the motives and object of his long residence in an obscure village and his occupation with matters of such little moment. It was of no use for him to elude the question by answering

> Pero yo hacer no sabía
> Otra cosa que pasteles.

The principal feature of Zorrilla's plot is of a very ordinary nature and has been used over-frequently. Melodramas at the end of which fathers discover daughters whom they had believed to be lost for ever can be counted by the score. As two acts of the play are placed in Valladolid and the author had no scruples elsewhere in making fundamental changes of fact with regard to the movements of royal personages, he might perhaps with advantage have lengthened the action and brought Don Sebastian into the presence of the King of Spain, justifying his action by reasons of state, which inexorably demanded the death of the inconveniently resuscitated monarch.

This drama was considerably less successful than its predecessors, a fact attributed by the author to the deficiencies of the famous actor Julián Romea in the part of the protagonist. Later, he tells us, in the provinces and in America—everywhere, indeed, but in Madrid—it became very popular, the part being given to another leading actor, Catalina, who, as a matter of fact, was best in comedy and never did well with serious drama at all.

"From that time forward," reports Zorrilla, in the *Recuerdos del tiempo viejo*, "I ceased writing for the stage."

V

It now only remains to speak of Zorrilla's *poema oriental*, entitled *Granada*. The story of the last days of Arab rule in this corner of Andalusia attracted the poet's attention, and inspired his fancy, from a very early period. Two of his first poems are *La Sorpresa de Zahara* and *El Último Rey Moro de Granada, Boabdil el Chico* ; never did his lyre yield tenderer and simpler music than in that lament of the Arabs as they left their homes :

> Y si huyendo de Noviembre
> Las arrecidas neblinas
> Vemos a las golondrinas
> De nuestra patria volver,
> Al dintel de nuestras tiendas
> A saludarlas saldremos
> Y de gozo lloraremos
> Mientras se alcancen a ver. . . .

Wearied of triumphs which no doubt he considered ephemeral, for he could not have predicted their long duration, Zorrilla was anxious to round off this central period of his career, which contains all his productions that are of interest to posterity, by writing a more extensive work than any he had yet published. This was to deal with the history of Arab rule in Granada, and was to cast an epic atmosphere round the characters of the final scene of that history and the conclusion of the long conflict between

Cross and Crescent which Spain considers to be her supreme
pride and glory.

No less than four years did Zorrilla spend in preparing and
writing the two volumes published in Paris in 1852. He
visited the places described in them, studied Arabic, read a
multitude of books and devoted greater care than ever
before to his language and versification. Unhappily, the
effort was not justified by the result, and the author reaped
neither the material profit for which he had had some reason
to hope nor the increase of glory desired for him by his
admirers.

He was able to complete but a small part of all that it was
in his mind to write and to which he had devoted long
preparation. Of the vast plan of a "Cuento de Cuentos"
on which he embarked, and which was to narrate the entire
history of Granada in the form of separate legends, he
composed only the first section, "La Leyenda de Muhamad-
Al-Hamar," in five books. The "Poema Oriental," devoted
to the last campaign of the Catholic monarchs, goes down
to the taking of Alhama. It may be doubted if, with all his
genius, Zorrilla had the energy, constancy and steadfastness
of purpose to accomplish so vast an enterprise. As soon as
he encountered the first difficulties with agents and booksellers, which, since he paid for his own printing and publishing, were of his own making, he became discouraged,
abandoned his entire project and determined to emigrate to
America in search of what he could not find in Europe.
During all the forty years of life that remained to him, he
neither published nor even completed a third volume.
In Spain the two elegant Parisian volumes were hardly read
at all. In America, where his renown was as great as in
Spain, or even greater, his dramas and short legends were
rated highly, but the bulk of these two volumes of poetry
merely inspired dismay.

Any would-be reader who picked them up, no matter
where he began, found passage upon passage that meant
absolutely nothing to him, but made him the most exquisite
music—a concert of vague, pervasive melody which lulled
and caressed the senses and rocked the mind to slumber.
Like Espronceda in the final pages of the *Estudiante de
Salamanca* or the introduction to the *Diablo Mundo*, Zorrilla
hardly leaves a single verse measure or metrical combination

unassayed. He has infinite rhythmic and constructional variety, but his phraseology is often insufficiently precise : his adjectives too commonly accumulate without in the least clarifying the sense, and his rhymes too seldom seem to spring, as they should, directly and spontaneously from thought or image. Zorrilla's mind was full of Arabic phrases, similes, allegories from the Koran and elsewhere and inscriptions from Moorish buildings, and these he sprinkles broadcast throughout his poem. He showed a particular enthusiasm for writing proper names in their original orthography, and to that end purposely disfigured them, as Leconte de Lisle in France disfigured names from the Greek. Leconte de Lisle, however, was an erudite of the erudites and made no pretence of writing popular poetry ; whereas Zorrilla's habitual readers, familiar enough with Boabdil, entirely failed to recognize him under the name of Abú-Abdil, a remark which also applies to other and similar changes. All this, together with the division of the *leyenda* of Al-Hamar el Nazarita into books with such Oriental titles as Libro de los Sueños, Libro de las Perlas, Libro de los Alcázares, Libro de los Espíritus, Libro de las Nieves, imparts to the book an artificiality and an appearance of straining after effect and deprives it of the charm of freshness and spontaneity which forms the principal attraction of Zorrilla's care-free narrative, and makes its diction even more verbose and redundant than it had appeared to be previously.

Let us repeat that there are delightful moments in the book—passages of incredible smoothness and beauty—especially in the part of it devoted to Moorish history. It is by these that it should be definitively judged, for its inequalities and its unfinished condition prevent the reader from appreciating its general plan or realizing the extent of its incompleteness ; it is principally suitable for anthologies and need be perused in full only by conscientious critics or editors of selected passages. Much the same may be said of the long poems of this type written by Sir Walter Scott.

Zorrilla makes no attempt to conceal the depth of the emotion produced in him by the tragic end of the royal house of Granada. Full of faith in his own powers, he evokes the shade of the Sultana Moraima and claims her royal patronage for his verses :

¡ Pálida sombra de Moraima ! Escucha :
Oye mi voz que te habla en las tinieblas . . .
Tú serás la sultana de mis cuentos,
Yo en mi laúd lamentaré tus penas,
Te llevaré conmigo a los alcázares
En donde tiene su morada regia
La noble, omnipotente poesía
Que sobre el mundo soberana impera . . .
¡ Adiós, sultana de las sombras ! Huye :
Yo me quedo cantándote en la tierra.

These lines, which occur near the end of the poem as we have it, increase our regret that any part of such sincere and generous emotion should be lost and such noble poetic intentions should remain unaccomplished. The more so still since this loss to art, and to the glory of the artist, was the result of an untimely and insensate journey in search of better fortune, which killed in its infancy what might well have been the best of all its author's productions.

# CHAPTER VII

## MANUEL BRETÓN DE LOS HERREROS

In 1828, there died in exile, at Paris, an illustrious writer of comedy, Leandro Fernández de Moratín. A few years earlier another exile had died at Orthez, in the person of that distinguished writer of tragedy, Nicasio Álvarez de Cienfuegos. The latter had been proscribed for his energetic resistance to the French invader in Madrid ; the former had been persecuted for having weakly bowed to the storm and accepted the title of Royal Librarian from Joseph Bonaparte. These facts are only typical of the anomalies and paradoxes of political life that succeeded each other rapidly during the first third of the nineteenth century.

Before his last years of sorrow and disillusionment came to an end, the unhappy Moratín must have heard of the great success which had been won at the Teatro del Príncipe in Madrid by a new prose comedy entitled *A la vejez, viruelas.* This comedy was the direct and legitimate outcome of Moratinian example and precept. It had been written as long previously as 1817 by a Riojan youth of twenty-one, called Manuel Bretón de los Herreros, who, for the sake of brevity and also in order to hide his Liberal antecedents, had refrained, during those troubled days, from using his full name. From his native town of Quel he had gone to live with his family in Madrid and here had pursued studies that were neither leisurely nor exhaustive before enlisting as a soldier in 1812. He fought against the French in Catalonia and Valencia, and at the close of the war had become a corporal. At the end of the year 1818 he went to join an army gathering in Andalusia, which it was hoped and believed would reconquer the colonies that had thrown off the yoke of Spain. The battle-cry of Riego in Las Cabezas de San Juan, first heard on January 1, 1820, and taken up in camp after camp by the troops that were quartered there with a view to the ill-omened enterprise, freed our author from a hazardous journey to America. Soon afterwards he obtained his freedom from the army.

He was successful in securing an administrative employment in the provinces from those who governed the country during the three years of the Liberal *régime* (1820–23). At that time he was so sincerely imbued with Liberal ideas that, when the men of 1823 found themselves about to fight the last battle against the royal army, with the aid of the hundred thousand soldiers led by the Duc d'Angoulême, he did not hesitate to re-enlist, and served under General Ballesteros, in Torrijos' defence of Cartagena, maintained until at last the city had to be surrendered. After a brief visit to his native town, he judged it safer to go back to Madrid, where he withdrew completely from politics and lived quietly with his mother.

Though the period of violent reaction which followed this Liberal *régime* hardly brought such odium on the Liberals as that which Moratín had incurred through being an *afrancesado*, nevertheless Bretón's comedies were represented in Madrid but seldom. Moratín's first disciples, Martínez de la Rosa and Gorostiza, had left Spain like their master. But in 1824 the hour had arrived for the recognition and proclamation of the triumph of Moratinian comedy, a triumph due to two young men, aged respectively twenty-eight and eighteen, both of them true followers and pupils of Moratín and soon to win the glory of successfully rivalling him. The elder was Bretón ; the younger, a native of Buenos Aires, educated in Madrid, called Ventura de la Vega. By a curious coincidence, on this night of October 14, 1824, when the Teatro del Príncipe was illuminated in honour of Ferdinand VII's birthday, and the first original work of Bretón was to be represented, the other play given in that theatre was "the first dramatic work of Ventura de la Vega."*

Neither the collection of Bretón's *Obras escogidas* (Paris, Baudry, 1853)—"approved and selected by their author," as the title-page has it—nor the completer posthumous edition of Madrid (1883), prepared according to Bretón's written indications, contains this comedy *A la vejez, viruelas,* in which its author's name first appeared, and this despite the fact that, according to Hartzenbusch, who was present at its

* Molíns : *Bretón de los Herreros* (Madrid, 1883), p. 33.

first performance, the reception accorded to it was very favourable.* The author considered it to be an "imperfect attempt," born of his inexperience,† and he was right. The best and happiest characteristic of the work is its title. Both plot and style are over-reminiscent of Moratín, and, if the verse of Bretón's comedies is far superior to that of his predecessor's, he lags far behind him in his prose. Of this he was himself perfectly aware. In spite of all the plays that he had translated into prose from the French over a period of many years, he wrote the huge majority of his original works in verse. According to the detailed list of his plays published in Molíns' biography, and the completer list in the 1883 edition of his works, he is the author of some 370 acts of original comedy, of which only about twenty-three are in prose.

Bretón was also an admirable verse translator. His version of Casimir Delavigne's *Les Enfants d'Edouard* is a good example of fidelity combined with ready elegance. If in prose he never attained to the airy grace of Vega's translations or of the *Crítica del "Sí de las Niñas,"* Vega is no more able to compete with him in the type of work represented by his perfect translation into Spanish of *Le Médecin malgré lui.* All critics unite in praising Bretón as the incomparable verse stylist and this praise he richly merited ; he had a perfect command of his own language, and in his light verse, as in his plays, every difficulty of rhyme or metrical combination that presented itself was only one more occasion for him to emerge triumphantly with some unexpected and brilliant solution. In prose he was never able to do this ; he profited little by his master's example and nothing that he ever wrote can be compared with those delightful private letters of Moratín, published in the *Obras Póstumas* (Madrid, 1867). It has been claimed that there is no collection of letters to equal this in the entire range of Spanish literature ; the only possible criticism of it is that the letters are too well written, the scrupulous purity of their style being surprising in such a private and intimate correspondence as that between Moratín and his old and faithful friend, Melón.

The period of over seven years which elapsed between *A*

---

* *Obras Escogidas de Don Manuel Bretón de los Herreros* (Paris, 1853), p. viii.
† *Obras de Don Manuel Bretón de los Herreros* (Madrid, 1883), p. lvii.

*la vejez, viruelas* and *Marcela o ¿ A cuál de los tres ?* (December 30, 1831) Bretón employed both in productive writing and in study. His education had been very defective and his scholastic attainments were small. In order to fill this gap, therefore, he devoted himself to an intensive course of self-education and at the same time wrote as ardently as ever for the stage to supplement his family's meagre income. During these seven years he turned out fifty-six plays, most of them translated from the French, for, as he himself tells us, translations were as well paid as original plays "and the task of translation was by far the easier of the two," apart from which a translator's reputation would suffer much less from any possible failure than would that of an original writer. Among Bretón's original works of this period are those in which he clearly revealed himself as the faithful disciple of Moratín, occasionally equalling him but never going beyond the limits of his master's inspiration. At the head of all these plays stands his first undisputed triumph, *A Madrid me vuelvo*, a three-act comedy written entirely in octosyllables with one assonance persisting through each act ; both the form and the content of this play fall strictly within the tradition and canons that had received the sanction of usage.

The artistically sculptured milestone that marks the point at which Bretón changed his literary direction and entered, by a new road, upon fresh fields, is *Marcela, o ¿ A cuál de los tres ? Marcela* is also the first, in chronological order, of five or six Bretonian masterpieces, models of their kind, which will probably always find a place on the stage and will certainly always be read with pleasure and admiration as immortal examples of language, versification and well-nigh inexhaustible wit. From this time onward, though Bretón always preserved his respect for Moratín, as for a former master, he no longer followed him, with a pupil's deference, as his sole model. He turned in every direction and underwent all kinds of new influences, including those of the foreign writers of whose works he was so assiduous a translator : Scribe and his collaborators, Victor Hugo in an act and a half of *Marion Delorme*, Schiller in *Maria Stuart* (or rather, Lebrun's unfortunate imitation of that play) and in a *Wallenstein* which was never performed but figures in the catalogue of Bretón's dramas already mentioned. The

masterly verse adaptation of *Les Enfants d'Edouard* surpasses
its original both in stylistic power and in poetical perfection.
Performed in 1835 by Concepción Rodríguez, Latorre and
Julián Romea—the foremost actors of the day—its triumph
was as great as though it had been Bretón's original drama.

The novel feature of *Marcela* consisted in the extraordinary rhythmical variety with which its creator endowed
it, his deliberate intention being to imitate the "feliz independencia, fecunda en primores" of Lope, Tirso, Moreto
and Calderón.   When he uses assonance it changes in each
scene, and elsewhere we find *redondillas*, octosyllabic quatrains, *quintillas*, *silvas*, a *letrilla*, a sonnet and a number of
*décimas*, all of them the perfect productions of an excellent
workman who was also an exquisite artificer.   The plot of
the comedy, on the other hand, is of the greatest simplicity,
hardly more complicated in its essence than that of a *paso* or
an *égloga* belonging to the early Spanish stage.   There is
merely an attractive young widow with three suitors, who
make their declarations by letter, and whom at the end of
the play she dismisses, one after the other, in a final interview to which she has summoned them all.   Larra, writing
on another of Bretón's comedies, *Un Novio para la niña*,
which has an identical argument, as has also *Un Tercero en
discordia*, made the acute observation that, while most
dramatists might have found it difficult to fashion a comedy
out of such a plot, "this author has written three different
dramas upon it."   The remark wounded Bretón deeply and
gave rise to an estrangement between the two, which was
ended some time afterwards by a public reconciliation,
famous in the literary annals of the period.   But evidently
the criticism did not serve as a lesson to him, for he increased
the number of his plays based on this theme from three to
five, by writing *Cuentas atrasadas* in 1841 and *Un Novio a
pedir de boca* in 1843.

Here we have the most serious defect in all Bretón's
dramatic productions, a defect for which there is no possible
compensation.   Within the narrow boundaries of his plays,
with monotonous and continually repeated symmetry, strut
ridiculous puppets, superficial as shadows and as vaguely
outlined as hastily sketched caricatures, of the types of
Marcela's suitors :   the melancholy poet, the pampered
glutton, the vain, talkative captain—Don Amadeo, Don

Agapito and Don Martín Campana y Centellas. None of his characters, men or women, old or young, are studied any more thoroughly than these. The engraver's chisel refuses to bite ; the artist's brush is too coarse ; the author's pen runs too freely ; the improviser abuses the gift which Nature has so generously bestowed upon him.

Such pronounced superficiality is one of those defects that have no remedy. In the last two or three years of his life, which he spent in the seclusion of his apartments in the Calle de la Montera, seldom going out and completely cut off from active occupations, Bretón set himself assiduously to revise and correct all his plays, one after another, with a view to preparing a definitive edition of them. His poetic diction became firmer, richer, less marred by repetitions, more impeccably correct in form. But his plots and characters could do no other than remain as they were. Yet to the end he was the conscientious artist, doing all that lay in his power to achieve perfection. On the evening of November 1, 1873, he was engaged upon a diligent revision of his comedy *El Cuarto de hora*. On the next morning he was unable to leave his bed ; a week later he died.

In the series of five plays which we enumerated above, *Marcela* and *Un Tercero en discordia* stand high above the rest by virtue of the richness and elegance of their versification. Never, we suppose, will they fall into oblivion ; they will not only be read but also acted as long as the Spanish language endures. In them, too, Bretón surpasses both his predecessors and contemporaries in this type of play as regards the airy grace of his wit and the brilliance of his diction. Neither Segovia, Fray Gerundio, Martínez Villergas, Rodríguez Rubí, Estébanez Calderón nor any other writer of that time can equal him in merit.

The Romantic breezes which, about 1834, began to blow with some vigour in Madrid at length carried Bretón along in the direction that, only a month before, had been successfully taken by Larra in his *Macías*. Bretón was not, however, as well prepared for this excursion as for his previous one. His oblation to the new cult—which he made perhaps, as he himself confesses,* not altogether voluntarily—was a five-act verse drama called *Elena*, in the writing of which he exercised all the freedom claimed by the

* *Obras*, etc. (Madrid, 1883), Vol. I p. 189, note.

Romantics. Its merit hardly goes beyond a modest mediocrity. Notwithstanding the lack of faith which he professed in the new doctrines, he relapsed into them more than once, but on none of these occasions did he produce anything worthy of remembrance.

The influence of romanticism on Bretón, however, was not limited to these various Romantic outbursts : it can be traced in a number of his best and most typical comedies, notably in *Muérete ¡ y verás !* which many consider to be the best of all. The argument of this play is based upon that of Alexandre Dumas' famous melodrama *Catherine Howard ;* but its background is quite dissimilar, its characters belong to a different type, the theme is treated in a tone of elegant comedy and the action is set in Bretón's own day, the scene being Zaragoza, and the date 1837, when civil war in Northern Spain was at its height. The action of Dumas' drama takes place in England, extends over the period during which Henry VIII was married to the fifth of his wives, Catherine Howard, and ends only with her death on the scaffold in full view of the audience. All this is in perfect harmony with the declamatory violence of an exaggerated romanticism. About a year previously, Madrid had seen and admired this melodrama as translated by Narciso de la Escosura ; and it occurred to Bretón that he might stage the same story as a comedy.

Don Pablo, Bretón's protagonist, is not, like Dumas' Ethelwood, an English peer, but only a mobilized Spanish officer who has gone to the wars, is believed to have died and, on returning to Zaragoza, finds (to use Dumas' antithesis) that the woman who should have forgotten has remembered and the woman who should have remembered has forgotten. The French melodrama is the description of an implacable vengeance which rushes rapidly towards a violent catastrophe, while the Spanish comedy, following the law of development of its type, ends in a carefully prepared but highly artificial scene in which Don Pablo appears, "like a ghost, swathed from head to foot in a white garment," in order to frighten those assembled in the very room for the signing of the marriage contract of the faithless woman with a friend of the supposed dead man. Don Pablo makes no attempt to carry the scandal farther ; he is satisfied by punishing the unfaithful one with a contemptuous forgiveness, and offering his hand, in the presence of all, to the silent but loving girl who has not forgotten him.

¡ Flor de mi tumba !   ¿ Por qué
Tan tarde te conocí ?

The most striking difference between these two plays is a purely literary one.  Dumas' melodrama is written in a very ordinary and a somewhat inflated prose, quite devoid of distinction and stylistically poor.  Bretón's comedy, on the other hand, is in excellent verse ;  its language is marked by diversity, clarity and vigour, and profusely sprinkled with epigrams and witty rejoinders.  Further, this is one of the most substantially constructed of Bretón's plays ;  the scenes progress in logical sequence and harmonize well with the general effect.  As is so often the case in his comedies, too important a part is played by the didactic purpose, suggested here by the title.  This is merely a common saying and the argument of the play is nothing more than an anecdote illustrating it.  "Die," it counsels, "and when you come back to life again you will see some surprising things."  There is really nothing unusual in the events of the play.  Such things are continually happening, save that as a rule a greater time elapses between the day of the deceased man's funeral and that of the wedding of his betrothed.

*El Pelo de la Dehesa* (1840), another of Bretón's most popular plays, is an excellent *comedia de figurón*.  As generally happens in such comedies, there is only one well and carefully drawn character, that of the *figurón* himself—Don Frutos Calamocha, the *nouveau riche* from the country who cannot adapt himself to the ways of Madrid.  The other personages are feebly developed characters or pale silhouettes, and the nature of the *dénouement* is from the very beginning of the story only too obvious.

Both before and after the performance of *La Batelera de Pasajes* (1842), there were animated newspaper discussions between the dramatic critics and Bretón's friends as to whether the play was a comedy or a drama.  The author first called it a drama, but when at a later date he included it in his collected works he gave it the title of comedy.  To our own mind, it is something of a hybrid, in which an excellent first act is followed by three very inferior ones.  The first act is placed in the port of Pasajes, during the Civil

10

War, when the English fleet sent to support the defenders of Isabel II was lying there ; the picture of the bay, with its busy life, its numerous *bateleras* and its vivacious *remeras*, is reproduced with the greatest delicacy and animation. The rest of the play, which takes place in the canteen tent of an Isabeline camp, is very poor ; and the detail of the plot is very improbable, because the author has determined that all his characters shall be brought together again by fair means or foul. The *dénouement*, too, is insufficiently prepared : it comes about through a challenge, the motive of which has hardly been mentioned, while the challenger has not been mentioned at all. It is one of those *dénouements* invented by an author purely and simply as a way of escape from a difficult situation.

In the second act, the respective positions of the *batelera* Faustina and Bureba, the captain who has deceived her, remind us of a similar situation between Isabel and Don Álvaro de Ataide, the captain in Calderón's *Alcalde de Zalamea*. It can hardly be said that there is direct imitation here ; there may not even be reminiscence ; but certain of Bretón's ideas, perhaps only by chance, recall Calderón's, as in the lines in which the *batelera* inveighs against her seducer and shows him that she has resolution enough to force him

> A cumplirme la palabra
> Que me distes a la faz
> Del cielo, y a que me vuelvas
> —¡ Que nada tuyo me das !—
> La honra que me robaste,

lines as apt and energetic as those similar ones in Calderón :

> . . . Un honor os pido
> Que me quitasteis vos mesmo,
> Y con ser mío parece,
> Según os lo estoy pidiendo
> Con humildad, que no es mío
> Lo que os pido, sino vuestro.

Before Bretón wrote this play, his previously unbroken popularity and success as a dramatist had been overshadowed by a black cloud which somewhat affected his character and marks the beginning of a second period in his work which was one of diminished fortune and happiness.

His muse now smiled upon him less kindly and the turbulent politics of his country helped to exert a malign influence upon his well-being.    Though he had not renounced the Liberal ideas of his youth, he began to find himself gradually left behind in the rapid forward march of Liberalism towards new conquests.    Like so many who, at Cádiz and during the famous "three years," had been ardent defenders of the most advanced ideas, he was now, with almost the whole of his friends, fighting in the ranks of the Moderate party. Espartero assumed government through the support of the Progressives.    Bretón's friends lost all influence in the country, and he himself was assailed by a storm of abuse when, in 1840, he published a short topical play called *La Ponchada*, which contained satirical allusions to ridiculous traits and defects, both very clearly evident, in the triumphant National Guard.    He was compelled to go into hiding, found himself dismissed from his post in the National Library and was so deeply moved by these events that he began to think seriously of emigration.

Gradually things grew calm again, but Bretón never regained the degree of popularity which he had enjoyed previously.    In no play written later than the *Batelera de Pasajes* does his style show the same striking combination of naturalness, fertility and charming wit which we continually find in *Marcela, El Cuarto de hora, El Pelo de la Dehesa* and the whole group of his delightful one-act plays, such as *Una de tantas, Ella es él* and *Mi Secretario y yo*.    Not only so, but Bretón's own character was becoming more and more embittered, until he came to stand as one more embodiment of that profound ill-humour which (to quote a bitter remark of Larra) so often characterizes "those who aspire to amuse others."

None of Bretón's twenty or more original plays staged between 1842 and 1849 awakened an interest comparable with that aroused by his plays in the past.    It was no doubt for this reason, largely attributable to the disfavour into which he had fallen, and in order, as he says himself, that "a play of his might be judged without personal prejudice, either adverse or favourable," that he conceived and executed the plan of writing his five-act play *¿ Quién es ella ?* (1849) anonymously.    When the curtain rose on the night of its first performance, the papers had devoted no previous attention to it, either flattering or the reverse, and the audience did not so much as suspect the name of its author.

It enjoyed no great success, except on its first appearance, when the curiosity of the audience and the atmosphere of mystery which surrounded it were both in its favour. Nor did it deserve more than fell to it on that occasion. It is on a far lower plane of merit than many other of Bretón's plays and its only attraction is that quality which to a greater or a lesser degree characterizes them all—*viz.*, skill and facility of versification. A leading part in the comedy is played by Don Francisco de Quevedo, yet Quevedo is not the protagonist and takes no very important place in the actual plot. He is introduced in old age, and the *milieu* in which he moves is that of one of the semi-tragic intrigues in which Bretón was never very successful. The third act takes place in a prison, where a person condemned to death is awaiting a pardon from Philip IV, whom he has grievously offended. The title of the play comes from the refrain of a *letrilla*—its best feature—in which Quevedo confesses his antipathy to women. In the last scene he proffers a public recantation in *quintillas*, a kind of final salvo on his big guns, or, to put it more appropriately, a grand set-piece crowning his display of fireworks. The *letrilla* is extremely witty, though we may suppose that the real Quevedo, the author of that famous satire in tercets upon matrimony, would have seasoned it rather more strongly and would not so easily have donned the white robe of repentance and uttered his recantation.

Bretón's extraordinary fertility was by this time diminishing or deteriorating with age. In the eighteen years separating ¿ *Quién es ella?* from his last play, *Los Sentidos corporales* (1867), he produced only a dozen more original pieces. One of these, however, *La Escuela del Matrimonio*, first given in January 1852, is generally considered to be among his best : Molíns even describes it as setting the pinnacle to his glory. It certainly combines all his principal dramatic gifts, while its deficiencies are nearly as well disguised as in his happiest days. The style is perhaps more compact and sententious than ever, though it may seem to be less gay and sparkling, and to display a less lively and scintillating wit. Three married couples indulge in mild disagreements—for none of their differences is irreparable,

or even really serious—and are pacified with no great
difficulty and set on the road to amendment by a young
wife who is the friend of them all, and who crowns the
fulfilment of her self-appointed task by pointing the moral,
as follows :

> Que miren cómo y con quién
> Antes de casarse dos,
> Y si no les sale bien
> ¿ Qué hacer ?   Llevarlo por Dios . . .
> Que cuando enferma un consorcio
> De achaques de desamor,
> Mal remedio es el divorcio
> Y el escándalo peor.

Undoubtedly there is more movement and complexity in
the three acts of this comedy than in the three of *Marcela*,
the four of *Muérete ¡ y verás !* or the five of *El Cuarto de hora*
and *El Pelo de la Dehesa :* the events of the plot are skilfully
linked together and the plot itself is freely and logically
developed.   As in so many of Bretón's other comedies,
however, the *dénouement* is artificial and the characters are
exaggerated types verging on the farcical.   Micaela, the
blue-stocking of the play, is a pedant developed to the point
of caricature ;   her husband is a fantastic simpleton ;   the
brusqueness of the General is altogether excessive ;   while no
banker on earth could possibly approach the depths of
ingenuous fatuity touched by Don Luciano.

At about this time Bretón wrote the chief of his non-
dramatic works, a serio-comic poem in twelve cantos entitled
*La Desvergüenza*, which was published only in 1856.    It
consists of over six hundred *octavas reales* and might well be
described as an amply filled storehouse of unusual and
difficult rhymes.    Some of these are dragged in from regions
far removed from the sense of the context and a whole
army of proper names is recruited from history and mythology by an author determined to vanquish his difficulties
of technique.    History and mythology, it may be noted, are
not infrequently abused by Bretón in his comedies.    Marcela,
for example, has a kitten called Clytemnestra, of which the
poet, Don Amadeo, says :

> Está postrada en su lecho
> La viuda de Agamenón.

This, in its context, may not be entirely ridiculous, though Marcela's choice of feline names might be considered so. But we open our eyes at Bureba's wooing of the simple *batelera*, who walks across the stage, "el bello pie desnudo," to be thus greeted :

> Así como tú eres,
> Debió surgir del Ponto
> La diosa de Citeres.

And, more surprising still, the uneducated girl understands the recondite allusion and deprecates the flattery :

> ¡ Vaya ! . . . Me da vergüenza
> Tanta lisonja. ¡ Calle !

In *La Desvergüenza* the obstacles are carefully sought out and accumulated, the solutions which the author finds for them being frequently successful and always highly ingenious. The most noteworthy feature of the poem is the undue good-nature of its satire, which neither wounds nor leaves a sting. Even in the canto devoted to politics, it fails to penetrate the surface, though politics had treated Bretón in a way which would have left any other writer permanently embittered. He tilts but little against the prevalent mania for office and not at all against the dominant militarism and the frequent *pronunciamientos* by leading generals, which in those days were the two running sores of the country.

*El Abogado de pobres* and *Los Sentidos corporales*, two plays produced when their author was over seventy, mark the end of his splendid career and the last flickerings of the divine fire which once had burned in him with such vigour. But he had still sufficient intellectual strength and activity to devote himself eagerly and unremittingly to the tasks of the Academia de la Lengua. Since Gallego's death, early in 1853, he had held the office of Secretary to the Academy, and no secretary of that body, always busy with new editions of its Grammar and Dictionary, can have surpassed him, before or since, in constancy of application. He played an important and indeed a predominant part, both in the discussions on the Dictionary when the Academy was in session and also in the final revision and the delicate task of combining the parts and giving the work its final form. It might have been supposed that work so much in harmony with his tastes and talents would have kept him happily occupied until the end of his life.   This would indeed have been the case but for the obstinacy with which he invariably maintained his own opinion at all costs, and his claim of infallibility for his views on matters of language—views which all his colleagues cordially recognized as those of an expert.   He would never give in.   When he saw that numbers were against him in a debate, he would endeavour to apply the closure and pass on to the next subject. According to Molíns, he would then add in an off-hand manner :   "I take it that nothing about this discussion will appear in the minutes."   And at the next meeting nobody would protest when it was found that he had in fact minuted none of it.

When the time came to work upon the preparatory material for the twelfth edition of the Academy Dictionary, it became clear that there was a profound disagreement between Bretón's ideas and the opinions held by the majority on the Academy's special committee.   At last, it seemed, the Secretary would be forced either to fall in with his colleagues or to bring about a final rupture with them. Not for a moment did he hesitate.   He appealed to the Academy in full session, and, finding himself in a minority, flung aside all considerations of personal interest and friendship that stood in the path of his inflexible character. Making the transparent plea of illness, he deserted the sessions of the Academy and allowed a temporarily appointed successor to take over his duties.   The Academy did its utmost to pacify him and even paid him the high compliment of accepting the reason which he gave for his absence and of considering him officially present at all meetings.   It was of no avail.   Though for more than a year he continued to occupy his official secretarial apartments, he never again, despite the repeated requests of many members, entered the hall in which the meetings were held and the door of which he had to pass daily.   Finally, he moved to another house some distance away and there spent the two and a half years that remained to him of life enveloped in a gloom of his own making and tormented by thoughts of purely imaginary grudges which he believed his former colleagues to be bearing him.   He died on November 8, 1873, a month before his seventy-seventh birthday.

# CHAPTER VIII

## VENTURA DE LA VEGA

Ventura de la Vega ("Buenaventura" is the name on the baptismal register) was born at Buenos Aires on July 14, 1807. His father, who held a post of some importance in his country's financial administration, died while he was still in his infancy, and, before he was twelve years old, the mother, an Argentine, sent him to Spain, to be educated by a paternal uncle. He was put to school at the Colegio de San Mateo, where among his teachers were Lista and Hermosilla, and among his classmates Espronceda, Felipe Pardo, Ochoa, Molíns and a number of boys who rose to high rank in the army. Among these last was Vega's life-long friend, Pezuela, Conde de Cheste, who composed the obituary oration delivered before the Spanish Academy in February 1866, comprising the best and most circumstantial biography of him that we possess.*

When his studies were over, Vega's mother was anxious that he should return to her and suggested to him a suitable boat and date of departure. At first, it appears, he agreed to the proposal, but the boat left without him and he settled (permanently, as it proved) in Madrid, expressing the reasons for his sudden resolution in a sonnet worth quoting both for its own merit and also because he omitted it from the selection of his own works published at Paris in 1866. It runs as follows :

> Surca sin mí los espumosos mares,
> Saluda ¡ oh nave ! de mi patria el muro,
> Y déjame vagar triste y obscuro
> Por la orilla del lento Manzanares.
> Si osa turbar la paz de sus hogares
> De extranjera ambición el soplo impuro,
> Otro defienda con el hierro duro
> Su libertad y mis nativos lares.

* Cf. *Memorias de la Academia Española* (Madrid, 1870), Tomo II, pp. 434, ff.

> Así exclamaba yo, cuando las olas
> Rompió la nave en que partir debía
> Y abandonó las costas españolas.
> Ella al impulso plácido del aura
> Voló a las playas de la patria mía,
> Y yo a los brazos me volví de Laura.*

For this Laura, whose real name is given us by Pezuela, Vega renounced his native country, which, despite the fact that his mother remained there, and outlived him, he never revisited. But he was not entirely forgetful of it, and, though it inspired none of his important works, either lyric or dramatic, he frequently wrote slighter verses, such as those addressed to a friend leaving for Buenos Aires in 1856, which indicate that, in thirty years, his feelings had undergone a radical change :

> ¡ Oh ! ¡ cuánto fuera mi consuelo, cuánto,
> Si en esa nave huyéramos los dos !
> ¡ Oh ! si a este suelo, donde sufro tanto,
> Pudiera darle mi postrer adiós ! . . .
> Mas ya que quiere mi fatal estrella
> Con duros lazos sujetarme aquí,
> Por mí te postra y con tus labios sella
> La tierra amada en que feliz nací.

Nevertheless, his literary tastes, ideas and aspirations were not those of a Spanish American, as he was apt to suggest, but of a genuine Spaniard. This was natural enough, since he was educated in Spain and spent the rest of his life there. Further, he was never attracted by politics, and, if he had returned to America, like his schoolfellow Felipe Pardo, "the satirist of Lima," he would not have scoffed as cruelly as Pardo did at its republican institutions and at the excesses committed by American democracy.

He arrived at man's estate, and became conscious of the full development of his powers, just as the exotic elements of romanticism, transplanted into Spanish soil, were beginning to blossom and bear fruit there. He was one of those who did most, in these early days, to keep them alive, translating and adapting from the French with great diligence— comedies, dramas and melodramas, in verse and prose, good,

---

* This is the version given in Ignacio Herrera Dávila's *Rimas Americanas* (Habana, 1833). Pezuela's (reproduced in the obituary oration referred to above) is slightly different ; no doubt he quoted the poem from memory.

bad and indifferent.    But all this he did solely as a means of
gaining a livelihood.    Romanticism never took root in his
affections.

> . . . de aquella fiera pesadilla
> Conseguí despertar con transudores
> A las voces de Lista y Hermosilla.

Soon Hermosilla's idol, Moratín, became Ventura de la
Vega's supreme model and literary deity.    No single critic
has spoken with more enthusiasm and admiration than he
of Moratín's five original plays—his "five stars," as he terms
them :

> ¡ Cinco no más ! pero de luz tan pura,
> De juventud tan fresca y tan lozana . . .
> Que vivirán, cuanto en la edad futura
> Viva la hermosa lengua castellana.

He himself wrote even fewer original works for the stage than
did his great master : three in all—a comedy, a drama and a
tragedy.

The drama, *Don Fernando el de Antequera* (1847), is, both in
content and in form, entirely Romantic, though its romanticism is of an insipid kind, fading into unreality even as it
comes from its creator's hands.    In each of the three acts of
the play the scene is in a different locality and the versification has considerable variety, though the *romance* of eight or
eleven syllables predominates.    The author is evidently
striving to give the play local colour, but his argument is
weak and devoid of interest.    Throughout the drama, Don
Fernando wavers between accepting and refusing the throne
offered him by the grandees of Castile, being unwilling to
dispossess the rightful heir, a child two years old, who is
under his guardianship.    There is no reason and no
dramatic necessity making either solution to the problem
inevitable, and the audience is supremely indifferent as it
watches the entrances and exits of persons completely
devoid of interest.    Only one of these, San Vicente Ferrer,
who plays no direct part in the action, can be said to have
any character at all.    The dialogue of the play is good, but
its general effect is simply that of an extract from some
national chronicle adapted for the stage, and that with no
great skill.

Ventura de la Vega's tragedy, *La Muerte de César*, which appeared in 1865, some twenty years after his other two plays, is the result of long and continuous effort. Despite its conservative scheme of assonances and its unvarying hendecasyllabic *romances*, it nevertheless has certain Romantic features, none too usual at the date at which it was written. It is chiefly the new characters it introduces— *i.e.*, those not in the plays of Shakespeare or Voltaire on the same subject, such as Servilia, Brutus' mother, and other minor personages—that give this neo-Classical work a vague flavour of somewhat hackneyed romanticism. The protagonist is neither Julius Cæsar, the egoistic tyrant of the eighteenth-century French Republicans, nor the *Imperator Cæsar*, outstanding and unique, as Mommsen puts it, in human memory. The machinery of Vega's tragedy includes a new element, to which no previous writer on the theme had given such prominence. Cæsar the dictator becomes, first and foremost, Brutus' father, being the seducer of Cato's sister Servilia, wife of Junius Brutus and mother of the future murderer of his own father. Quite early in the play we are introduced to this unknown Cæsar, tender and melancholy, his soul full of love for this son whom he cannot openly acknowledge yet whom he would fain make his heir before he leaves for the Parthian wars. The mother hesitates long before she can resolve to confess her fault and her dishonour. Cæsar reproaches her :

> Tú no amas a tu hijo . . .
>                        . . . Por conservar intacta
> Esa opinión en que tu orgullo goza,
> Porque tu vida obscura y solitaria
> Sus encantos no pierda, a Bruto quieres
> En ella consumir, cortar las alas
> A su impetuoso genio, de su padre
> Ahogar las halagüeñas esperanzas,
> Y lo que es más, el porvenir de Roma.

These sentiments, so completely unnatural in such a man and in such a situation, the hesitations of Servilia, her final resolution to sign the parchment recognizing the paternity —a parchment which decides the Dictator, notwithstanding omens and warnings to the contrary, to go to the Senate on the Ides of March, and which, when he falls to the ground murdered, he is still clasping in his hand—all these devices

are certainly ingenious, but they belong rather to melodrama, making it impossible for the play to attain the severe
majesty of such other similar works as Corneille's Roman
tragedies, *Cinna* and *Horace*. Nor has *La Muerte de César* as
much life and movement as other dramas inferior to it in
style, such as Alexandre Dumas' *Caligula*, in which there is
at least an appearance and a fair illusion of exact local
colour.

So much for Vega's tragedy. We now come to the
comedy, which completes his threefold dramatic legacy, for
apart from these three plays he composed nothing but
topical pieces, only a few of which (notably the *Crítica del
"Sí de las Niñas,"* a favourite with all lovers of Moratín) can
be called well-constructed trifles. The comedy, however,
*El Hombre de Mundo* (1845), is Vega's most notable production ; it stands alone among his works, his one real masterpiece, a solitary monument to his greatness.

The three plays—drama, tragedy and comedy—have to a
very high degree one quality in common : elegance, correctness and nicety of literary form. If with formal perfection
they fail to combine the infinite variety and fluency of
Bretón, they far surpass anything Bretón ever wrote in
purity and Attic grace. Vega, it must not be forgotten,
composed his plays with great deliberation, taking years to
complete work that his productive contemporary finished
in as many weeks, and minutely revising everything that
he wrote before publishing it. It must be allowed that,
when a work that has been thus polished, revised and
improved turns out to be as perfect in style and versification
as *El Hombre de Mundo*, it calls for unqualified praise and
admiration. In this comedy Vega surpasses even the verse
comedies of Moratín ; and Moratín could (as in the prose
of *El Sí de las Niñas*) achieve a formal excellence which,
considering the age in which he wrote, is really marvellous.
It must not, of course, be forgotten that during the forty
years between Moratín and Vega Spain had won for herself
a flexibility and freedom of expression that was unknown in
the literature of the beginning of the century. Nevertheless,
it remains true that he did in fact outstrip his master.

In other equally important respects, however, the master
keeps the advantage. Vega's moral lesson is no loftier than
Moratín's, nor are his characters any profounder. His

"hombre de mundo" is simply a former seducer of women, now married and retired from business, who fears to be treated as he himself, with unthinking cruelty, has so often treated others. The plot is developed on a low and undistinguished level, attributable to the unduly important part played in its development by the servants of the house. Such familiarity between master and servant in these serious and intimate matters may or may not have been acceptable and true to life at the time when the comedy was written ; to-day it is certainly surprising, and even offensive, though hardly to such a degree as to tarnish the play's excellence. *El Hombre de Mundo* had an immediate success upon the stage, which was maintained long past its own day, for the stage effects are excellently prepared, succeed one another with commendable promptness, and carry the piece at a rapid pace to its natural *dénouement*.

What, then, does it lack that it cannot be called a work of the very first order ? Menéndez y Pelayo answers the question thus :

> Si algo se echa de menos en ella . . . es un modo más elevado de considerar la pasión y el deber . . . el hábito de tomar la vida por lo serio, que es en el fondo el modo más poético de tomarla.*

It is only thus, indeed, that truly great comedy is written ; only thus could the immortal Molière place in the centre of his graphic picture of the gay, frivolous and empty court society of the age of Louis XIV the unforgettable figure of his Misanthrope—"one singular figure," as John Morley says of him, "hoarse, rough, sombre, moving with a chilling reality in the midst of frolicking shadows."†

Bearing in mind Vega's gifts and limitations as a dramatist, we should hardly expect that any unusual good fortune would have attended his lyric poetry. He was by nature too much inclined to inactivity and indolence to know anything of the ardour and acquire the impetus without which neither lyrical rapture nor the essentially personal accent of the lyricist is possible. Not one of Vega's verse compositions has that delicacy and sonority of tone which vibrate with such power in the lyrics of Espronceda, nor even the elo-

---

* *Antología de poetas hispano-americanos* (Madrid, 1895), Vol. IV, p. clviii.
† *Studies in Literature* (London, 1901), p. 90.

quence and wealth of imagery of the verses of La Avellaneda and of García y Tassara.  The best of them, *La
Agitación*, a poem written at the age of twenty-five, in those
days of ever-increasing Romantic enthusiasm, expresses with
some vigour the unrest and uncertainty of the writer's spirit
at a critical moment in his life, but suffers from confusion in
plan, and, despite drastic revision, contains over-affected
passages in which excessive ornateness of phraseology leads
to obscurity.  An example of this is the stanza :

> Mi planta no, mas de mi pecho ciego
> Llegó un lamento a penetrar su oído,
> Y en sus trémulos labios tocó el fuego
> De mi ardiente gemido.

Vega also wrote in prose, as we have said, with the
greatest elegance ;  those of his numerous dramatic translations from the French to which he devoted any care are
models of excellence in diction.  In his *Crítica del "Sí de las
Niñas"* he sets up as a stylistic rival to Moratín, and comes
out not greatly the loser.  Various of the characters of *La
Comedia Nueva* and other of the master's works figure in the
*Crítica*, and it really seems at times as though we were
listening to the same admirable prose, now somewhat rigid
and excessively polished but always distinguished by purity,
gentle irony and abundance of wit.

Like Bretón, and indeed like most people, Vega found
literature hardly a sufficient means of livelihood ;  like others
he had to seek and accept remunerated public employment ;  and like them, too, he was ruthlessly deprived of this
so soon as the political party which had appointed him fell
from power.  In 1856, however, he managed to obtain the
Directorship of the Conservatory of Music and Declamation,
a post which was in close harmony with his tastes and
talents.  This appointment he succeeded in retaining to the
end of his life.

He was always on excellent terms with the higher circles of
Madrid society, his pleasant and courtly manners making
him *persona grata* everywhere and his great gifts of reading
aloud and declamation giving him the *entrée* to great houses
as well as to aristocratic functions organized by amateurs in
drama.  In one of these functions, to his keen satisfaction,
he appeared on the stage with the Condesa de Teba, after-

wards Empress of the French ; and it is not hard to imagine that the well-known ideas of Napoleon III on Julius Cæsar and the Imperial democracy of Rome inspired the similar opinions to be found in *La Muerte de César* and other of his writings.

Never too robust, Vega broke down in health while still in middle age, and died, after a painful illness, in November 1865. Only three months previously, he had completed the preparation of an edition of his principal works, which a Spanish-American friend had agreed to subsidize. He did not live to see its publication, but it appeared in the year after his death, finely printed, though marred by numerous errata.

Some four years later appeared his translation of the first book of the *Æneid*,* which had provided him with pleasant occupation during the last part of his life, and received the same cordial welcome as had long been the lot of whatever came from his pen. It adds nothing, however, to his reputation. Written in unrhymed hendecasyllables, well constructed but often somewhat prosaic, it has little of the divine beauty of its original. Annibal Caro's Italian translation in the same metre is far superior to Vega's and Miguel Antonio Caro's Castilian *octavas* preserve and communicate much more of the spirit of Virgil's poetry.

* Cf. *Memorias de la Academia Española* (Madrid, 1870), Vol. II, pp. 468–97.

# CHAPTER IX

## GERTRUDIS GÓMEZ DE AVELLANEDA

I

La Avellaneda is generally considered to have been the greatest woman writer of Castilian verse in the history of literature and it is difficult to see how the opinion can be disputed. No other such woman can equal her in lyric poetry or drama, and during the Romantic period she has the further distinction of being in the front rank of lyricists irrespectively of sex. Like Ventura de la Vega, she was a Spanish-American—much more properly so, indeed, for, whereas Vega left Buenos Aires as a child and received the whole of his education in Spain, La Avellaneda lived in Cuba until she was twenty. By that time her tastes and character were already formed, and for her first master and model she chose a great Cuban poet, José María de Heredia, cousin of that other poet of the same name who wrote in French and has become justly famous for his sonnet-collection *Les Trophées*.

Like Vega, La Avellaneda had a Spanish father, her mother being a Cuban. She was born in the year 1814 at the inland town of Puerto Príncipe, the capital of a central region in the island, at that time still sparsely populated. The father, a naval officer, held a post of some importance in the military organization of the district but died while Gertrudis was a child. The mother re-married, her second husband being an army colonel and a native of Galicia, whither the whole family moved in 1836. The girl-poet bade farewell to her native land in a sonnet more affectionate, and of no less merit, than that of Vega (p. 152). Neither poet forgot the mother-land ; but, whereas Buenos Aires was the capital of a republic which had won its independence after sanguinary fighting and had not as yet established diplomatic relations with Spain, Cuba, bound to Spain as a colony, had perforce to maintain constant trade and intercourse with it : thus La Avellaneda found herself in uninterrupted contact with men and affairs in the country of her birth. From La Coruña she went with her brother to Andalusia, to visit the home of their paternal grandfather, and at Cádiz, in 1839, she published her first poems under the patronage of a man who, though never distinguished for his initiative, afterwards became a celebrated critic : Manuel Cañete, then director of a periodical entitled *La Aureola*. Gertrudis, who still thought of herself as something of a foreigner in Spain, adopted the pseudonym of "La Peregrina."

Towards the end of 1840, she went to Madrid. Spain was then at the height of the literary renaissance which began with the Romantic Revival. The Civil War had but recently come to an end and the activity and freedom of thought which accompanied it had not subsided. With the single exception of Larra, all the leaders of the literary revolt were still writing, and there also survived a few of the more venerable authors of the preceding century, such as Gallego and Quintana, who had kept the esteem of the new and reigning generation through their attachment to mediæval literature. The girl-poet, newly arrived from Andalusia, where she had won honours in literary contests, had before her arrival also become known to literary men in Madrid through the poems which she had published in Cádiz. They now found that with poetic talent of a high order she combined youth and beauty ; and, as one would expect, both the cultured society of the capital and its various literary circles received her with open arms and enthusiastically sang her praises. Only a year after her arrival in Madrid, she published the first collection of her poetry in a small volume to which Gallego contributed a preface of not exaggerated eulogy. From that time her reputation was assured and her name coupled with those of the greatest writers in the country.

These poems of 1841, slightly retouched and improved, but not greatly changed, reappeared with many others in 1850, in a volume of larger format which contains all the necessary material for the formation of a judgment on La Avellaneda's merits as a lyricist. Indeed, such a judgment ought properly to be based on this edition alone, since in the edition incorrectly described as "complete" (*Obras*

*Literarias*, Madrid, 1869–71, 5 vols.) various of the best of her poems were disfigured and weakened through an unhappy desire to improve them. She did, of course, continue to write after 1850 and this last edition contains many new works the style of which maintains the same high level of ability, but is clearly indicative of a diminished inspiration. Never again, however, did her genius shine with such brilliance as in the excellent collection of 1850, the last poem of which, it may be noted, bears the mournful title : "El último acento de mi arpa."

No poet ever conceived, or maintained, a higher ideal of literary art and a deeper respect for it than La Avellaneda ; and this ideal and respect she expressed in magnificent language and at a very early age in her ode *A la Poesía* and in the eloquent *octavas* dedicated to Gallego and entitled *El Genio poético :*

> La gloria de Marón el orbe llena,
> Aún suspiramos con Petrarca amante,
> Aún vive Milton y su voz resuena
> En su querube armado de diamante.
> Rasgando nubes de los tiempos truena
> El rudo verso del terrible Dante,
> Y desde el Ponto hasta el confín Ibero
> El son retumba del clarín de Homero.

Espronceda, no doubt, could write lines of this temper whenever he pleased, and even García y Tassara occasionally attained to their standard. Few of their contemporaries, however, reached it at all. Yet in La Avellaneda such lines recur with considerable frequency.

In the history of the nineteenth-century Spanish lyric, La Avellaneda represents the complete and skilful fusion of the Classical art of Quintana and Gallego with the Romantic lyricism of Byron, Lamartine and Victor Hugo. One feels that she has an equal affection and admiration for both ideals of poetry and that she studies and follows both with equal sympathy. From the Classicists she takes the lofty tone, the firm line and the well-rounded form ; from the Romantics, the note of intimate individuality, the profundity of emotion and the infinite variety of colour which enriches their palette. What she creates is therefore highly personal, and yet bears a close resemblance to the brilliant

work of her contemporary García y Tassara and her somewhat greater successor Núñez de Arce.

The ode of La Avellaneda entitled *La Cruz*, like Quintana's odes *Al Mar* or *A la Invención de la Imprenta*, is a rapid
and eloquent historical generalization in which, along the
broadest lines and with penetrating vision, she follows the
most celebrated stages of the journey of humanity down the
centuries.  Perhaps in the Spain of those days not even
Quintana would have been bold enough to venture her
serene and magnificent allusion to the separation of the
colonies :

> Dió un paso el tiempo, y a su influjo vario,
> Que tan pronto derroca como encumbra,
> No es ya de un mundo el otro tributario . . .
> Mas inmutable al signo del Calvario
> El sol del Inca y del Azteca alumbra.

And quite certainly Quintana would not have had the
audacity to make a sudden change of metre in the middle of
his poem, and to bring it to a close with stanzas composed
of lines of nine syllables as La Avellaneda here succeeds in
doing with such striking effect.

A number of her other poems suggest comparison with
Quintana.  A gravely melancholy elegy, *A una Acacia*,
reveals a solemn sadness, neither very intimate nor very
deep, much as does Quintana's beautiful *Despedida de la
Juventud*.  Both poems have a kind of sober charm, which
makes an ineffaceable impression.  The conclusion of one
stanza :

> La suerte
> De tu pompa fugaz también alcanza
> A mis dichas mezquinas,
> Y el astro sin calor que alumbra inerte
> Tus míseras ruinas,
> Imagen es del pálido recuerdo
> De aquel amor que para siempre pierdo.

is a reminiscence of Byron's poem *Sun of the sleepless*, which,
a year after writing her own poem, she translated very aptly,
under the title of *A la luna*.

> ¡ Oh, cuánto te semejas
> De la pasada dicha
> Al pálido recuerdo, que del alma
> Sólo hace ver la soledad sombría !

Verse translation was a pastime which La Avellaneda thoroughly enjoyed and of which she was a brilliant exponent. She frequently exercised her talents, not only on Byron, but also on Hugo and Lamartine. For Lamartine she had a great predilection and she translated him as skilfully as did Andrés Bello, though in quite a different style. Lamartine's meditation entitled *Bonaparte* might almost be considered to have been improved by its translation into Spanish. The form of the original—a series of stanzas metrically identical—is no doubt more artistic than the *silvas* of the translation, which have no fixed rhyme-scheme. But the sonority of La Avellaneda's diction, the sustained impulse of the lyrical movement and the vigour of the expression give greater brilliance to the Spanish version and enliven the somewhat monotonous effect of the original ode, which, after all, as Cesare Cantú observed in his *Reminiscenze*, is nothing but a paraphrase of Manzoni's *Cinque Maggio*. La Avellaneda's revision of her first version, which appears in the 1869 edition of her works, is an example of the way in which she altered her original lyrics without improving them.

The note of tenderness and deep pathos which can just be heard in *A una Acacia* and is so clearly perceptible in such a poem as Espronceda's *A una Estrella* is apt to be muted on the lyre of La Avellaneda. It is no doubt for this reason that her work has so often been described as masculine ; the reason, however, is inadequate and the description unjustifiable. She was essentially womanly, both in her published writings and in her private correspondence— indeed, in her whole life. But her womanliness was of a kind of which there must be many other examples : she was proud, high-minded, thoroughly sincere, unable to adapt herself readily to gentle and peaceful emotions. She had not sufficient passionate love to engage her entire soul and dominate her will ; it could never become the inspiration of the whole of her poetry, as it was of Sappho's. That ardent, compelling human love, which characterizes the deep experience and the chaste expression of such women as Marceline Desbordes-Valmore and Elizabeth Barrett Browning, in no way suggests or resembles the love revealed by La Avellaneda in the very few of her compositions which may be called true love-poems. The allusions to love

scattered elsewhere throughout her works are generally
vague and impersonal ; if one sets aside their high artistic
qualities, they are of a kind that might have been the work of
any other person, either man or woman.

Only two of La Avellaneda's poems can properly be called
love-lyrics.* Both these have the same title, *A Él,* and an
interval of five years separates them.  The first has so little
reality, and so little feeling, in its expression, that there are
two completely different texts of it :  the first is that of the
1841 and 1850 volumes ;  the second, that of 1869, is altered
to the point of transformation into something completely
new.  The latter is a genuine revision undertaken by La
Avellaneda at the age of fifty-five ;  its length is double that
of the first version, and the two have in common only three
or four short phrases and a rather differently worded simile.
We can hardly learn much from this of the true feelings of
La Avellaneda at the age of twenty-five.

The second of the two lyrics, first published in 1850 under
the title, *A . . . . .,* re-appears in the last edition, completely
unchanged, save in the title, which is now that of the preceding poem, *A Él.*  Since its author desired neither to add
to it nor to subtract from it, the natural inference would be
that it is the sincerer of the two and a truer representation
of a condition of her mind.   Never has a despairing woman
met disdain or betrayal (for the motive inspiring the poem
is not clearly indicated) with language of greater indignation,
vibrating with more concentrated energy.   Abandoned by
her lover, she cries :

> Te amé, no te amo ya, piénsolo al menos ;
> ¡ Nunca si fuere error, la verdad miré !
> Que tantos años de amarguras llenos
> Trague el olvido ;  el corazón respire !
> Lo has destrozado sin piedad :  mi orgullo
> Una vez y otra vez pisaste insano ;
> Mas nunca el labio exhalará un murmullo
> Para acusar tu proceder tirano.
> .    .    .    .    .    .
> No era tuyo el poder que irresistible
> Postró ante ti mis fuerzas vencedoras.

---

* We may omit *Amor y Orgullo,* as being disqualified by its author's own
scepticism as to the efficacy of the heroine's sacrifice :

> ¡ Feliz si en el sepulcro de su gloria
> Su amor también no deja sepultado !

Quísolo Dios y fué : ¡ gloria a su nombre !
Todo se terminó : recobro aliento ;
¡ Ángel de las venganzas ! ya eres hombre ;
Ni amor ni miedo al contemplarte siento.

The feeling which gives life to these lines is in no way
suggestive of the fragments that have come down to us under
the name of Sappho or the sonnets of Vittoria Colonna.*
La Avellaneda is not a woman immortalized by passion like
Eloïse or the "Portuguese Nun." She was a greater literary
artist than the first and had nothing at all in common with
the second. In the ode, in the elegy, and, most of all, in
the field of her chief glories, the drama, her vigorous inspiration, energetic diction, grandiloquence and love of the
noble and the beautiful succeeded in combining and
establishing themselves in works that will be immortal.
But on the other hand she does not belong to the select
body of patient craftsmen of the written word, faithful lovers
of perfect and exquisitely chiselled form, a class of writer
none too well represented in Spanish literature. Her style
is robust rather than delicate ; her sense of diction is too
easily content with meaningless or unsatisfying words, weak
rhymes, vague expressions. Such blemishes as *cadáver frío*,
*silencio mudo, humo leve* have persisted, despite careful revision,
in the definitive versions of some of the best of her poems,
and it is only right to draw attention to these when one
eulogizes her extraordinary merits.

Of one notable modern poetess alone are we reminded in
reading La Avellaneda : Louise-Victoire Ackermann. In
both these women energy, vigour and eloquence are pre-
dominating gifts, and even in style they are not entirely
dissimilar. But La Avellaneda sought and found in religion
consolations which the French poetess, like her English
contemporary, George Eliot, considered a mere narcotic
and as such incompatible with her gloomy philosophical
pessimism.

La Avellaneda's life in Madrid, where she was treated with
uniform respect and admiration, and where on several
occasions she enjoyed great successes on the stage, was
nevertheless not entirely happy. More than her share of

* For a contrary opinion, which seems to me to contradict the evidence of La
Avellaneda's life and writings, see Juan Valera : *Juicios Literarios*, Madrid,
1890.

human calamity fell to her, and this weighed the more heavily upon her because her mind was naturally addicted to pessimism, though, thanks to her profound and unalterable confidence in the counsels of the Church, she bore all her troubles with resignation. At thirty-two, inspired less by love than by a heroic sentiment of duty, she married a promising young politician. Shortly before the ceremony she addressed her future husband in some quatrains replying "to some lines in which he endeavoured to draw his own likeness" :

> Yo como vos para admirar nacida,
> Yo como vos para el amor creada,
> Por admirar y amar diera mi vida,
> Para admirar y amar no encuentro nada.
>
> . . . . .
>
> Yo no puedo sembrar de eternas flores
> La senda que corréis de frágil vida ;
> Pero si en ella recogéis dolores
> Un alma encontraréis que los divida.

But the year which saw her married left her a widow. The first months of her widowhood she spent in a convent at Bordeaux, where she bewailed her lot in two pathetic, grief-laden elegies. A few characteristic lines may be quoted from the first of them :

> ¡ De juventud, de amor, de fuerza henchido,
> Su porvenir cuán vasto parecía ! . . .
> Mas la mañana terminó su día !
> ¡ Ya del tiempo no es !
> Al golpe atroz que me desgarra el pecho
> No quiere Dios que mi valor sucumba ;
> Mas con los restos que tragó esa tumba
> Se hundió mi corazón.

Nine years later she married again, her second husband being a colonel of artillery. Once more the bride found herself a nurse, for her husband was treacherously stabbed, in broad daylight, when he was walking to the Congress of Deputies, of which he was a member. The wound was serious, and for a long time he hung between life and death, but eventually he reached the stage of convalescence, though never again becoming completely strong. Then husband and wife accepted the invitation to go to Cuba with General

Serrano, who had been appointed Captain-General of the island.

So, after an absence of twenty-three years, La Avellaneda returned to her native country. She was well received by her compatriots and honoured by a public "coronation" at a great theatrical function organized for the purpose by a popular literary society. But even the kindly climate of Cuba was unable to prolong her husband's life, and soon she found herself once more a widow. The blow was an even heavier one than before and she returned to Spain in the depths of sorrow and depression. From that time onward she wrote nothing more of importance. During her journey to Europe she improvised some stanzas entitled *A vista del Niágara*, and in these there are a few good lines, together with a generous apostrophe to José María de Heredia :

> ¡ Oh, si la esquiva musa,
> Que al desaliento su favor rehusa,
> Por un instante me otorgara ahora
> Del gran vate de Cuba el plectro ardiente ! . . .

After this she composed little but religious poetry and her dejection increased daily. "My sole ideal," she wrote to her friend Cecilia Böhl (the novelist Fernán Caballero) in a letter dated September 17, 1866, "is to end this sad life in a convent. If I have not long ago attempted to fulfil this desire, it is probably only because I have hesitated to cast away my final illusion and my last hope of happiness upon earth." New troubles embittered her life still further. First came the death of her only brother, for long (as she wrote in a letter) her "inseparable companion." Then followed the revolution of October 1868, which led to the dethronement and flight of Queen Isabel, and imperilled the situation of La Avellaneda's close friends the Duke and Duchess of Montpensier, which, with the critical condition of her adopted country, was a source of great grief to her. "Le aseguro," she wrote to a friend in February 1869,

> Le aseguro, mi estimado amigo, que va entrándome gran-dísimo desaliento respecto a la cosa pública, pareciéndome que este pobre país español lleva en lo más íntimo de su naturaleza el germen mortal. . . . Mucho desearía arreglar aquí mis negocios para poderme marchar a Portugal o Francia, aunque a decir verdad no creo que en este último punto se vea el horizonte más claro que por acá.

She sought distraction from her troubles in revising and correcting her literary productions, but was unable to bring the task to completion. At the end of the fifth of the six volumes, her strength failed her, and, after a brief illness, she died on February 1, 1873, a few weeks before her fifty-ninth birthday.

II

*Alfonso Munio*, a four-act tragedy first given in 1844, was La Avellaneda's great *début* in drama, where so many successes awaited her. It is only a sketch, quite imperfect in itself, but full of poetic life, giving promise of greater things to come. The plot, though interesting, is hardly substantial enough to occupy the four acts : it is merely the skeleton of a tragedy, and, with the exception of Munio and his daughter Fronilde, the characters are mere indications, lightly sketched in outline ; the last act but one, however, which ends with Fronilde's death, produces a striking impression. The dramatic illusion has been skilfully prepared, and the uneasy sensation is abroad that something dreadful is about to happen ; when at last, amid thunderings and lightnings, Munio re-appears, emerging from the room into which he has followed his daughter in order to kill her, and cries, beside himself,

¡ Horrible tempestad, desata un rayo !*

the audacity of the effect produced is sublimely Romantic.

The chief distinction of the drama consists in its poetic style, marvellous both for its power and its spontaneity as well as for the eloquence and vigour of its versification. Unhappily, however, this quality, which is indisputably its chief merit, was greatly diminished in the author's revised version of 1869. The plan of the play she left completely untouched and the details of the plot almost entirely so ; while, in changing the title and the protagonist's name to Munio Alfonso, she followed historical tradition more closely. But she also quite unnecessarily disfigured the style and language of the play, transforming the vigour and youthfulness which had given so much delight at its *estreno* into her debilitated manner of a quarter of a century later.

* So the 1869–71 edition.   The original version has "¡ Mándame un rayo !"

She omitted, for example, those fine lines near the end of the play :

> Con el riego
> Que prepara mi mano, la cosecha
> De invictos héroes brotará abundante
> Tu suelo venturoso . . .

and substituted the following four lines, all of inferior quality and the last positively execrable :

> Marchemos a aplacar los caros manes
> Con torrentes de sangre sarracena,
> A cuyo riego—¡ el alma me lo anuncia !—
> De héroes la España cogerá cosecha. . . .

With *Alfonso Munio*, in its original form, La Avellaneda had made a good beginning.   This she followed up, a year later, with two plays which she termed, not "tragedias," a name she did not again use, but "dramas trágicos" : *El Príncipe de Viana* and *Egilona*.   These two plays show no advance upon their predecessor, but they had a good run on the stage, and, if their author gained no ground with them, she certainly lost none.

*Saúl* (described as a "Biblical tragedy" in its first edition, and as a "Biblical drama" in 1869) was read publicly at the Liceo de Madrid in 1846 and was presented in revised form at the Teatro Español three years later.   It had only a moderate success, but none the less it is a play of the loftiest inspiration, in which the author consciously challenges so great a predecessor as Alfieri and, in the lyrical part of her work, surpasses him.   She acknowledges that she was inspired to write her play by the tragedies of Alfieri and Soumet, based on the same theme, very strangely placing them on an equal level, and attempting in this drama to harmonize their different qualities.   Her play has nothing of Alfieri's severe simplicity and systematic sobriety, but it is more attractive than his, for it makes an irresistible appeal through its fresh, penetrating, poetic perfume, its rich melody and its variety of rhythm.   The lyric passages in La Avellaneda's *Saúl* are very noteworthy : one of the finest, unfortunately mutilated in the 1869 edition, is the wonderful lament of Saúl's daughter Micol, David's wife, in the last act, with its prophecy of ruin and death.

La Avellaneda continued to write for the stage in the

years which followed. In 1852 she produced a comedy, *La Hija de las Flores*, which was greatly applauded, and bears witness to the flexibility of her powers. Then come two curious but well-written verse translations from French originals : Emile Augier's *Aventurière* (*La Aventurera*, 1848) and a prose drama by Alexandre Dumas and A. Maquet, entitled *Catilina* (1867). In 1852, again, she produced a happy dramatic adaptation of an historical theme to which she gave the rather less happy title of *La Verdad vence apariencias* ; this theme is the same which served Byron for his *Werner*. The action of La Avellaneda's play takes place in the fourteenth century, first during the night after the battle of Nájera between Peter the Cruel and his brother Henry, and then after the battle of Montiel, during the latter's reign. It is cleverly constructed, keeps the interest at its height to the very end and has more local colour than many Romantic and semi-Romantic plays of this period.

Finally, in 1858, appeared La Avellaneda's supreme dramatic effort, *Baltasar*, the best play she ever wrote and one which not only placed her high among the great dramatists of the period but will maintain her reputation at that level.

*Baltasar : drama oriental* was the full title of the play, both in the first edition and in succeeding editions, until that of 1869, where, to our surprise, we are informed by the list of *errata* that the adjective has all the time been a misprint for *original* ! The change is certainly justified, for the fact that the action of a play takes place in Asia hardly suffices to define it as "oriental," especially when its orientalism is merely historical. As La Avellaneda was well acquainted with the works of Byron, had translated some of his poems and had made use of the plot of his *Werner*, it was only natural that some similarity should be suspected between her *Baltasar* and Byron's *Sardanapalus*. The resemblance between them is unmistakable but there is nothing in La Avellaneda that can be described as genuine and direct imitation. If, as is most probable, it was Byron who gave her the idea of staging this oriental monarch, immersed in pleasures and contemptuous of his fellows, yet, despite all his egoism and effeminacy, displaying enough courage and energy in his last hour to meet his end like a hero, the similarity goes but a little way beyond these general traits, and the dramatist develops her theme in her own way and with her own resources, without any loss of originality.

In *Sardanapalus* the interest is more human and consequently more pathetic. In the dedication to her own play La Avellaneda describes its inspiration as religious. It ends with the prophecy of Daniel, the period of the seventy weeks and the announcement of the rebuilding of the temple, which "shall hear the voice of the Messiah." Baltasar, doing battle against Divine Omnipotence, has been compelled to yield ; the catastrophe, which has been predicted, and is inevitable and independent of the will of man, turns Baltasar's death and the final conflagration into a detail of minor importance. Nitocris, as he flings the torch with which he sets fire to the palace in order that he may perish there with the mortal remains of his dead son, is a pale figure compared with Byron's compelling creation, Myrrha, the Greek slave who with a similar gesture kindles the pyre and throws herself into the flames that she may die in the embrace of the Assyrian monarch. There was, of course, no place in the plan of *Baltasar* for any scene equivalent to the long and magnificent one in which Myrrha and Sardanapalus complete their funeral preparations and bid life a melancholy farewell—a grandiose and truly poetical scene, one of the finest in the entire range of Byron's tragedies. But the Spanish play, considered as a whole, is less monotonous, and is certainly richer and more varied in form. Baltasar, again, is no abstraction but a living person. In this he resembles Sardanapalus, who, as he moves through the play, is torn by feelings which, if at times they seem over-modern and over-Romantic, are not untrue to the situation in which he finds himself and leave a deep impression of barbarity combined with greatness.

We have said nothing as yet of La Avellaneda's work in prose, though it fills two volumes of the 1869 edition. These volumes consist principally of novels and tales ; of the articles which she contributed to periodicals they include only a single short series dated 1860 and collected under the title "La Mujer." These make pleasant reading, but are superficial in the extreme, their object being to prove that "the intellectual and moral power of woman is *at least* the equal of that of man." They reflect their author's disillusion in her encounter with the Spanish Academy.

When the death of Juan Nicasio Gallego caused a vacancy in its ranks, La Avellaneda came forward, in response to many suggestions from her admirers, as a candidate for the honour of election. By a narrow majority, however, the Academy rejected her, passing a resolution that it would not elect women to membership.

Among the novels in this collection we miss the three earliest : *Sab, Dos Mujeres* and *Guatimozín*. The first and the third of these are based on American subjects. *Sab* is of particular interest, the hero being a mulatto slave in Cuba, whom adversity provides with the opportunity to display the feelings of a hero. But the picture of the odious *régime* that exploits and humbles him has not the tragic force of *Uncle Tom's Cabin*, a vigorous novel on a similar theme by a famous American woman writer which became an outstanding success ten years later. The brilliance of La Avellaneda's talent is seen in poetic tales and *leyendas* rather than in full-length novels, and is never displayed as strikingly in prose as in verse. But in both media, though using different methods and attaining different results, she sounds the same note of sincerity.

# CHAPTER X

## RAMÓN DE CAMPOAMOR

In the same year as Zorrilla, García Tassara and Rodríguez Rubí (the *annus mirabilis*, as we have already called it, of 1817) Ramón de Campoamor y Campoossorio was born in a little village of Asturias. He was destined to outlive all his literary colleagues, and to die, full of years and eulogies, in 1901. Like Zorrilla, he left school and grew into adolescence just as romanticism in Spain was reaching the climax of its success, and his first poems appeared about the same time as Zorrilla's.

Before proceeding farther, it may be as well if we answer a question which will certainly come to the mind of every reader. "How," we shall be asked, "can Campoamor be included among the Romantics?"

The answer is that, though he was not a Romantic for long (for, while still a young man, he deserted a movement which was so clearly unable to hold public opinion), his life and works have a very definite place in the history of the Romantic ideal in Spain. He was a man of his age, keenly sensitive to the impressions of the moment, and in his first two verse collections, *Ternezas y Flores* (1840) and *Ayes del Alma* (1842), sang plaintively in the Romantic strain. At that time the reading public was captivated by Zorrilla, for whom it reserved all its enthusiasm. Around the pale forehead of this true Romantic, crowned by its head of abundant black hair, his odes, dirges, ballads and dramas formed a luminous halo which gave him a distinction surpassing that of any of his rivals. Campoamor found it as impossible as the rest to avoid imitating Zorrilla, adopting the same tone and seeking to convey his effects by exactly the same methods. Such lines as these, for example, from *Ternezas y Flores*, might well have belonged to Zorrilla in his less inspired moments :

Errante sol de aromas circundado,
Tu ardiente lumbre tenue debilita,
Que ya mi corazón de arder cansado
Negro sus alas moribundo agita.

And Zorrilla would gladly have sponsored such *quintillas* as those of *Tu boca* or *La Beata de máscara*.

But Campoamor soon realized that if he was to stand out from the crowd he must branch off in a new direction, for he could not compete with such an adversary as Zorrilla on his own ground. At about the end of the fourth decade of the century, then, he set out resolutely upon a fresh road, facing almost diametrically the opposite way to that of the road which he had been taking previously. He abandoned Zorrilla—the "divine bard," as he calls him—and with him his picturesque Romantic world of light and colour, and set out to write "philosophical" poetry, to tread what he calls "the field of subjective, intimate and completely personal impressions." This rather surprising *ex post facto* description of his new ideals, which we purposely quote in his own words, is given in a book entitled *El Personalismo*, which he published in 1855. He hewed out his own path, explored new ground and did all that he could to break with romanticism. Gradually he became convinced that in making the change he had found the true bent of his natural talent and the secret of his own poetical power. Accordingly he thought that he might invent something new— if only a new word for something that already existed. And so he invented the *dolora*, and a number of other types of verse which, when all was said, proved to be of much the same character, distinguished from one another chiefly by variation in length—the *pequeño poema*, the *humorada*, the *cantar*. Armed with the first of these inventions, he set out upon his career with a high heart and supreme confidence, and it was not long before he reached the coveted goal of an enviable reputation and heard the applause which was so sweet to him—the just reward, it must be allowed, of his determined and persevering labours. And the loud applause and the glorious reputation lasted as long as even he could have wished.*

---

* See Bibliography, *sub* Campoamor (p. 243, below) for an idea of the extent of his reputation.

In the first edition of the *Doloras*, that of 1846, Campoamor defined the *dolora* thus :

> Una composición poética, en la cual se debe hallar unida la ligereza con el sentimiento y la concisión con la importancia filosófica.

This conveniently vague definition, which could be applied with sufficient propriety to many of the verses actually included in the collection, was equally applicable to some of Campoamor's earlier fables and to a large number of epigrams, lyrics or even German *Lieder* well known in Spain before the *dolora* was so much as thought of.

The best and fairest criterion by which to judge the *Doloras* is that which we apply to any other collection of verses—their intrinsic worth. The new *genre* as such, if new it is, may be left to take care of itself—to find its place, or lose itself, in history. Titles and definitions, after all, are details of small importance. No great weight has been laid on the precise sense of the term *Orientales* as used by Victor Hugo for a collection of poems which have certain traits in common but are by no means limited in subject to the Orient. Yet the title was accepted by everyone, unquestioningly, and later *Orientales* of a vaguely similar kind were written by Zorrilla, Arolas and other Spanish poets.

Well or ill named, the *Doloras* are not, nor did they ever claim to be, Romantic poetry : so much was made clear more than once by their inventor himself. They are in open contradiction with Romantic doctrine, which deprecates any tendency to be prosaic in style, and, often for lack of ideas (which we cannot all possess), attempts consistently to keep for poetry all its prosodical devices, its wealth of music and its essential lyricism. These things take quite a subsidiary place in the *Doloras*, the chief preoccupation of which is with philosophizing ; with presenting, whether in semi-dramatic or dialogue form, or as apologue or narrative, moral reflections, lessons from experience and philosophical judgments. Thus the *dolora* becomes a kind of fable, in which there is nothing to compensate for its lack of naturalness and simple *bonhomie* when compared with the fables of La Fontaine—a quality, it may be added, which such professed Spanish fabulists as Samaniego, Iriarte and Hartzenbusch failed to achieve likewise.

The chief fault of the *Doloras* is their prosaism. Campoamor's poetic diction, which often has ingenuity or sobriety, though seldom originality, almost invariably fails, for lack of power, when it attempts to soar. On the other hand Campoamor has generally something to say : he certainly thinks for himself, plans his verses with care, and occasionally, when he has made himself master of his inspiration and when his form and his thought are therefore in perfect consonance and harmony, produces masterpieces. Such are *¡ Quién supiera escribir !* the *Gaitero de Gijón* and four or five more really noteworthy poems of the same type, to say nothing of such vigorous and varied descriptive poems as *El Tren Expreso* and a few more of the *Pequeños Poemas*.

Yet it was not for nothing that Campoamor was born in 1817 and not without significance that he lived and grew up among Romantics and breathed the atmosphere of the Romantic Revolt. There came a time when his literary evolution seemed complete. He was hailed as leader of the new anti-Romantic movement in poetry. He added precept to example by bringing out his own *Poética,* which ran clean counter to the ideals of Espronceda and Zorrilla ; upon this *Poética* he lectured publicly in the Madrid Ateneo and afterwards published it in book form. Yet he never entirely lost the traces of his first literary impressions and of the lessons learned in his youth. There is abundant testimony in the productions of his maturer years that he was a frequent and careful reader of Victor Hugo. A large number of phrases and ideas taken from these productions and shown to have been copied almost literally from Hugo were collected and published in 1873 in a Madrid periodical called *El Globo.* The result was a long and heated discussion, in which Campoamor was alternately abused and defended ; but the actual fact of the plagiarisms was recognized, implicitly or openly, by all, including Campoamor himself in his *Poética.**

The discussion itself, though it did no good to Campoamor's reputation, is not historically of great importance. The significance of the matter is that he was a man of his age—*i.e.* of the age in which he was brought up—only as far as the point at which he could not be otherwise ; that he

* On this question, see Juan Valera, *Disertaciones y Juicios Literarios* (Madrid, 1890), p. 190.

rebelled very early against the influences of his *milieu* and of the time at which he had happened to achieve his first successes ; and that his energy of will, his industry, his laudable insistence upon creating a *genre*, leading a movement, and utilizing his peculiar literary gifts transformed him into the poet of the *Doloras*. From this time forward he wrote in effect nothing but *doloras* (though these were of widely different dimensions and bore different names), thus revolutionizing, in his own words, both "the content and the form of poetry,"* but remaining always—again in his own words—"a lover of letters rather than a professional writer."†

Campoamor both foresaw and actually witnessed the reaction which could not but succeed the wordy lyricism often carried to such ridiculous exaggeration by Zorrilla, and still farther by Zorrilla's imitators. He was shrewd enough to choose the right moment to lead the reaction, profiting by the state of mind of a public wearied to extinction by such abuse of mere melody devoid of sense or significance ; but unfortunately he went to the opposite extreme, and in his eagerness to flee from the vague jinglings of his predecessors, began almost immediately to write in rhymed prose. In the very first of the *Doloras* in chronological order, a poem entitled *Cosas de la edad*, there are premonitions of this danger ; write down the lines of its first *quintilla* just as they stand, without observing the metrical divisions, and you have a paragraph of prose. So Campoamor began and so he went on ; the process just described can be applied to any number of his other poems with the same results. No one, for example, but for the rhymes, could say if the first lines of these ingenious and celebrated stanzas were verse or prose :

> ¡ Pobre Carolina mía !—¡ Nunca la podré
> olvidar !—Ved lo que el mundo decía,—
> Viendo el féretro pasar.

It is altogether too facile a task to write "poetry" in this fashion, yet, securely if slowly, success came to it. When, about the year 1850, the glory of Zorrilla was seen to be paling, the brilliant star of Campoamor was rising on the farther horizon. Edition of his succeeded edition rapidly, both in Europe and in America ; it would be a difficult task

* *Poética*, p. 35.                    † *Poética*, p. 126.

to-day to make a complete list of them. Campoamor himself, according to his biographer, gave any bookseller who wished to publish either his earlier or his later works generous permission to do so. And they took full advantage of his liberality, especially to re-publish the *Doloras*, which of all Campoamor's collections was easily the favourite.

It was clear, however, that admirers of what Lope de Vega might have called the "Arte Nuevo de hacer versos líricos" were not precisely those who had so eagerly read the poems of the great Romantics and had applauded them with such enthusiasm. The same person could hardly have an equal admiration for Campoamor and Espronceda, two poets representing the opposite poles of literature ; Campoamor's public, which, both in Spain and Spanish-America, was continually on the increase, seems to have been largely recruited from among persons who had no real love for poetry at all. In every modern society there are classes and individuals who can endure reading verse only if it contains material far removed from the essence of poetry, something which it cannot offer without debasing its own character, something which quenches its exquisite perfume. They demand oracular expositions of homely philosophical truisms or maxims of apparent profundity clothed in language of affected simplicity. The reader who would find copious examples of both these types of verse has only to glance at the table of contents of a volume of *Doloras*, and, without going beyond the first five-and-twenty, he will discover *Quien vive olvida, No hay dicha en la tierra, Vanidad de la hermosura, Todo se pierde, Quien más pone pierde más,* and so on.

Among Campoamor's particular literary bugbears were the poets Herrera and Quintana, and we may suppose that he had no greater attachment to Espronceda, or to any great lyric poet, either Classical or Romantic. It is not merely the studied simplicity of his language that puts a gulf between Campoamor and these models ; he is equally far removed from them by the defectiveness of his versification. He never succeeded in completely mastering subtleties of metre and accentual rhythm and in using them with any variety or grace. So competent a judge as Miguel Antonio Caro could say, in a note to Andrés Bello's *Poética*, that he hardly knew whether the Asturian pronunciation or some peculiar mental deafness must be held responsible for such unpronounceable combinations as :

> Me dijo el Redentor : "Presente o ausente . . ."

> Engañosa o engañada hasta aquel día . . .

Both these lines belong to the poem entitled *El Drama Universal*, which contains many similar ones. This poem is a long work in five acts, or cantos, published in 1869, and certainly of greater interest than the languid and almost unreadable *Colón*, which had appeared ten years earlier. *El Drama Universal* is a fantastic poem of vast proportions, something after the style of the second part of Goethe's *Faust*, containing a complete philosophy, summarizing the entire history of the human race and expounding some strange ideas on the transmigration of souls and the origin of worship, but containing no character of the stature of a Faust, a Helen or a Mephistopheles. The chief personages of the poem—Honorio, Soledad, Palaciano—are mere names, or rather shadows. They have no life or interest ; they owe the poet no thanks for endowing them with the immortality of art. The style of the poem is very careless and unequal and many of its lines, like those cited, are weak or inharmonious, though others, it must be admitted, are vigorous in the extreme. Such are the lines quoted by the Colombian critic Rafael Pombo :

> Y es siempre para el alma la materia
> De su eterno pecar eterna excusa.

> En torno de lo claro y definido
> Vuela algo indefinible y misterioso.

> Como el castigo a toda falta llega,
> Le llega a cada pena su esperanza.

> Por no turbar, la madre, resignada,
> Tal vez el sueño o la quietud del hijo,
> Al umbral de la puerta, acurrucada,
> *Hasta mañana aguardaré*, se dijo.

We may add a few lines from Pombo's criticism of this poem, the most considerable piece of work that Campoamor has left us. "If to our way of thinking *El Drama Universal* is neither poem nor drama, it is nevertheless the work of a poet : weak in construction but rich in precious ore, which may well be mined by poets of the future. . . . We must recognize in it a clear perception of a worthy ideal, a notable talent, a none too common interest in content and moral aim ; at times we can even discern genuine inspiration produced in the poet by incidents of true sublimity. It is greatly to be deplored that an author combining such gifts should have been at pains to convince us that he lacked instinct for form, plasticity of language, and the gift of going straight to the sources of his ideas and of opening a pure, natural current to flow serenely through a chaos of verbiage."*

Such was Pombo's judgment of a fellow-poet in the year 1872 ; and, though Campoamor lived for nearly thirty years longer, our considered judgment upon his work as a whole can hardly be very different.    It was natural that his powers should decrease in old age ;  the last of the *Pequeños Poemas*, for example, are markedly inferior to the *Tren Expreso*, which was the first of them.    But fortunately it is needless to go into these in detail, our task in this chapter having been to show the relation of Campoamor to the Romantic movement and to his own Romantic contemporaries, which task may now be considered at an end, or, at least, in no way advanced by a detailed study of his declining genius.

It must not be supposed, however, that, because we have so limited ourselves in accordance with the subject of this study, we are minimizing the importance of the place earned by Campoamor, both as to his prose and as to his verse, in the history of the evolution of modern Spanish literature. At times, when we read his *Personalismo*, his *Polémicas* and his *Poética*, so elegant, so completely unaffected and so full of ease, we wonder if his prose has not rarer and more enduring qualities than his verse.    In the *Poética*, more particularly, from its first line to its last, we find a portrait of the man Campoamor himself, drawn with a precision of feature, a vividness and an intensity of characterization, such as can never be found in the *Doloras* or the other verse collections.

* *El Mundo Nuevo* (New York, 1872), Vol. I, p. 274.

# CHAPTER XI

## TWO PROSE-WRITERS : DONOSO CORTÉS AND BALMES

### I

We have just been speaking of prose, and we remarked, it will be remembered, in an earlier chapter, that, next to Larra, the most original and brilliant prose writer among all those who were born or flourished during the so-called Romantic period was Juan Donoso Cortés, also known as the Marqués de Valdegamas. It seems to us indisputable that there is no Spanish prose of high rank, in the early nineteenth century, other than that of Larra and Donoso Cortés. The best poems of Espronceda and Zorrilla can stand in an anthology beside the eclogues of Garcilaso and the odes of Herrera. The best dramas of Rivas, García Gutiérrez and Hartzenbusch or the best comedies of Bretón are comparable in quality with those of Lope de Vega and his successors. But who can speak of Toreno, Alcalá Galiano, and Pidal, or even of Estébanez Calderón, Mesonero Romanos or Fernán Caballero in the same breath as of the great chroniclers and historians of the Golden Age, the host of ascetics and mystics or the initiators of the novel from the early Picaresque writers to that supreme artist, Cervantes?

Larra, for all his youth, may stand unabashed amid so great a company, and Donoso Cortés, in a literary sense, belonged to the family of Larra. He made a particular contribution to the prose of the Romantic period, working out for himself a style which, while entirely typical of his personality and entirely Spanish, brings to the mind a vivid recollection of the brilliant yet substantial prose of Chateaubriand, Xavier de Maistre, Lamennais and Lerminier. Oratorical, ornate, replete with images, this style might well have served to inaugurate a school. At a later date Emilio Castelar went far towards popularizing it, but unfortunately he fell a victim to exaggeration, and finally, amid the trash of hyper-lyricism, it disappeared.

Born in an Extremaduran village in 1809, Donoso Cortés was educated at Salamanca and distinguished himself in legal studies at Seville. His precocity and industry, however, were of little practical use to him, for according to the regulations of the day his youth prevented him from obtaining the title of *abogado*, which he took only in 1833. His great eloquence, which also showed itself when he was still a young man, gained him employment as a teacher of literature at Cáceres, and, for want of a more congenial field, his active mind found scope and stimulus in literary activity, while he awaited the disappearance of Ferdinand VII and that deadening political *régime* which suffocated and consumed all the vigour of Spanish youth.

In the poems which he wrote at this time there is something more than the ardour and spontaneity common in *juvenilia*, as may be seen from two of them : an elegy on the death of the Duquesa de Frías and an attempt at an epic entitled *El Cerco de Zamora*, written for an Academy contest. This last is the only piece of verse included in the five large volumes of his works published by Tejado (Madrid, 1854). The elegy is to be found in the volume where it first appeared, a *Corona Fúnebre* published in honour of the Duchess, in 1830. In the epic there are a number of descriptive passages of merit. The elegy is naturally far inferior to the three by Gallego, Quintana and Martínez de la Rosa in the same *Corona*, but it is probably better than any of the others. Despite its Classical reminiscences and the artificial tone in which it opens, there are suggestions, in several stanzas, of the impassioned vehemence of the future orator. "Alto prócer de Iberia," runs the peroration, addressing the Duque de Frías, who was himself a poet :

> Alto prócer de Iberia,
> La musa es el dolor, vate el que llora.
> Cuando en torno a su frente laureada
> Nube espantosa pálida se mece,
> Y del rayo humeante acompañada
> El mortal que la mira se estremece,
> Alza la voz, y el sublimado acento
> Lleva sonando el viento
> Hasta el abismo obscuro :
> El abismo le escucha ensordecido :
> La destrucción le inspira :
> ¡ La destrucción también suene en tu lira !

Hardly was Ferdinand VII dead than Donoso Cortés embarked boldly upon a political career with the aim of supporting Isabel's claims to the throne and her mother's regency.  At that time, as a result of his apprenticeship to Quintana, he was an ultra-liberal, and his historical studies had convinced him that only through liberty could Spain find regeneration and the effects of the past *régime* be destroyed.  This was his first theme, developed in one of his early essays, dated 1834, in which he maintains the freedom of the citizen to rise in revolt, and upholds the rights of "revolutions, which would be the greatest scourge of nations if tyrants had not made them necessary." The Holy Alliance he describes as an "alliance of tigers, made to teach men how to form an alliance of b.ethren." The Spanish Revolution of 1820 he justifies in the following striking passage :

> España desenterró el estandarte que había tremolado en Cádiz, que libre e independiente había conservado en otros días el depósito de la existencia nacional y el esplendor inmaculado de su gloria.  La revolución, abandonando después la escena del mundo a la Santa Alianza, no había renunciado ni a la existencia ni a la victoria, y se refugió en las entrañas de las sociedades para crecer en silencio, para aparecer espontáneamente en el día señalado por la Providencia.  La aurora de este día había ya brillado en el horizonte de España y su luz se dilató como por encanto por otros países, dispuestos también a saludarla, porque en la escuela del infortunio habían aprendido a conocerla, y entre los hierros que la oprimían le habían erigido un altar.*

A year later, in 1835, still retaining his steadfast faith in liberty, he studies history in the light of liberal opinions :

> En el seno de las Universidades, ligado, pero no vencido, por el yugo de Roma, crecía el principio de la razón independiente, Hércules que había de purgar la tierra de monstruos y a quien la tierra había de llamar su soberano y ceñir una diadema, cuando subiese al trono que le tenían preparado los que ya le adoraban en su cuna.

Elsewhere, in a single phrase, he summarizes the opinions he then held of the French Revolution.  It was to him the conclusion of the drama of the emancipation of the world, "el

* *Consideraciones sobre la diplomacia y su influencia en el estado político y social de Europa.*  Madrid, 1834.

gran drama que comienza en la crucifixión de Jesús para concluir con la expiación de Luis."*

Many of these ideas of his had undergone some change as early as 1837. The mutiny of La Granja, with its unhappy consequences—"el aterrador carácter del movimiento revolucionario de las provincias," as it was called by Donoso's friend Pacheco†—left an ineradicable mark upon his spirit. He lost much of his earlier confidence in the practice of liberty and from his *cátedra* in the Ateneo he began publicly to proclaim the necessity of resistance :

> La historia de los gobiernos que resisten es la historia de los gobiernos tutelares : la de los que, en vez de resistir, invaden, es la historia de los gobiernos tiránicos : la de los que en vez de resistir, ceden, es la historia de los gobiernos imbéciles. Los primeros, al pasar, dejan en pos de sí una huella luminosa : los segundos, una huella de sangre : los últimos, una huella de lodo. Sobre el sepulcro de los primeros cantan un himno las naciones : sobre el de los segundos, escriben los hombres una maldición indeleble y un anatema terrible : sobre la losa funeral de los últimos se deposita el desprecio de todas las generaciones que pasan.‡

But in philosophy and religion his opinions changed more slowly. In the lecture from which this last passage is taken, he speaks eulogistically of Wyclif and John Huss, and finally describes Luther as "not beginning, but concluding, the great work of secularizing the human intelligence." He had still a vast way to go, in the space of a few years, before reaching the position of his *Ensayo sobre el catolicismo, el liberalismo y el socialismo*, and delivering himself of those stern negatives, carved out in phrases of the utmost plasticity, like medals on which are still discernible the clear imprint of his own irreconcilably ascetic profile. In the aphorisms of this, his principal work, we still seem to hear the vibrant tones of the orator, the accents of the enlightened pessimist and the prophet of misfortune, which so often resounded within the walls of the Congress of Deputies.

> Entre la verdad y la razón humana ha puesto Dios una repugnancia inmortal y una repulsión invencible. . . . La razón

* *La Ley electoral considerada en su base y en su relación con el espíritu de nuestras instituciones.* Madrid, 1895.
† Joaquín Francisco Pacheco : *Discurso en la Academia Española*, November 27, 1853.
‡ *Lecciones de Derecho político.* Madrid, 1837.

sigue al error a donde quiera que va, como una madre ternísima sigue a donde quiera que va, aunque sea el abismo más profundo, al fruto amado de su amor, al hijo de sus entrañas.*

That long period of fifteen years which separates opinions so different, and points of view so dramatically opposed, Donoso spent in supporting the Moderate party, and fighting loyally against the Progressives for the Queen Regent, Cristina, with whom he spent some time in exile as private secretary. Two very different events, both unexpected and both equally painful, precipitated this final phase of his life, this final incarnation of his restless spirit : the lingering illness and Christian death of a favourite brother in 1847 and the French Revolution of 1848.

The evolution, when completed, was extraordinary in its thoroughness ; like Lamennais, Donoso Cortés passed from one extreme of thought to the other, though in the contrary direction. Lamennais, at one time the most valiant and intrepid champion of Ultramontanism since the mediæval popes and doctors, the author of that celebrated *Essai sur l'indifférence en matière de religion*, found himself in 1848 among the most advanced Republicans and Socialists on the benches of the Montagne, as the extreme left wing was called in France. At about the same time, Donoso Cortés, once the friend and pupil of Quintana, became the fiery controversialist of the *Ensayo*, no less eagerly intent upon the task of pulverizing and destroying the moderate ideas of the doctrinaire Liberals, whom formerly he had supported, and the bold affirmations of Proudhon, Lamennais himself and other Socialists. At the end of their careers, at the summit of the ascent which each made toward peaks so unlike, each believing with perfect good faith that he was climbing toward the light of justice and truth, they viewed life from very different aspects. Donoso was loaded with honours and found himself the possessor of a peerage, an important post in the diplomatic service and regiments of friends. Lamennais, on the other hand, though greater both as a writer and as a thinker, had to purge the sincerity of his convictions in prison and ended his life in poverty, alone in an old house and in an obscure suburb of Paris, abandoned by all and persecuted to the last by Napoleon III's police and by the

* *Ensayo sobre el catolicismo, el liberalismo y el socialismo considerados en sus principios fundamentales* (Madrid, 1851), p. 137.

rancour of the Ultramontanes, who had succeeded in imposing their will upon the country.

It is far from our purpose here to discuss the ideas contained in Donoso's *Ensayo*, our concern being only with its literary value as one of the monuments of Spanish prose in the early nineteenth century, and the most interesting work of its kind in our whole period.   The style of Donoso Cortés, as we can see throughout the *Ensayo*, and even in the passages excerpted from it above, is an oratorical style, with all the merits and defects inherent in that *genre*.   Brilliant and grandiose, it abounds in poetic images, but is apt to become monotonous and merely declamatory ; it lacks half-tones and delicate *nuances ;* the prophet's serious countenance is seldom illumined by the most fleeting smile and there is nothing to give relief to the monotony of his lugubrious intonation.

Donoso Cortés is always master of his style, and has much of the force and inspiration of the polemist who believes himself possessed of absolute and incontrovertible truth. What he lacks is the power to forge that vivid, penetrating and persuasive type of argument which has no idea of overwhelming its adversary by pulverizing him with a formidable bludgeon, but harasses him with pinpricks directed at the most vulnerable part of his defence, while all the time preparing to deal him that final thrust which will bring the duel to a conclusion and leave the spectators astonished at the victor's dexterity and skill.

At its outset the book is described as aiming in particular at refuting the doctrines of Proudhon—"citizen Proudhon" as Donoso often calls him with aristocratic disdain.   At the time of its appearance, Proudhon, like Lamennais before him, was undergoing a three years' imprisonment as a result of one of his writings.   Few in France still remember the once redoubtable author of the *Philosophie de la Misère*, and, if Donoso's attack upon it is read in Spain to-day, it is chiefly for the brilliance of its style.   Figures of speech, for example, as eloquent and as well sustained as this, will always find admirers wherever Spanish is spoken :

Tended los ojos por toda la prolongación de los tiempos, y veréis cuán turbias y cenagosas vienen las aguas de ese río en que la humanidad viene navegando . . . en el ancho buque que no tiene capitán, con espantoso y airado clamoreo, como de tripulación sublevada. Y no saben ni a dónde van ni de dónde vienen, ni cómo se llama el buque que los lleva, ni el viento que lo empuja. Si de vez en cuando se levanta una voz lúgubremente profética, diciendo : ¡ Ay de los navegantes ! ¡ Ay del buque ! ni se para el buque ni la escuchan los navegantes, y los huracanes arrecian, y el buque comienza a crujir, y siguen las danzas lúbricas y espléndidos festines, las carcajadas frenéticas y el insensato clamoreo, hasta que en un momento solemnísimo todo cesa a la vez, los festines espléndidos, las carcajadas frenéticas, las danzas lúbricas, el clamoreo insensato, el crujir del buque y el bramar de los huracanes. Las aguas están sobre todo, y el silencio sobre las aguas, y la ira de Dios sobre las aguas silenciosas.

Donoso Cortés died in Paris on May 3, 1853, and his seat in the Academy was awarded to Rafael M. Baralt, the Venezuelan historian and author of a well-known *Diccionario de Galicismos*. At the reception of the new Academician, both his own speech and the reply to it read by Joaquín Francisco Pacheco were wholly devoted to the work of Baralt's predecessor—a somewhat rare occurrence. Certainly there is no more complete, shrewd and impartial study of Donoso than this of Baralt's, one of the finest *discursos*, to our thinking, that have ever been read in the Academy.

It is curious that an authority on gallicisms should have been called upon to pronounce judgment on one who had for so long resided in France, whose principal education had come from French books—notably from Bonald, his true master, and also from all the French neo-Catholic writers from Chateaubriand and Joseph de Maistre down to Veuillot. Baralt shows no great desire, however, to comment upon Donoso Cortés' gallicisms, though naturally enough he discovers much influence of French authors upon the texture of his language and the qualities of his style. He seems to be hinting at this, if not directly asserting it, in his description of Donoso's style as "not possessing that delightful naturalness which gives great and genuine Spanish prose so much of its value."

The chief interest of Pacheco's reply to Baralt's speech is the additional detail which it furnishes about Donoso's life, Pacheco and Donoso having been fellow-students at Seville and lifelong friends. Pacheco believed that the germs of that physical malady which cut him off at the early age of forty-four had been in his system from his youth and that to this may be attributed much that seemed morbid or violent in his ideas and the expression of them, as well as "the secret of his apparent changeableness."

Outstanding talent combined with a natural timidity of character and a weak and sickly constitution : this seems to be the explanation of a great part of the life as well as of the writings of the distinguished orator, the fiery controversialist and the indefatigable fighter, who entrenched himself behind strict Catholic doctrine literally interpreted, and during the latter part of his life was too strongly influenced by Veuillot and the writers in the Parisian *Univers*. Much of the aggressiveness and intolerance of his last book was the result of his relations with that militant sect, which went from one exaggeration to another, with the impassioned Veuillot at its head. These writers flattered and eulogized him, translated his *Ensayo* and encouraged and impelled him to the top of their bent, only too glad to have the support of so well known and distinguished an official personage in that troubled year of 1853 when it was already possible to predict the *coup d'état* of Louis Napoleon and with it the triumph of the Cæsarean restoration.

## II

"Jaime Balmes, Presbítero"—to describe him as he almost invariably described himself in letters and books—was born at Vich, in Catalonia, in 1810. Nearly two years younger than Donoso Cortés, he died five years before him, leaving a remarkable reputation for a man of thirty-eight, not only in Catalonia but throughout Spain. In spite of the dates just given, however, Balmes may almost be considered as a precursor of Donoso Cortés, for when, in 1847, Donoso turned towards traditionalism and neo-Catholicism, Balmes' books were already written and he himself had been stricken with the mortal illness which led to his death in the following July. The thought of the two men is at bottom very similar, but apart from this their intellectual life has little in common. Balmes was a deliberate and studious Catalonian, with no resplendence of imagination and no outward title or dignity save his priest's garb, his journalistic skill and his reputation as a Catholic philosopher. Donoso was an ardent and brilliant Extremaduran, eloquent both in his speech and with his pen, who, by means more particularly of the pen, exercised a direct and constant influence, both within and without Parliament, on the government and progress of the country. The opinions of both—of Donoso, that is to say, in his last years and of Balmes throughout his life—though they never completely dominated authoritative circles, continued their gradual penetration of them and led the monarchy, under Isabel II, through palace intrigues, to the lamentable reactionary excesses which precipitated the catastrophe of 1868.

It is curious to recall the opinions of Balmes upon Donoso Cortés' oratory. We find these expressed in 1845, with relation to the parliamentary debates upon the return of their possessions to the clergy. Donoso was not entirely in favour of this proposal ; he pleaded for certain attenuations of it, defending the vested interests which had arisen with the progress of time. For this reason we commonly accept Balmes' judgment on this occasion with a good deal of reserve, but he was incapable of committing a conscious injustice in literary matters and the judgment itself is a perfectly fair one :

> En todo lo que habla o escribe el Sr. Donoso hay osadía de imaginación, hay exuberancia de ingenio, hay pompa de estilo, hay énfasis y solemnidad en el tono. Sus palabras no son nunca vacías, siempre envuelven un pensamiento ; la lástima está en que a veces este pensamiento envuelto en la palabra no es más que una imagen hermosa o la brillante chispa que brota de un contraste . . . Es tal la afición que tiene a la magnificencia y esplendor de las formas que con frecuencia se olvida del fondo . . . No sabe qué hacerse con una idea, por grande que se la suponga, si está sola ; necesita otra que contraste con simetría.

Balmes himself could never be accused of indulgence in grandiose images and unlike Donoso he was quite unable to obtain dazzling effects by the skilful handling of antithesis. To be perfectly frank, without wishing to do him the slightest injustice, one must admit that Balmes' style is sometimes heavy, is redundant to the point of entirely sacrificing elegance to clarity, tautological simply through being analytical and continually needing both revision and condensation, as though he were so completely dominated by the impassioned sincerity of his own reasoning that he had no time to polish what he had written.   His influence in Spain and Spanish America, both as thinker and as prose-writer, has always been considerable and his books have been read and studied in many universities ; if he is seldom invoked as an example of good composition, his admirable little book *El Criterio* has certainly served as an aid to thought.   It is a short treatise on logic, well within the range of the youngest student, conceived by the clearest of thinkers and eminently readable.

Balmes' career as a philosopher and publicist lasted, unfortunately, only for some nine years, from the time of his first work, on clerical celibacy, which, like Rousseau's first work, was written for a literary contest, and won a prize, until his untimely death in 1848.   Such was his indefatigable industry that he left more than twenty volumes, none of which is without interest.   In the last year of his life he was elected an Academician, but his health was already failing, and, being completely immersed in the Latin translation of his *Filosofía Elemental*, he was unable to take his seat, or even to revisit the capital.   The only honour, therefore, that he obtained in his whole life, he never enjoyed.   When quite young, he had applied for a canonry at Vich Cathedral, but his application was unsuccessful and he remained all his life a simple priest.

His principal scientific work, the *Filosofía Fundamental*, published in four volumes in 1846, reveals its author's constant endeavour to bring about the greatest possible degree of harmony between his firm Catholic convictions and the doctrines of modern philosophy, chiefly of the Cartesian and Scottish schools, though he does not hesitate to attack Descartes fiercely when from his own standpoint this becomes necessary.   His treatise, therefore, in its general lines, is eclectic, though not of course in the same way as are the works of Victor Cousin.   It is written with greater impartiality and breadth of outlook and with greater temperateness than are the works of many other expounders of these thorny and controversial questions, though it cannot be said that he avoids problems which many writers treat with extreme circumspection.   The same doctrines in briefer form are contained in the treatise entitled *Filosofía Elemental* (1847), which, however, is neither sufficiently simple nor rigorously methodical enough for a text-book. Its style is far too discursive, so that no part of the book leaves a clearly defined impression, and the last part, which is devoted to the history of philosophy, ancient and modern, is extremely defective.

The work generally hailed as Balmes' masterpiece, which has been translated into several languages, and to which he owes his reputation outside Spain, is entitled *El Protestantismo comparado con el Catolicismo en sus relaciones con la Civilización europea* (1844). This book was inspired by a desire to refute certain opinions of François Guizot expressed somewhat provocatively in lectures given at the Sorbonne between 1828 and 1830, and published about the same time, on the history of civilization in Europe. Balmes' work was published in 1844.

Any present-day reader of both the French book and the Spanish will at once realize that the divergence between their authors' points of view is so great as to be quite insurmountable. Each author traces along broad lines a philosophical picture of the history of the human race since the time of the establishment of Christianity, interpreting the events it describes in accordance with his own preconceived opinions. The one defends the pure Catholicism of Popes and Councils ; the other eulogizes the Lutheran Reformation. Each author, in his rapid and brilliant historical survey, insists only upon such facts as correspond with his own opinions and to a certain extent sees everything through his own particular spectacles. All this, however, in no way diminishes the purely literary value of the two works, but, if anything, increases it. This is particularly true of Balmes' book, every page of which is inspired by such faith and enthusiasm and dominated by such genuine and sincere conviction that it will always be of interest to a reader with no previous knowledge of the subject, though he can hardly fail to observe the superficiality of the author's historical attainments and the general impression which he gives of improvization. The same tone is found in Guizot, and is the more noticeable from the contrast between the easy style of the lecturer and the vast and profound erudition of the scholar. Donoso's *Ensayo*, part of which is also directed against these same lectures of Guizot, is considerably more successful in preserving its artistic unity. For our own part, we confess that there are other works of Balmes which, old-fashioned though they be, we read with greater interest. Such are his contributions to two reviews, *La Civilización* and *La Sociedad*, and the long series of political notes and dissertations comprising a bulky volume of 808 pages published in 1847 under the title *Escritos políticos*. These consist chiefly of Balmes' contributions to *El Pensamiento de la Nación*, a weekly paper of which he was the leading spirit and which was published in Madrid from January 1844 to December 1846. During these three years, whether he was in Barcelona, Brussels or Paris, he never once failed to send this paper his weekly article, which became its chief attraction.

The style of these articles is neither more careful nor more elegant than that of the books which we have been considering ; it is more animated, however, as befits the style of a journalist who strives hard to adapt himself to the political situation, to oppose the Government temperately and fairly and to be guided by practical necessity and the spirit of the age. The fact that Balmes had to complete each article in a brief and limited period, often without books and generally far from Madrid, served him as a spur, and gave him, not only a greater capacity for rapid work, but freshness, variety and vigour, without ever robbing him of the seriousness and moderation habitual to him. Thus his articles deserved, and have attained, a somewhat longer life than the fleeting and ephemeral existence which is too often the unhappy destiny of the products of journalism.

It is a vivid and by no means unfaithful picture of Spanish political history from 1844 to 1846 that we obtain from these editorial articles. Balmes pursued a determined campaign in favour of the marriage of Queen Isabel with the eldest son of the Don Carlos of the Civil War, because, like the Vatican and like the vast majority of the Spanish clergy, he was anxious to keep intact the interests of the Church which were provided for in the Carlists' programme, while at the same time hoisting the Liberal banner beneath which Isabel's supporters fought and conquered. The marriage campaign was pursued with great determination and ability, but it was foredoomed to failure ; its success would have been equivalent to the destruction of the only practical and permanent result of a sanguinary seven-year conflict. When the question was settled, the Queen having married a

Spanish prince and her sister a son of Louis Philippe, the *Pensamiento* ceased publication. The long article dated December 31, 1846, in which Balmes takes leave of his readers, is a masterly exposition of the political condition of the country which no historian of the period could fail to find of utility.

We append a specimen of Balmes' journalistic style, taken from an article in *La Civilización* for August 1, 1841, describing the conspiracy of the generals who in that year had attempted to seize the person of the Queen and overthrow Espartero's regency :

> El general Concha, al frente de algunas compañías sublevadas que ha sacado del cuartel, llega a Palacio, acuden al mismo punto varios jefes, y entre ellos el general León con su gallarda presencia y su corazón de treinta años. Va vestido de húsar, de grande uniforme, lujosamente ataviado, como si fuera a una magnífica parada. En el momento decisivo, al salir de su casa diciendo *Vamos allá,* ¿ quién sabe lo que le diría su corazón ? Aquellas marciales galas con que se adornaba, ¿ habían de servir para realzar su triunfo, o para hacer más trágico su suplicio ? ¡ Desgraciado ! ¡ Se ataviaba para marchar al cadalso ! . . .
>
> Pero todo se deshizo como el humo : el general León había creído que la estrella de Espartero se eclipsaría en la noche del 7 ; que le abandonaría la fortuna que de muchos años a esta parte le está prodigando sus favores ; pero el general León se engañó ; Espartero continúa Regente y él perdió la vida en un suplicio. ¡ Triste resultado de los trastornos políticos, que así perezcan los hombres, aun después de conseguido el triunfo de la causa que defendían ! ¡ Quién se lo dijera al general León en Villarrobledo y en Belascoaín ! : "A poco tiempo de concluída la guerra con Don Carlos, reinando en Madrid Isabel II, ¡ serás arcabuceado !"

These and other paragraphs of equal or greater merit prove that, besides being the sole Spanish philosopher of note in this period other than Donoso Cortés, Balmes was surpassed by few in the period as journalist and essayist.

# CHAPTER XII

## DII MINORES—I

### Francisco Martínez de la Rosa

Something has already been said, in connection with Larra and his *Macías*, of Martínez de la Rosa's play *La Conjuración de Venecia*. A few words must be added on the not too well sustained Romantic element in the works of this eminent writer, which in his own day were famous but have now fallen into fairly general oblivion.

Born at Granada in 1787, Francisco Martínez de la Rosa was brought up in the straitest sect of the Classicists, at that time supreme in Spain, and became an admirer of Meléndez Valdés, an imitator of Moratín and a translator and commentator of Horace's *Ars Poetica*. During the last part of the reign of Ferdinand VII, political vicissitudes compelled him to live for some years as an exile in Paris, and there, in the midst of the tempestuous literary revolution which at that time was revivifying every form of art, his flexible and cultured mind was subjected to powerful new influences. These could not penetrate to the very depths of his being, for so strongly had his original ideas become rooted within him that in essentials they remained the same to the end of his days. Nevertheless, this dramatist who from his youth up had written comedies and tragedies began to look with the curious interest of a student at these innovations which in Paris were the subject of general discussion and by many were considered something of a scandal.

Unfortunately, however, though perhaps inevitably, after living for more than forty years in a different environment, he concentrated all his interest upon novelties which were merely superficial. He may be compared with Casimir Delavigne, who, in *Louis XI* and *Les Vêpres Siciliennes*, was overlaying his plays with a light coating of history, and tincturing them with a few drops of essence extracted from Ducis' and Letourneur's versions of the plays of Shakespeare, and a few more from the tragedies of Byron. A similar proceeding gave Spain two semi-Romantic prose dramas, *Aben Humeya* and *La Conjuración de Venecia*, which alone make it essential to include Martínez de la Rosa in any survey of the Spanish Romantics.

In the preface to a volume of lyrics which he published in 1832, the year after his return to Spain, Martínez de la Rosa formulated his own profession of faith, declaring that he felt "disinclined to enlist in the ranks of either Classicists or Romanticists" and that he "looked upon it as an established fact that either side is right when it censures the exaggerations of the other, but at once commits the same error as its opponent when it endeavours to exalt its own system." In these words we have the programme of his whole life, in literature as in politics. Just as he dabbled in Romanticism without abjuring Classicism, so he found himself dubbed *pastelero*, or political hedger, by the Liberals of 1821 and at the same time looked upon with disfavour by Ferdinand. Yet neither in his literary nor in his political career do we find any reason to doubt the sincerity and nobility of his character.

*Aben Humeya*, which he wrote in French for performance in the Parisian theatre of the Porte Saint-Martin, was received with respectful interest, for its author was well known, either personally or by reputation, to all journalists and public men in Paris and to the majority of its men of letters. They knew, too, that the honour of representing Granada in the Cortes of 1812 had brought him several years' imprisonment in Africa, and that he had then been a Liberal minister and was one of the leaders of the revolution of 1820 that temporarily checked Ferdinand's despotism, emigrating to France before its effect came to an end three years later.

When, in 1836, almost two years after the *Conjuración de Venecia*, *Aben Humeya* was staged in Spain, it seemed to have come too late. Larra, who had welcomed the earlier drama with such cordiality, treated the later somewhat harshly, though perhaps not altogether unjustly. It is more carefully worked out than the episode of the Venetian conspiracy, but its plot is less dramatic and has not the same interest. In style it is naturally of considerable elegance, for its author was most meticulous in his use of prose ; but it tends to be affected, and, even at its best moments, lacks the conciseness and energy which one demands of the theatre. The most familiar phrase in the entire play affords a good example of this affectation :

¿ Ves este reguero de sangre ? . . . Ese es el camino del trono.

Another example comes from Aben-Humcya's speech before the battle :

Tenemos que vengar *en breves instantes* medio siglo de esclavitud.

where the three words italicized add nothing to the sense and would be better omitted. Neither here nor elsewhere in the play can we detect the deeply impressive tone of the finest scenes in the *Conjuración de Venecia*.

Martínez de la Rosa invariably adapted his versification to the precepts and practice of Classicism, but in certain passages of his *Edipo* (a pallid reflection of Sophocles) his natural gentleness and sensibility of temperament, more marked in him even than in Meléndez Valdés, inspired him with verses full of the deepest melancholy, some of them well worthy of inclusion in anthologies. Such are those free hendecasyllabics which Martínez de la Rosa addressed to the Duque de Frías

Desde las tristes márgenes del Sena.

This epistle and those which Gallego and Quintana wrote for the same *Corona* of 1830 (cf. p. 183) are the work of three poets who are Classicists by taste and upbringing, yet there is something indefinable in them which announces the approaching change in Spanish lyric poetry. Martínez de la Rosa's poem is in no way inferior to that of either of the others : it has more pathos than the solemn, eloquent poem of Quintana and is less declamatory than the fine, virile one by Gallego. These three poets, whose genius illumined the end of a literary age, infused into these poems—perhaps unwittingly, possibly even in spite of themselves—a suggestion of that peculiar "Romantic" melody which from various directions was now entering Spain.

### ANTONIO GIL Y ZÁRATE

Gil y Zárate was a man who, almost without aid and by sheer perseverance and energy, carved out for himself a considerable reputation as a dramatist, and certainly a greater one than he really merited. Furthermore, he exercised a great influence on his country's progress in his capacity as Director-General of Public Instruction and organizer of a scheme of University studies. His education, in the academic sense, was better than that of Bretón, García Gutiérrez and a large number of his contemporaries. Education in this sense, however, to the creative artist is not everything.

The son of two popular actors, Gil y Zárate was born at San Lorenzo del Escorial in 1793, received his elementary education in France, and returned to France again as a young man in order to complete his higher studies in science and letters. He had certain gifts as a playwright but was neither a poet nor a stylist, either in verse or in prose. All his work strikes one as being a product of his will-power, the result of violent and persevering effort, aided but little by inspiration. Yet two of his plays, *Carlos II el Hechizado* (1837) and *Guzmán el Bueno* (1842), enjoyed an extraordinary popularity ; at a time when the prevailing Romantic fervour made unbiassed judgment difficult, and they were considered by many to be the equals of *El Trovador* and *Los Amantes de Teruel*, they were given as frequently, and with as much success, as *Don Álvaro* or *El Zapatero y el Rey*. To-day, having lost the interest of novelty, they have found their proper level, the more easily since part of their appeal was made to the political passions which inflamed men's minds during the period of Isabel II's minority. *Carlos II*, in particular, is now recognized as being a violent melodrama which fed the unusually violent passions aroused by a passing crisis by disguising Claudio Frollo, the Archdeacon from Hugo's *Notre Dame de Paris*, as Froilán Díaz, the confessor of the "bewitched" monarch, an historical character who seems to have been nothing like as evil and libidinous as the author here makes him.

The play is full of movement and its author was evidently well acquainted with stage technique. Even without the tremendous fillip given to it by revolutionary enthusiasm, it would have been appreciated and applauded as a sincere attempt to show the infamy of one aspect of the most odious kind of fanaticism by means of an ably conceived historical and Romantic picture. It is not because of its disfigurement of an historical character nor because of the exaggerated violence of its plot that the play has quickly passed out of date and become forgotten, but because of the inequality of its style and the mediocrity of its versification.

Gil y Zárate was no mere youth when this drama was first produced, but a man of over forty. The moment at which he produced it, however, was one of those periods of history which posterity thinks of as eminently youthful : periods of excitement and audacity in which politics and literature tend to outgrow their own development and to fling down every barrier which has been set up to restrain them. In politics, the masses were struggling to overturn the oligarchy which since the death of Ferdinand had governed the country almost continuously in the name of his daughter. In literature, the excesses of romanticism had invaded the stage, and shattered the last bonds of classicism. Thus *Carlos II el Hechizado* met the demands of the moment and as a result was acclaimed by spectators who were looking for powerful and sensational drama and cared little for the graces of artistic form.

It is not surprising, therefore, to learn that, later in his life, the serious and sensible Director of Public Instruction, alarmed by the persistent influence of his play, is said to have regretted writing it and to have petitioned the Ministry of the Interior to prohibit its performance. This seems to be a well authenticated fact* ; not so, however, the supposed death-bed retraction, which was given great prominence by the religious press after the dramatist's death in 1861 and promptly denied by those most intimately connected with him.

*Guzmán el Bueno* is a better play than *Carlos II*, less melodramatic and also more carefully written. The famous story of the loyal father who, rather than betray his king and surrender a besieged town in order to save the life of his son, throws his own dagger over the wall to the enemy has, for once in a way, found a very acceptable stage rendering. It was given an excellent reception and continued to be successfully played whenever popular patriotism demanded some dramatic outlet. Gil y Zárate took care that there should be no half-heartedness about the

---

* Marqués de Valmar : *Autores dramáticos contemporáneos* (Madrid, 1882), Vol. II, p. 224.

applause by lavishing on his characters passages like the
well-known

> ¿ Españoles no sois ?  pues sois valientes.
> A fuer de castellanos sois leales . . .

He might well have done better in comedy than in drama,
had he not been completely overshadowed here by Bretón
and thus been obliged to cultivate a field less completely
monopolized.   Like Rivas, Martínez de la Rosa, Bretón and
Vega, he belonged to the Moderate party and went in and
out of office with it perseveringly.   O'Donnell's triumph in
1858 brought about his retirement.   "Demasiado altivo,"
he writes in his autobiography, "para hacer súplicas y
gestiones que me habrían rebajado . . ., no he querido
volver a tomar parte ni en la política ni en la literatura."
Some three years after writing these words he died.

### ENRIQUE GIL Y CARRASCO

Enrique Gil may be taken as exemplifying that love of
melancholy which characterized a number of Spanish poets
during a period in which either a genuine or a pretended
*tristeza* was a common trait in poetry all over Europe.   Of
these Spanish poets he is at once the gentlest and the most
sincere.   His life, from beginning to end, was in perfect
harmony with the plaintive tone of his verses.   Fate dealt
him many years of trouble and privation.   From his birth he
lived in poverty, a trial to which, as soon as he came to
manhood, was added ill-health.   He died at thirty-one years
of age, far from his home and country, and was buried in the
Catholic cemetery of Berlin, where a sympathetic friend
carried out his last wishes by erecting a tombstone to his
memory and planting his humble grave with flowers.   These
were renewed, more than once, by brother poets from Spain,
who visited the cemetery for that express purpose.   One of
them, Eulogio Florentino Sanz, tells us how, as he searched
for the Spanish inscription among the German ones, he
recalled Gil's own verses "A la Violeta" :

> Quizá al pasar la Virgen de los valles,
> Enamorada y rica en juventud,
> Por las umbrosas y desiertas calles
> Do yacerá escondido mi ataúd,

Irá a cortar la humilde violeta
Y la pondrá en mi seno con dolor
Y llorando dirá : "¡ Pobre poeta !
Ya está callada el arpa del amor."

Gil was born in 1815 in a village in the province of León, near the Galician border. His early education he received in what his brother and biographer* calls "the gloomy city of Astorga" ; he then spent a short time in Valladolid before proceeding to Madrid, where he completed his studies. Soon after his arrival here he made the acquaintance of Espronceda, who encouraged him to send his verses to the papers. One of his early poems, *Una Gota de rocío*, published in *El Español* at the end of 1837, succeeded in attracting attention and was spoken of very favourably by men of letters. Like nearly all Gil's poems, it has metrical ingenuity and variety and at times achieves the most delicate effects of rhythm and harmony. It begins thus :

Gota de humilde rocío
　　Delicada,
Sobre las aguas del río
　　Columpiada ;
La brisa de la mañana
　　Blandamente,
Como lágrima temprana
　　Transparente,
Mece tu bello arrebol
　　Vaporoso
Entre los rayos del sol
　　Cariñoso.
¿ Eres, di, rico diamante
　　De Golconda,
Que, en cabellera flotante,
　　Dulce y blonda,
Trajo una sílfide indiana,
　　Por la noche,
Y colgó en hoja liviana
　　Como un broche ?

Espronceda's example had a direct and favourable effect on Gil's diction, and, despite the great temperamental dissimilarity between the two poets, some of Gil's verses are not at all unlike Espronceda's "Serenata," his verses in *Sancho*

* The biography will be found in *Obras de Enrique Gil, Poesías Líricas*. Madrid, 1873.

*Saldaña* and the well-known *A una Estrella*, an agreeable poem, though not one of the first order.

It must be remembered that Gil's poems were not collected and published in book form until more than a quarter of a century after his death and that he never had the opportunity of revising them. Even as we have them, they are considerably superior to the work of other writers, such as Selgas, who cultivated exactly the same type of poem and enjoyed a much greater reputation. Neither as a Nature artist nor as a poet of intimate emotions or melancholy impressions did the author of "La Primavera" and "El Estío" reach the same height as Enrique Gil. Selgas' diction is more correct and as a rule his style has a more sustained elegance, but he has seldom as much to say and never sounds the depths of Gil's intensity of feeling.

In his invariable modesty, Gil did not stray beyond the unambitious field in which he believed himself qualified to labour, and scarcely ever aspired to loftier lyric flights, save once, when his grief at the death of Espronceda inspired an elegy of greater force and volume than was usual with him yet sounding the same characteristic note of desolation. He compares Espronceda to an eagle soaring upwards toward the sun to quaff its streams of light ; then, giving a personal note to his lament, he exclaims :

> ¡ Y yo te canto, pájaro perdido,
> Yo, a quien tu amor en sus potentes alas
> Sacó de las tinieblas del desierto,
> Que ornar quisiste con tus ricas galas,
> Que gozó alegre en tu encumbrado nido
> De tus cantos divinos el concierto !

Enrique Gil is also worthy of mention as a writer of prose. Next to Larra's *Doncel*, his novel, *El Señor de Bembibre*, is the best in the period. There are certain resemblances between this story and the *Bride of Lammermoor*. The title alone recalls the form of address used by Scott of his hero, the Master of Ravenswood. The main lines of the argument are similar, and an identical situation constitutes the crisis of the action. It is neither fair nor correct to say that Gil has imitated Scott ; his plot might perfectly well have occurred to him independently, and he might never have been aware of its similarities with Scott's novel. On the other hand, the *Bride of Lammermoor* was popular in Spain and must therefore

certainly have been known to him, especially since Doni-
zetti's opera of the same name was at this time continually
being given in Madrid.

A comparison of Gil's novel with Scott's would be almost
entirely to the former's disadvantage. The qualities which
give distinction to Gil's poems—their sustained melancholy,
the delicacy of their thought, the continual recurrence of
their muted melodies—have no place in a novel, but rather
tend to rob it of power and interest, and cause it to languish
precisely where the plot demands greater vigour. Doña
Beatriz de Ossorio yields to maternal pressure and fails to
keep the word which she has plighted to her absent lover and
to wait for him during the full length of the term to which
she has agreed, and for this she has none of the reasons that
break down the resistance of the unfortunate Lucy, the
victim of her dominating mother's inflexibility. Upon the
return of Beatriz' lover, Don Álvaro Yáñez, all the actors in
the tragedy meet, by chance, in the open air, but the scene
has none of that concentrated energy which adds such
emotion and effectiveness to the appearance of Ravenswood
at the moment of the signing of Lucy's marriage contract.
From that stage onward, the progression of *The Bride of
Lammermoor* to its inevitable catastrophe has all the terror and
fatalism of an Æschylean tragedy, whereas in *El Señor de
Bembibre* the interest decreases progressively till the novel
reaches its laborious end. It contains nothing to rival the
heart-rending pictures of Lucy's funeral and of Edgar's
disappearance and death.

Gil, on the other hand, looked with tear-veiled eyes upon
the melancholy landscapes of autumn and winter evenings
in his native country, on the banks of the Sil, in the shadow
of the distant mountains of Galicia—landscapes which he
reproduced in passages abounding in the truest poetry.
Indeed he frequently suspends his narrative in order to
paint these lovely natural pictures with the fine skill of the
miniaturist, adorning them with phrases each as soft as a
caress. Rarely in Scott do we find a passage as exquisite
as this, which we select from Gil's novel as one example
among many :

Las primeras lluvias de la estación, que ya habían caído,
amontonaban en el horizonte celajes espesos y pesados, que
adelgazados a veces por el viento y esparcidos por entre las

grietas de los peñascos y por la cresta de las montañas, figura-
ban otros tantos cendales y plumas abandonadas por los
genios del aire en medio de su rápida carrera.   Los ríos iban
ya un poco turbios e hinchados, los pajarillos volaban de un
árbol a otro sin soltar sus trinos armoniosos, y las ovejas
corrían por las laderas y por los prados, recién despojados de su
yerba, balando ronca y tristemente.   La naturaleza entera
parecía despedirse del tiempo alegre y prepararse para los
largos y obscuros lutos del invierno.

A number of Gil's literary articles have found a place in
the collected edition of his works, and these are so full of
sound judgment and excellent observations that they can still
be read with pleasure and advantage.   He has left shrewd
studies of Hartzenbusch's *Doña Mencía*, García de Villalta's
translation of *Macbeth*, the poems of Espronceda antedating
the *Diablo Mundo*, and various other notable works of the
period : his is a true poet's criticism which penetrates below
the surface to the writer's intentions and is able to recognize
genuine inspiration.

Gil left Spain in May 1844, sailing from Barcelona to
Marseilles and proceeding thence to make a tour of the
different states of the Germanic Confederation in order to
report at length to the Foreign Minister in Spain upon the
mutual political relations of these states and their social,
industrial and intellectual situations.   As he had only his
writing to live upon, this diplomatic mission was very
welcome to him, the more so as it fell in with his own
interests, for he had long had a keen desire to make a detailed and first-hand study of German literature.   Unhappily, however, he was already in an advanced state of
pulmonary phthisis, which was aggravated by the cold
northern climate.   He died in February 1846, less than two
years after he had left his own country.

### GABRIEL GARCÍA Y TASSARA

García y Tassara has come down to posterity purely and
simply as a lyric poet.   It is true that he wrote much in
prose, but he confined himself to political articles of a kind
that seldom finds its way into book form.   If we may judge
from the only piece of his prose with which we are personally
acquainted—his preface to the 1872 (Madrid) edition of his

poems—these articles were probably dogmatic, pretentious and more than a little obscure.

At one time it seemed as though his poetry also ran the risk of remaining unpublished, or, at least, of not being disinterred from the periodicals in which it had all been published until after the death of its author. A collection, it seems, was first made at Bogotá, without the author's collaboration, consent or even knowledge. A circular describing this projected edition is said to have reached him by pure accident. "So in South America," he exclaimed, "they consider me a poet ! Evidently nobody is aware of that in Spain !"*

At the time of this remark, García y Tassara was Spanish Minister at Washington. Fortunately for literature, there came a moment when he retired from politics and diplomacy, or rather when he ceased to take an active part in them, and he then found tranquillity and leisure to collect, revise and publish his poetry.

García y Tassara is one of those poets who are happy in having no history. He was born, at Seville, in 1817 and died in 1875. His ideas changed little and both they and the chief events of his life are reflected in his verses, which, like his political articles, reveal him as an energetic fighter, always ready for the fray. Three important historical events occurring during his lifetime were highly distasteful to him and he wrote of them with red-hot indignation : the Revolution of 1848 in France and all its consequences down to the *coup d'état* of Louis Napoleon ; the Spanish Revolution of 1868 ; and the Franco-German War of 1870. The impression left on his spirit by each of these transcendental events is duly recorded in his poetry ; each served as a powerful stimulus to spur his genius to greater heights.

He was a really great lyric poet ; until the very end of the nineteenth century scarcely any surpassed him save Bécquer and (at his best) Núñez de Arce. His political satires in verse have the lyrical fervour of Victor Hugo's, or, to speak more aptly, of Auguste Barbier's. This kind of writing expressed the natural tendency of his talent ; with it his career began and ended. As early as 1839, when the ambition and the audacious pride of Mehemet Ali—the "excelso Bajá," as he calls him—had kindled war in the

* Cf. Rafael Pombo in *El Mundo Nuevo* (New York, 1872), Vol. I, p. 23.

East and this war was threatening to involve the European Powers also, he composed a vigorous *canto*, of which he published a number of splendid fragments, eulogizing the Egyptian chief and expressing indignation that he should be described as a rebel and Europe should be leagued against him :

> Esta Europa sin fe, que al recostarse
> En la tumba de cien generaciones,
> Quisiera inocular en las naciones
> . El germen de su propia destrucción . . .
> .        .        .        .
> El ruso y el inglés, los dos colosos
> Que aprietan a la Europa entre sus brazos,
> La Francia tricolor que hace pedazos
> Cuanto la empresa de los siglos fué,
> En pos caminan al fatal despojo . . .

This method of presenting past and contemporary history —a searching for motifs of indignation and despair—took a yet greater hold on him between 1848 and 1852. As he says of himself in the preface already mentioned, he was a born Conservative, and troubles in France and elsewhere in Europe stirred all his Conservative instincts to their very depths. He poured out his soul in some well-known verse epistles, which he calls "a kind of poem" ; it might rather be described as a copious and magnificent torrent of lyricism, charged with humour and overflowing with eloquence, expressing the compassion, misgiving and wrath inspired in him by the revolution. Like another Dante—a "mísero Dante," to use his own modest term—he thinks of himself as called to sing to Europe of "the Divine Comedy of her death," and to cry in God's name

> A los pueblos que su brazo alcanza :
> ¡ Lasciate ogni speranza, ogni speranza !

The inscription over the gate of hell, as it appears in the work of the Italian poet, is the source to which he repairs to nurture and refresh his irremediable pessimism. This same poem, which he first entitled *Luzbel* and later *Un diablo más*, has some robust tercets addressed to Dante, of which we here give an example :

> Tu infierno es este mundo ¡ oh padre Dante !
> Encima del dintel de nuestra vida
> La tremenda inscripción ya está delante.

El mal hizo en la tierra su guarida ;
El bien no es más que idealidad suprema
Entre obscuros crepúsculos perdida.
　　Víctima de un recóndito anatema,
Huérfana, de su Dios abandonada,
Como las sombras de tu gran poema,
　　La humanidad ¡ oh Dante ! desespera,
Dobla la sien en la doliente mano,
Y abandona el timón a la onda fiera.
　　No inquiere ya el arcano.　No hay arcano.
No pide ya venganza.　No hay venganza.
No hay más que el himno del dolor humano
Y el sempiterno adiós a la esperanza.

After the dethronement of Isabel II in 1868, his depression grew still greater.　He attempted to return to public
life, was a candidate for the *diputación*, but was (to use his own
words) "desahuciado en Sanlúcar y en Carmona, muerto
electoralmente," whereupon his gloomy presentiments became darker still :

　　¡ Ah !　La patria otra vez, la patria cara
Que, a la merced del popular sufragio,
A optar hoy se prepara,
Como entre el rudo escollo y el naufragio,
Entre la dictadura y la anarquía . . .

The Franco-German War seemed to him a terrible confirma-
tion of all his predictions :

　　¿ Ni qué añadir podría
Si cumplida ya está la profecía ?
¿ Si vino Atila, si murió la Francia,
Si tras la Francia morirá la Europa . . .

As long previously as 1851 he had foreseen and prophesied
the rising of a new Attila :

　　Cuya guedeja hirsuta,
　　Cuya férrea armadura mal enjuta,
　　Aun la sangre magnánima destila
　　Del romano universo debelado.

As we read them to-day, however, these poems once alive
with fierce invective and these gloomy prophecies have lost
much of their force and expressiveness.　Europe has passed
through the convulsions of the Great War, so much more
gigantic than any known to García y Tassara either in his

history or his experience.  Spain, after enduring half a century more of misgovernment, has had seven years of dictatorship, followed by a new revolution and the establishment of a second Republic.  In the light of these transcendent events it is hard to re-capture García y Tassara's indignation at what by comparison are unimportant ones. Yet we may still be captivated by his poetic style and the artistry with which he dominates his lyre and draws from it rich and ample harmonies.

Continually he gives us new phrases, original thoughts and unforgettably vivid images, touches of colour which add light and brilliance to the vigour of his style.  In his poem to Mirabeau, solid and compact as beaten steel, which begins by that striking description of its hero

> A un tiempo Cicerón y Catilina,

and goes on by likening him to Napoleon, he has a fine passage, ending :

> Sus linderos guardando de consuno
> Como dos centinelas inmortales,
> Os alzáis en robustos pedestales
> El grande Emperador y el gran Tribuno.

García y Tassara can frequently create peculiar effects by the skilful blending of vowels.  Take, for instance, his use of the vowel *a* in this description of the patriotic odes of his model and master Quintana

> Con versos como espadas
> De España las entrañas ulceradas.

Sometimes, it is true, he abuses the device of alliteration, and, still more frequently, that of repetition, so that his style often becomes monotonous.  Hardly one of his poems but bears his trade-mark—a word repeated twice in the same line. For all their grandiloquence his poems are often rude, harsh and uneven.  He seldom for long sustains such a level of technical perfection as we find in the poems of Quintana. La Avellaneda, equalling him in brilliance of form, surpasses him in smoothness.  Espronceda, in all but his worst moments, outclasses him completely.

The majority of his poems were written between 1839 and 1842.  It was in 1851, however, when he was stirred by the political events of the past three years, that he produced perhaps the best of all his poetry, including that already described, and also three poems which alone justify his reputation. These are the *Recuerdos* of his youth, dedicated to his old friend Salvador Bermúdez de Castro, and the odes to Quintana and Mirabeau. The *Recuerdos* have the fragrance of a melancholy and a deeply personal emotion which are none too frequent with him ; even in one of the best of his poems, *A Laura*, he is not so profound or so communicative. Seldom did he achieve a poetical description of such exactitude and sobriety as in this passage :

> Volemos, ¡ ay ! volemos
> A aquellos campos de la edad primera :
> Naturaleza nos dará un abrazo :
> ¿ Quién sabe, Salvador, si aún no hallaremos,
> Flor de aquella celeste primavera,
> Palpitante de amor algún regazo ?
>    Mira el feliz ribazo,
> Los bellos sauces, la enramada umbría,
> La barca leve, las serenas olas.
> ¿ Qué falta allí de cuanto fuera un día
> Sino *ellas dos* con nuestro amor a solas ?
>    Sombra, silencio, calma,
> La blanca luna, Aznalfarache al lejos
> Y el aura que recorre las colinas.
> Amor, misterio, inspiración . . .

A poet who could sing thus even while declaiming against the socialistic affectations of Louis Napoleon and making the hero of the famous second of December exclaim

> De pie sobre el cadáver de las leyes :
> "Yo soy Proudhon, Emperador de Francia,"

is far too original and interesting a figure for either his verses or his name to be forgotten.

### TOMÁS RODRÍGUEZ RUBÍ

Among all the Spanish dramatists of the first half of the nineteenth century, Rodríguez Rubí, if we may accept the authority of Hartzenbusch, was the most popular—"el más aplaudido de todos."* The critic sets down this remark

---

\* *Obras de . . . Bretón de los Herreros* (Madrid, 1883), vol. I, p. lvi.

14

quite simply, without commenting upon it ; we may suppose, however, that he was conscious of its irony, for from the purely literary standpoint Rodríguez Rubí is one of the weakest of all the dramatists who had any success on the stage whatever. The audiences of the early nineteenth century must certainly have been considerably more indulgent than were those of the early seventeenth. Lope de Vega, in his *Arte Nuevo*, had written :

> Y escribo por el arte que inventaron
> Los que el vulgar aplauso pretendieron,
> Porque como las paga el vulgo, es justo
> Hablarle en necio para darle gusto.

But some of the plays which these latter-day audiences seem to have applauded and enjoyed were unworthy even to be compared with what Lope de Vega produced and described as "necio" in order to please (*darle gusto*) the audiences of his day. The explanation of this is probably that among the frequenters of theatres there were (and are still) persons drawn from strata of society below any that went to the playhouses two centuries before, that the theatres were more numerous (and are now more numerous still) and that the custom of going to them became much more widely extended. However this may be, we must perforce respect the voice of the people and give Rodríguez Rubí a place among the lesser deities of Spanish Romanticism.

Deplore it or deny it as we may, one fact is indisputable : *La Rueda de la Fortuna, Borrascas del Corazón, Isabel la Católica,* plays which to-day are considered to be mediocre and even worse, were in their own day more vociferously applauded and brought more profit to their author than any play written by Bretón, Vega, Hartzenbusch or Gil y Zárate. Rodríguez Rubí achieved a complete triumph. He created, so to speak, the public that he needed and perverted its taste so completely that when he was succeeded by another dramatist, Francisco Camprodón, combining much the same merits and defects as his own, but with the defects more strongly marked and the merits much less so, the latter secured an even greater success with *Flor de un día*, an intimate drama after the style of *Borrascas del Corazón* or *La Trenza de sus Cabellos*. This play had innumerable performances both in Spain and in America, was continually reprinted and won applause and eulogies everywhere.

From the personal standpoint, both as a public man and as a private individual, Rodríguez Rubí was very popular ; and his numerous friends united in singing his praises as a very perfect gentle dramatist. In this way he reached as great heights as he could desire, both in politics and in literature, after a comparatively short novitiate in either profession.

Born at Málaga in 1817, he was still very young when he went to settle in Madrid. His early reputation he owed to his Andalusian origin, for he began by writing humorous verses in the Andalusian dialect which were widely quoted for their exact and witty reproduction of the vocabulary and pronunciation of that region. As a politician he joined the Moderate party, with nearly all the outstanding literary men of his day, from Larra to Campoamor. The latter described the party as an "oligarchy of the intelligentsia" and declared that he himself had joined it out of sheer fastidiousness. Before the dethronement of Isabel II, Rodríguez Rubí went from one administrative post to another, becoming at length Colonial Minister, a portfolio which seems to have been reserved for neophytes in the Cabinet, and in particular for poets, since at a later date it was awarded to López de Ayala and Núñez de Arce. After the restoration of the Bourbon dynasty, an event which, in company with the Conde de Valmaseda, Rodríguez Rubí did all he could to bring about, he was sent to Havana with the title of Royal Commissioner, charged with the task of rehabilitating the finances of Cuba, which was in the midst of an insurrection. This was a strange mission on which to send a dramatist ; and he seems to have accomplished nothing. When, therefore, shortly after his arrival, his friends in Madrid fell from power, he very properly resigned. He died only in 1890, but long before his death he had ceased to take any active part in politics.

Like Gil y Zárate, Rodríguez Rubí achieved dramatic success chiefly through his own determination. By dint of long application and perseverance in battling with difficulties, he succeeded in mastering the art of verse composition and in acquiring a certain superficial facility. But he never managed to write with any distinction ; even in his best pages there are obvious signs that he has had to go back over his work and fill up gaps and there are also inequalities of diction due to other causes. In his play *Borrascas del Corazón*, described in its dedication as "la más querida de cuantas se elaboraron por mi pobre ingenio," there occurs an important scene between the two principal characters— the Marqués de los Vélez and the woman whose heart is the scene of the *borrascas*. The Marqués proposes to deliver himself of a panegyric to love. This is how he does it :

> . . . . . Amor es conjunto
> De lo bello y es también
> De las glorias del Edén
> El más cumplido trasunto.
>
> .        .        .        .
>
> Es la fuente de venturas,
> Y el amor en conclusión
> Es la primera pasión
> De las pasiones más puras.
>
> Mas con prendas tan divinas,
> Si le contemplamos bien,
> Ese amor tiene también,
> Como las rosas, espinas.

The unfortunate author was no more skilful in comedy— only here the familiarity of tone characteristic of the *genre* does something to conceal the triviality of his thought and the vagueness of its expression, or, at least, prevents them from becoming evident at the very beginning of each play. Comedy also provided him with a field for the display of the talent for observation and the gift of humour of which he had given such excellent examples in his Andalusian tales. He could not, however, compete profitably with Bretón in a sphere in which Bretón had won so many triumphs before he himself came on the scene at all. Little by little he made explorations and began to discover a new field in which he could establish himself without fear of finding a rival there already. This was the field of so-called "high comedy" (*alta comedia*), which starts from either an historical or a pseudo-historical basis (as in *La Rueda de la Fortuna, Bandera Negra*, incorrectly termed "drama," *Dos Validos* and others) or from a political situation, the author setting out in this case, with frankly satirical intentions, to ridicule scenes from contemporary life, which he does unscrupulously, to the point of caricature. An excellent example of the latter type of play is *El Gran Filón*, his last triumph, and, as many think, his best comedy. The field of his activities lay between these two extremes and for over thirty years he kept the theatrical companies furnished with material. No doubt he produced less than Scribe, but, on the other hand, save very rarely, he worked entirely without collaborators. Further, he generally wrote in verse rather than in prose, and his verse, pedestrian as it is, is hardly more so than the verse and the prose alike of the author of the *Verre d'Eau, Bertrand et Raton* and the *libretti* of Meyerbeer's operas.

Accidental circumstances contributed to the increase of his prosperity. His best pieces were written in the fifth decade of the nineteenth century, when the star of the great Bretón was beginning to pale and the public was treating him with growing indifference. This was also the period of the culminating success of the comedies and *vaudevilles* of Scribe, which were continually being translated and represented in the Madrid theatres. The public, therefore, which, like every Spanish public, much preferred verse drama to prose, took a particular fancy to the works of this "Spanish Scribe" which had the advantage of being pleasantly brief and also of being melodious to the ear. Finally, Rodríguez Rubí was fortunate enough to find an actress in Matilde Díez, and an actor in Julián Romea, both of whom were of exceptional talent and well suited to his style of comedy. Without the former, it is very improbable that either *Borrascas del Corazón* or *Isabel la Católica* would have seemed as good a play as each did at the time of its *estreno*, nor would their author have written *La Trenza de sus Cabellos* and a number of other plays constructed to the exact measure of Matilde Díez' powers.

We have given some of the reasons why Rodríguez Rubí wrote several types of play so different from one another, and why he succeeded, and even triumphed, in them all. It must not, however, be forgotten that, though he had none of the highest gifts of artistry, he had two other qualities of inestimable value : sincerity and conviction. He aspired to the realization of the best that was in him and he believed that his dramas really contributed to the improvement and the reformation of society. All this is quite clear from the

speech which he made on taking his seat in the Spanish
Academy on June 17, 1860, and which of all his works is
certainly not the least worth reading.


## EULOGIO FLORENTINO SANZ

Eulogio Florentino Sanz, whom, if we judged by the date
of his birth—March 1825—we should consider the last of our
Romantics, is celebrated principally as the author of the
notable verse drama *Don Francisco de Quevedo* (1848). Besides writing this very interesting play, he translated some
poems from the German, chiefly from Heine, wrote original
lyric poetry, which, like his translations, he never collected ;
and also produced a second drama, *Achaques de la Vejez*
(1854), inferior to *Don Francisco de Quevedo*, but better than
anything of Rodríguez Rubí's, although its plot is none too
solidly constructed and has no great interest.

Though he lived till 1881, Sanz produced no other
dramatic works than these. It is said that he was disappointed at the reception given to them, and, considering
himself unjustly treated and neglected, disdained to continue
writing and spent the last twenty years of his life in the most
profound embitterment and disillusion.*

Sanz was never elected to the Academy, because he would
not condescend to comply with its rules and present himself
as a candidate for admission : he therefore joins Larra,
Espronceda, García y Tassara, Enrique Gil and the rest of
the little group which stands outside the company of the
official immortals. It is clear that, besides his late but
notable contribution to the glories of Spanish romanticism,
Sanz brings an original temperament to distinguish him
from his contemporaries—unless it was an early impoverish-
ment of genius that stopped him from writing and not the
enigmatical pride and independence with which he is
credited.

*Don Francisco de Quevedo* is a somewhat unusual play
standing noticeably apart from the ordinary Romantic
formula, but its inspiration is too purely literary for it to be
described as realistic. The portrayer of Quevedo does not

---

* See the speeches read before the Spanish Academy "en la recepción pública
del Excmo. Sr. D. Antonio M. Fabié." Madrid, 1891.

to an excessive degree transgress the bounds of probability
nor contradict too violently what we actually know of that
author either from the external evidence of history or from
the internal evidence of his writings. Yet he transforms him
into a highly poetical character, a man of supreme distinction, with none of the habits of buffoonery which others so
mercilessly attribute to him, including Bretón in his ¿ Quién
es ella ?

The play was represented by an excellent caste, including
Julián Romea, Matilde Díez and La Lamadrid. From its
first performance it obtained considerable success, though it
cannot be said ever to have become really popular. It was
too carefully written to be entirely to the taste of a public
which at that time awarded its chief applause to the impressive but unequal versification of Rodríguez Rubí. But
it gained the keen and decisive appreciation of all true lovers
of literature and this appreciation it never lost. Sanz'
poetical style, occasionally laboured but always robust and
strong, with no superficial charm or melody of diction won
at the expense of meaning, recalls that of Hartzenbusch in
his best moments and never descends to those lower levels of
art occupied by Rodríguez Rubí's successors—Camprodón,
Eguilaz, the younger Larra, Olona and the *zarzuela*-librett-
ists, so popular and so vociferously applauded. His unusually rich vocabulary and the vigorous temper of his
phraseology allow him to create a special kind of form, more
sober, concise and expressive than that generally favoured
by the Romantics ; in dialogue, however, he is apt to
indulge in excessive artifice and in abuse of epigram and
irony.

A few lines from the admirable *Canción moral*, composed by
Quevedo a few months before his death, serve as epigraph to
the drama :

> Yo soy aquel mortal que por su llanto
> Fué conocido, más que por su nombre
> Ni por su dulce canto.

The quotation is a very apt one, as Sanz' hero is a gloomy
and a melancholy Quevedo, whose jests

> gotas son
> De la hiel del corazón
> Que les escupe a la cara ;

a Quevedo continually worried and irritated at the false idea that posterity will form of him, a fear that in another part of the play makes him exclaim, "con risa sangrienta,"

> Sí, Quevedo, los hombres ¡ oh ventura !
> Allá en la edad futura,
> Te honrarán . . . ¡ con chacota y alborozo !
>     Y al ver tu calavera, alegre risa
> Llamarán a su gesto, y, por laureles,
> Al son de un tamboril, después de misa,
> Ceñirán a su frente blanca y lisa
> Corona . . . de juglar . . . ¡ con cascabeles !

This heightened insistence on gloom, sadness and sarcasm in the drama is a strikingly Romantic trait, as is also the depth of the hero's passion and the hopelessness of his love for the Infanta Margarita,

> Dama de la sangre real . . .
> Por el Rey gobernadora
> Del reino de Portugal,

so infinitely above him in social position and so far removed from him in virtue.

Sanz' respect for history in this play is, of course, no more scrupulous than was usual with the earlier Romantics from the time of Dumas and Victor Hugo. Even were we to allow the true Quevedo to have had many of the characteristics attributed to him, we must also grant that Olivares was certainly not as evil or as devoid of acuteness and intelligence as he is here represented to be, nor was his fall from power so ignominious. At the time of that fall, Quevedo, very far from being in Madrid, was an old and infirm prisoner in a convent of the Order of Santiago at León. The favourite's disgrace brought him his liberty but he was already sixty-three years old and "like one who has played his part in the world, he did no more than pine away. His health was ruined ; his wounds were aggravated by his privations and the humidity of the dungeon. He lived but for two years longer."*

The patronage of Romea brought to this youth of twenty-three what he describes at the beginning of the play as the "honrosa deferencia" of seeing his first attempt at drama

---

* Ernest Mérimée : *Essai sur la vie et les œuvres de Francisco de Quevedo* (Paris, 1886), p. 121.

staged immediately.  Undoubtedly it bears witness to his
limited experience.  The two principal *motifs* or springs of
the plot—the conflict between Quevedo and Olivares and
the love of Quevedo and the Infanta—are not faultlessly
interwoven and fused together in the action of the play ;
they are developed independently and eventually require
different scenes for their resolution.  One of these scenes is,
of course, the great *coup de théâtre* of the play : the King's
dismissal of his favourite by means of a letter in which
he treats him as a criminal and speaks of sending him his
executioner.

> Olivares . . . si estuvieses en mi alcázar a mi regreso el
> amigo te dará sus brazos . . . el rey . . . su verdugo.

This scene is violent, insufficiently prepared and, in its
essential details, not in conformity with historic truth.  The
resolution of the other part of the plot makes some amends
for it.  This is the pathetic and delightfully poetical scene
between these two generous platonic lovers about to say
farewell and to part for ever :  he to return to his *villa* and
she to enter a convent.

| QUEVEDO. | Y allí con honda querella |
| | Diré a mi suerte cruel : |
| | ¿ Por qué me separas de ella ? |
| | Y vos . . . |
| MARGARITA. | Yo diré a mi estrella : |
| | ¿ Por qué me separas de él ? |
| QUEVEDO. | (*Con amargura*) |
| | ¡ Adiós ! |
| MARGARITA. | ¡ Adiós ! |

It is here that the play should have ended.  There was no
need to bring back the "varios caballeros," headed by the
inevitable trio of courtiers, who have been continually
appearing on the stage and always saying more or less the
same things ;  they have certainly nothing of importance to
add on this last occasion.

As a young man's first attempt at drama this was a work of
fine proportions, as full of promise as the first dramatic
attempts of García Gutiérrez and Hartzenbusch.  Unfortunately, Sanz went no farther.  It cannot be said that he
was entirely without friends able to help him rise and
prosper in the literary world ;  after the Liberal triumph of

1854 he was sent as *chargé d'affaires* to Berlin, where, being still young, he was able to enlarge his horizon and to cultivate German letters, as it is clear that he did from his verse translations. He was living in Berlin in 1836 when he wrote that epistle to Calvo Asensio, describing the abandoned grave of Enrique Gil, to which we have already alluded. Well deserving of quotation are the tercets in which he condemns the miserable, barren Spanish graveyard of the time, with its rows of coffins sealed up in niches, so different from the lovely garden-cemeteries which he saw in Germany and in other countries. The lines give some adequate idea of the style and talent of this potentially great writer, who, through his own fault as it would seem, never fulfilled the promise of his early manhood.

Dentro de nuestros muros funerales
Jamás brota una flor . . . Mal brotaría
De ese alcázar de cal y mechinales,
    Índice de la nada en simetría,
Que a la madre común roba los muertos
Para henchir su profana estantería . . .
    De tierra sobre tierra levantadas,
Más solemnes quizás por más sencillas,
Las del santo jardín tumbas aisladas,
    Con su césped de flores amarillas,
Se elevan . . . no muy altas . . . a la altura
Del que llore, al besarlas, de rodillas.
    Mas sola allí . . . sin flores . . . sin verdura
Bajo su cruz de hierro se levanta
De un hispano cantar la sepultura . . .
    ¡ No tienes una flor !—¿ Ni a qué dolores
Una flor de tu césped respondiera
Con aromas y jugos y colores ?
    Sólo al riego de lágrimas naciera . . .
Y de tu fosa en el terrón ajeno
¿ Quién derramó una lágrima siquiera ?

# CHAPTER XIII

## DII MINORES—II

After the theatre, the means of self-expression most favoured by nineteenth-century romanticism in Western Europe was prose fiction. In Spain, however, as preceding chapters have shown, the Romantic novel, in Larra, Espronceda, Enrique Gil, García de Villalta and Escosura, reached only a mediocre level, and it was not until the Romantic movement was over that there began the Golden Age of the novel, which even to-day is not completely at an end. Three writers of prose fiction, though somewhat later than any whom we have treated, should find a place in this concluding chapter. They bridge the gulf between the ineffective Romantic novelists of the first half-century and the great Romantic, Realistic and Eclectic novelists of the second.

The first of the three—first in date, fame and merit—is **Fernán Caballero.** This was the pseudonym of the daughter of the erudite German writer, Johan Nikolas Böhl von Faber, Consul for Hamburg in Cádiz. At a very early date, Böhl von Faber brought to the Peninsula something of the fragrance of that Romantic essence which was being so freely distilled by contemporary writers in Germany. He was anxious that in Spain's literary studies and allegiances she should cease to follow the eighteenth century and go back to the seventeenth, at any rate in drama ; it is true that some enlightened Spaniards had long been doing this, but none the less Germany probably had a greater appreciation of this drama than had Spain. The same also applies to the respective attitudes of Böhl, his fellow-countrymen and the Spaniards to the rich treasures of mediæval Spanish poetry, especially to the anonymous *cantares* and *romances* which so graphically and vigorously depict the life of the nation. Many of these great literary monuments were unknown in Spain, though Böhl, Grimm, Depping and others were making them popular by editing them in Germany.

Cecilia Böhl von Faber was born, in Switzerland as it chanced, in 1796 ; she spent her whole life in Spain and died at Seville in 1877. In her tastes, sympathies and type of genius as well as by virtue of her upbringing and the fidelity with which she resided in Andalusia, she was an Andalusian to the backbone. Her novels and short stories, together with the songs which she herself collected from the country people, form the most exact picture imaginable, if not the most artistic, of the life and customs of that part of Spain, with no trace either of caricature or of verbal pedantry. In their clarity and their delightful naturalness they surpass both the early verses of Rodríguez Rubí and also the *Escenas Andaluzas* of Estébanez Calderón. Had Fernán Caballero paid as much attention to her style as she did to her material, she would probably never have been superseded in this type of semi-realistic novel and popular story. But she cared less than any artist should for literary perfection and elegance and as a result her simplicity too often becomes carelessness or even triviality. Later in her life she attempted to enlarge her horizon and sought out other subjects, including somewhat more complicated arguments, "which she invented without stopping to observe," like that of *La Gaviota*, or created characters which are "expressionless puppets, like the Sir George Percy of *Clemencia*."* To many readers, nevertheless, these two novels are among the best she ever wrote. Her eagerness to teach moral and religious lessons and to give sound instruction carried her farther and farther from pure and independent art. She might well, without making any secret of her religious faith and devotion, have become a Spanish George Sand ; as it is, she appears in modern literary history as a figure already vague in outline and becoming less and less distinct as time goes on.

**Manuel Fernández y González** (1821–1888) was both more productive and more popular than Fernán Caballero. With his fertile imagination and his tireless industry, he should have become a kind of Spanish Alexandre Dumas. Like Dumas, he organized a novel-factory, with rather fewer collaborators ; nearly all his novels were historical and a few

---

* J. Fitzmaurice-Kelly : *Historia de la literatura española*, translated from the English by A. Bonilla. Madrid, n.d., p. 517. [These criticisms are modified in later editions.]

of them have real interest.  He was accustomed to boast of
having a number of works on the stocks at the same time,
which would be published simultaneously, and it is certain
that the various instalments of them all were awaited with
eager curiosity, though he never made his millions or built
palaces of Montecristo.  He has few readers to-day, not
because his particular type of fiction has gone (or ever goes
permanently) out of fashion, but because his works lacked
the robustness indispensable to long life.

**Antonio de Trueba,** though born, according to the
baptismal register, in 1819, is said to have considered himself
to be "a year or two older" than this.  He died in 1889.  A
native of Biscay, he wrote regional tales like Fernán Caballero, and, with some emotion and intense sympathy, described the *costumbres* of his native province.  Another
contemporary, the Salamancan **Ventura Ruiz Aguilera**
(1819–1881), wrote stories and verses of much the same kind,
as well as narratives in the form of *Proverbios*.  Both these
authors had the advantage over Fernán Caballero that they
could write equally well in verse and in prose.  In their
verse they often show some resemblance to Campoamor, for
which reason they appear to stand apart from the Romantic
group, but they had no idea of creating or adhering to any
such new type of verse as the *dolora*, nor of forming a poetic
style in opposition to the style then in fashion.  All three
were alike in cultivating the field of poetry at a spot very
near its boundary with the prosaic.  Campoamor is the
most successful in keeping on the right side of the boundary,
thanks both to his superior intelligence and to the fact that
he almost always has something to say which is worth saying.
Ruiz Aguilera, on the other hand, has much deeper feeling ;
he is endowed with greater breadth and generosity of ideas,
though he has neither the variety nor the philosophic
purpose of the *Doloras* and the *Pequeños Poemas* and he
certainly never had sublimity enough to rise to some of the
heights of the *Drama Universal*.  Campoamor, on the other
hand, lacked that elegiac gift which enabled Ruiz Aguilera
to write with such inspired grief in his *Elegías* on the loss of
his daughter, nor did he ever rival the sorrow-laden melody
of those lines from "La Limosna," beginning :

> Ayer cuando la nieve
> En copos muda y lenta descendía,

or of those others from the same poem describing the effect
produced on him by the discordant notes of the instrument
which the old beggar was playing as he pleaded for charity :

> A su triste armonía,
> A ese rocío de dolor sediento
> Mi corazón se abría . . .
> Así el agua de Mayo el campo inunda
> Y los dormidos gérmenes fecunda.

In the *Cuentos* of Trueba, especially in those entitled
*Cuentos de color de rosa* and *Cuentos de varios colores*, there is an
absence of "bite" or of anything imparting vigour to their
author's optimism and bringing it into harmony with life's
realities. His observation rarely penetrates far below the
surface, save when some personal emotion is touched, as in
his protests against the continual emigrations of the Basques
in search of fortune, which he deplores as testifying to a
weakening of their national character.

The author of *Escenas Andaluzas*, **Serafín Estébanez
Calderón** (1799–1867), better known by his pseudonym of
"El Solitario," gained a reputation in his lifetime as a
*costumbrista*, which his nephew, Antonio Cánovas del Castillo,
strove to perpetuate in his biography.* Estébanez' language,
now over-archaic, now over-Andalusian, is obscure and
artificial, while his style is affected in the extreme. A want
of naturalness is obviously a deadly sin in any *cuadro de
costumbres*. At the same time, he had an excellent command
of Castilian, and was one of the foremost combatants for its
purity. On the day of his death, Cánovas del Castillo tells
us, when he had received Extreme Unction and it was
known that the end could not be far off, "he asked to have
some pages of *Don Quijote* read to him, before rendering his
soul to God." Besides his *Escenas Andaluzas* (1847), he wrote
some poems, a historical tale called *Cristianos y Moriscos*
(1838), and a history entitled *La Conquista y Pérdida de
Portugal*, which Cánovas del Castillo published in 1885.
None of this work, however, is of the highest merit.

**Roca de Togores, Marqués de Molíns** (1812–1889) was
as important a figure in politics as in literature—perhaps
more so. On the one hand, he was elected to the Spanish

---

* *El Solitario y su tiempo.* Cf. p. 247, below.

Academy as early as 1837 and for many years was one of its most active members. On the other hand, with the exception of Cánovas del Castillo and Martínez Campos on the civil and on the military side respectively, none contributed more effectively than he to the breakdown of the reign of Amadeo and the Bourbon restoration.

Though his literary output was considerable, he will probably be remembered less in literature than in politics. He composed every kind of lyric—*leyendas* like Zorrilla, *romances históricos* like Rivas, *doloras* like Campoamor—and all of them have a certain facility and considerable elegance, though often also an incongruously archaic flavour.

His best known, most notable, and most successful work was a verse drama, *Doña María de Molina* (1837). The argument of this play is fundamentally the same as that of Tirso de Molina's *La Prudencia en la Mujer* ; it is more scrupulously adjusted to the old traditions and chronicles but has no higher degree of poetic verisimilitude. Molíns' position with regard to his predecessor's work is similar to that of Martínez de la Rosa with regard to Sophocles' *Œdipus*. One can understand that Martínez de la Rosa, writing in another language and at a distance of so many centuries, should wish, like Voltaire, to re-tell the Greek story to a public belonging to so different a type of society. But Molíns, by comparison, was almost a contemporary of his famous model ; further, he was writing in Tirso's own language and using a similar system of versification ; and finally, his public and Tirso's belonged to the same country. Inevitably, therefore, his drama is somewhat in the nature of a *refundición*, although technically it must rank as an original play, and he even assures us that he was not acquainted with *La Prudencia en la Mujer* when he wrote it. He made a scrupulously careful study of thirteenth-century Castilian history, in which he was thoroughly immersed when he began to write his drama. *Doña María de Molina* has considerably less intrinsic merit than *La Prudencia en la Mujer* ; but, in relation to the development of Spanish historical drama during the Romantic period, it represents something particular and characteristic, and, in certain of its traits, so distinct from the achievements of García Gutiérrez and Hartzenbusch that its author's name will never be completely forgotten. When his drama was first staged, before an audience very few of whose members could have read Tirso's play, the loftiness of its historical argument sufficed to kindle public enthusiasm. It is now no longer represented on the stage, and is only read by curious amateurs and critics, who can hardly refrain from making an invidious comparison in which it inevitably suffers.

Three other poets of this period, one of them also a notable prose-writer, have hardly been mentioned in these chapters, yet it is impossible to omit them entirely from our survey.

**Juan Arolas** (1805–1849), a Valencian priest whose poems were published, in a collected edition, posthumously, deserves in particular to be remembered for his *Orientales*, though, like Zorrilla, he also wrote *leyendas*, on traditional themes, which are still read with interest. In the *Orientales*, he goes behind Zorrilla and Zorrilla's model, Victor Hugo, to the Eastern poets themselves, who give him such characteristic themes as the "encendido amor de Sacuntala," and highly luminous and resplendent images, surpassing even those of Zorrilla, at any rate in his pre-*Granada* poems. Sensual love, ardently conceived and expressed, an atmosphere laden with the perfume of the seraglio, the monotonous existence of imprisoned beauty and the constant disdain for life engendered by a fatalistic creed : all this gives these poems—to our mind the poet's best—considerable local colour and an exotic Moorish flavour. Balaguer's description of Arolas' poems as "bells cantars lamartinians" has no precise meaning ; it is hard to detect any close resemblance between the author of the *Orientales* and the elegiast of the *Meditations* and *Jocelyn*.

**Nicomedes-Pastor Díaz** (1811–1863) was fond of literature but had little time to devote to it, being a distinguished statesman who in the course of a by no means long life was Plenipotentiary for Spain in Piedmont and Portugal and twice a minister of the Crown. His poems have pomp and colour, and, though sometimes over-gloomy, abound in magnificent images. Being written almost exclusively in one tone and one key, they tend to monotony, but they also frequently attain a singular degree of resonance and brilliance. Perhaps no reader of his poem *La Sirena* can forget that final stanza which so much enchanted Hartzenbusch when he heard it declaimed by the author in the Madrid Liceo :

> No más oí de la gentil sirena
> El concierto divino,
> Sino el tumbo del mar sobre la arena
> Y el bronco son del caracol marino.

This was one of Díaz's first compositions to attract attention. Many of his subsequent poems contain purple passages of equal sonority and beauty. Nevertheless, to our own mind, his best work was done in prose.

His outstanding production in this medium is entitled *De Villahermosa a la China. Coloquios íntimos.* The first part of this book was published in a periodical ; the next three parts followed it ten years later ; and the whole appeared in book form in 1858. Its author purposely refrained from describing it as a novel, for the plot develops very slowly and the characters are few in number. It is more properly a prose poem, steeped in the profoundest melancholy, in which the author pours out his most intimate feelings without displaying any affectation of scepticism, or any excess of world-weariness. Javier, the protagonist, is a Werther or a Jacopo Ortis, but more virile than either ; instead of committing suicide, he stands by his faith, goes to China as a missionary and dies there as a martyr, after doing all in his power to repair the consequences of that ardent passion which he has awakened but cannot return.

The book is beautifully written and wrestles successfully with the many obstacles of language which it encounters in its attempt to express the most delicate shades of passion with clarity and precision and to analyse deep and subtle feelings. A passage from a letter of Pastor Díaz to Antoine de Latour, which he sent him with the book, will give some idea of what the effort cost the wrestler :

> Esta lengua española no está hecha al análisis íntimo del corazón ; nuestros autores antiguos, los prosistas digo, eran exteriores, objetivos, no descendían al examen íntimo de la conciencia. Ustedes los franceses tienen la frase hecha para todas esas medias tintas y su lengua es menos exigente y más servicial. La nuestra es indómita, como un órgano de muchos registros. Ella, es verdad, canta y llora, suspira, gime, aúlla, silba, grita, murmura y se presta a todos los tonos como a todos

15

los afectos ; pero se revienta uno al manejar esas teclas de piedra que corresponden a tubos de bronce, siempre se oye un poco del teclado, y el fuelle. Además yo escribí ese libro enfermo y luego no le pude corregir.

On its first appearance, in spite of its real merit and its author's celebrity, the book attracted hardly any attention. Díaz was bitterly disappointed. "Why should I write anything further ?" he wrote to Latour. "You alone sent me congratulations when I published my book ; yet, when I am given some decoration or appointed to some political post, I receive hundreds of adulatory letters." He lived only five years more, being carried off in his prime by heart trouble, after a long illness.

**Antonio Hurtado** (1825–1878) attained distinction both as a lyricist and as a dramatist. In the *Romancero de Hernán Cortés* (1847) he showed himself to be one of the most inspired of those who carried on the tradition embodied by the Duque de Rivas in his *Romances históricos*. Nor is his merit far below that of his model in his collection of *leyendas* entitled *Madrid Dramático* (1870). In this work events from the life of Lope de Vega, Cervantes, Quevedo, Villamediana and Moreto alternate with other episodes of a more or less historical nature based on the national tradition. Hurtado also had some success on the stage. Both his first play *El Anillo del Rey* (1852) and *La Maya* (1869) exhibit the traits of romanticism in a state of decadence. Towards the end of his life Hurtado abandoned romanticism for spiritualism, which he brought on the stage in a play called *El Vals de Venzano* (1872).

**Manuel de Cabanyes** (1808–1833) a Catalonian poet, had a shorter life even than Larra, and his early death, as well as his outstanding talent, is responsible for the reputation which he has won in Catalonia. His poems are neither entirely Classical nor truly Romantic, and, though it seems probable that, had he lived longer, he would have been an out-an-out Romantic, we can only judge him with any propriety upon the body of work that he has left. This consists of one small collection, the nature of which is indicated by its title, *Preludios de mi lira* (1833), and of a few fragments. It contains sufficient material to reveal him as a fervent admirer of Horace, on whom he modelled himself with marked ability.

A number of Catalonians, Cabanyes' contemporaries, formed a group in which the central figure is that of Jaime Balmes. The most remarkable of these is **Pablo Piferrer**, who died, as it chanced, in the same month and year as Balmes, at the even earlier age of thirty. Piferrer wrote verse of a mediocre quality but much better prose—a picturesque, Romantic prose which suggests that he might easily have become a Spanish Ruskin. He was unable to complete his monumental work, *Recuerdos y Bellezas de España*, in which with an exuberant wealth of style he describes and interprets the artistic ruins and monuments of the Balearic Islands and Catalonia : the Catalonian section he left in an unfinished state and progressed no farther with the rest of his scheme, which was to have embraced the entire country. José María Quadrado, a Mallorcan writer, also a friend of Balmes', describes Piferrer's chief work, in an article on Piferrer and Balmes, as a poem, an artistic *Childe Harold*. Its young author did in fact travel all over the parts of Spain of which he wrote, and not only formed æsthetic judgments but also evoked historical memories and brought to light the feelings which lay deep beneath the surface of all he saw. In this way he composed what was at once a work of art and a work of great erudition. In Piferrer, as in Cabanyes, Spanish Romanticism lost genius of surpassing promise.

The seat in the Spanish Academy that Balmes never assumed was offered, after his death, to **José Joaquín de Mora** (1783-1864). A native of Cadiz, Mora became as well known in Spanish America as in Spain, chiefly on account of his *Leyendas Españolas*. These were begun in 1835, when he was living at La Paz, in Bolivia, were concluded during his return journey to Europe in 1838 and were published in London and Paris in 1840.

The first part of Mora's life was a succession of wanderings and adventures which it is impossible to detail with any brevity. During the Napoleonic Wars he was for some years a prisoner in France and left his country on the fall of the constitutional *régime* in 1823, settling in London, which was then a refuge for Spanish Liberals and a centre of activity for Spanish Americans who were striving for the independence of their respective countries. Like the famous Blanco White, Mora publicly embraced the cause of American separatism, placed his talent at its service, lent it the active aid of his pen, and, three years later, embarked for Buenos Aires at the invitation of President Rivadavia. A year later, Rivadavia and the Liberal party had fallen, and Mora, who had been devoting his time to the support of this party, had to leave the country. Accepting a similar invitation from the Chilean government, he then set out for Santiago, where he resided for three years. Here, however, he was suspected of complicity in a plot against the Republic and his position eventually became untenable. He had done much to improve Chilean education, but his adversaries were implacable, and, as they were also in power, he was first imprisoned and then ignominiously expelled from the country. No doubt, however, the same fate would have overtaken his rival, Andrés Bello, if the opposite party had been victorious.

The next seven years Mora spent in Peru and Bolivia, until he sailed for London as Consul-General of the Peruvo-Bolivian Confederation. When, after a few months, the Confederation was defeated by Chile, he returned to Spain, where, considering that he had sided with the rebel colonies, the welcome he received was encouraging. The wars were over, the colonies had won their independence and no one had now any desire to rake up the ashes of dead controversy. For some time he was principal of a college at Cádiz, but eventually settled in Madrid. Here he wrote freely for the press, was elected to the Academy, published a collection (1853) of his other poems, and lived quietly, unattracted by politics and hence unmolested by enemies, till his death in January 1864.

In the judgment of posterity, all Mora's poetical work is contained in the *Leyendas Españolas*. Here alone he is a poet at all ; in the large volume of *Poesías* published in 1853 he is simply and solely a maker of verses. In the *Leyendas* he brought truly original gifts to a type of work not in itself new ; interwoven in its very texture we find the humorous wit and sarcasm of *Beppo* and other works of Byron, traits which, however, in no way diminish the sustained interest of the narrative. Like Byron, he is prodigal of digressions, sometimes very happy ones, which he utilizes to drive home lessons learned by experience, often the bitter lessons of disillusionment. He has not the gift of expressing his feelings with Byron's eloquence, nor has he the inspiration of Espronceda. He is content, however, to walk on a humbler level, and he does his utmost to give his narrative an individuality of tone and accent which successfully distinguishes him from his contemporaries. He tilts happily against the most formidable difficulties of versification, as in the five octosyllabic *octavas* of the *leyenda* entitled *Pedro Niño*, which Andrés Bello, his Chilean rival, applauded in the very year of their publication.* Bello also picked out various other poems of Mora for approval in his excellent *Principios de Ortología y Métrica*.

After Larra's death, no literary critic remained in Spain with either his shrewdness or his assiduous devotion to his profession. Critical articles, of course, appeared regularly and frequently in the papers, but, as a widely read and authoritative writer, Fígaro had no successor. Politics absorbed the greater part of the press, and it was only in the field of drama that people took any great interest in the evolution of the new tendencies in literature. Still, though no critic appeared of outstanding merit, there were many who can be described as estimable : Gil y Carrasco, García de Villalta, Ochoa, Ferrer del Río are typical examples. Nor must we forget Lista, who, without renouncing his own canons of criticism, endeavoured, as we have said, not always successfully, to see the best in more modern ones, and never forgot that Espronceda and some of the lesser Romantics had been his pupils.

**Antonio Alcalá Galiano** began by being more intransigeant than Lista, and did battle with Böhl von Faber over the latter's Schlegelian eulogies of Calderón and Golden Age drama. During the period of his political exile, however, he became converted to the new opinions, and wrote the lengthy anonymous preface to the Duque de Rivas' *Moro Expósito*. This is a kind of literary manifesto, something after the pattern of Victor Hugo's preface to *Cromwell*, but without the militant and youthful tone of that work and without its wealth of ideas and images and splendour of style. Its tone is that of mature didacticism, its argument is deliberately and laboriously developed and it reaches an un-

* In the periodical *El Araucano*, 1846. Cf. *Obras Completas de Don Andrés Bello* (Santiago de Chile, 1884), Vol. VII, pp. 301–311.

distinguished climax in its unnecessarily timid proclamation
of principles which were already conceded, even in Spain.
Turning to the *Moro Expósito* itself, Alcalá Galiano then
declares that here is a work neither Classical nor Romantic
and that its author has no belief in the existence of such
arbitrary divisions. To write this was simply to thrust
evidence aside and to refuse to credit it. The unanimous
testimony of contemporaries of all shades of opinion assures
us that, while Alcalá Galiano was a marvellous orator and
improviser in political life, he takes a much lower place as
critic and historian.

Another historian and critic was **Antonio Ferrer del
Río,** who indulged in an affected style and sometimes displayed incredibly bad taste, but whose books have real
interest and rest on a solid basis of knowledge. The series of
contemporary biographies entitled *Galería de la Literatura
Española* (1846) has few of these defects, no doubt because of
the rapidity with which, as its author tells us, it was written.
Badly chequered, however, are his two historical works :
*Las Comunidades de Castilla* (1850) and the *Reinado de Carlos III*
(1856–7). In the rising of the Comuneros under Charles V
Ferrer del Río saw what he believed to be the beginning of
Spain's decadence, an opinion which he expressed in the
title of his book, no doubt in order to make it appear sensational. The *Reinado de Carlos III* was a work which he took
many years to write, with the intention of its being the crown
of his labours as a historian. It was published under the
auspices and patronage of the King Consort and it has an
undisguisable flavour of court historiography, particularly
in the epilogue, where it enumerates the blunders and
offences of the epoch of Charles IV without so much as
mentioning the scandalous favouritism lavished upon Godoy.
Yet little, if anything, better and more complete has been
written upon this period—the one relatively bright passage
in the gloomy annals of the reign of the Bourbons in
Spain.

**Salvador Bermúdez de Castro** (1814–1883), the friend
of whose verses García Tassara speaks so warmly,

—Tus versos, Salvador, que amé cual míos—

published a biography of Antonio Pérez (1841), four years
before Mignet's *Antonio Pérez et Philippe II*—a biography full

of incident which can be read with all the interest of a novel. Although, as Mignet points out, it assumes or invents explanations of doubtful points which are often quite untenable, Bermúdez de Castro was undoubtedly a careful student of the period and made use of documents which had not previously been known. In 1862, the **Marqués de Pidal** (1799–1865) published an extensive *Historia de las Alteraciones de Aragón* covering the same period, less dramatically written but substantial in their construction—composed, however, with the declared object of whitewashing the character of Philip II and defending his actions.

The only full and important general history of Spain published in this period is that begun by **Modesto Lafuente** (1806–1866) in 1850 and completed fifteen years later in twenty-nine volumes. The author, a native of Aragon, was a satirist in verse and prose before devoting himself to the study of history and writing this work. His comic vein, which he exploited for many years, brought him a reputation and a popularity far above what he could ever have achieved as a historian. Fray Gerundio and Tirabeque, characters of his own creation in whose mouths he placed jests and satire, mainly political, clothing them in ordinary language well within the comprehension of the people, came to be considered as personages belonging to real life, and for some time Lafuente's periodical (issued in two weekly broadsheets) had an extraordinary success. His satire is common, coarse and devoid of lofty purpose, but it is also pointed and witty. He has no sense of poetry and none of the inspiration so often evident in Larra ; to-day it is difficult to take any interest in him or even to understand how his contemporaries could ever have rated him so highly. But he wrote on the level of the masses, his influence during the tensely absorbing period of the Civil War was considerable and he championed the cause of national liberty and regeneration. Furthermore, this periodical often reveals him as a most ingenious versifier.

It was patriotism that inspired Lafuente with the project of writing a history of Spain. Such a work was greatly needed at this time, for there was none save that of Mariana, which had been written in the last years of the sixteenth century and was only recommendable for the classical excellence of its diction and the vigour of its magnificent style. But the task of writing such a work in Lafuente's day was as formidable as the planting of an oasis in the middle of the Sahara. There were not sufficient collections of documents and there were no proper catalogues in the archives ; nor were the necessary monographs available in any great abundance. Lafuente himself, unfortunately, had had no adequate preparation for the work into which, unhesitatingly and dauntlessly, he now flung himself. For fifteen years he worked on with indefatigable perseverance, and never once took his hand from the plough until he reached the date of Ferdinand VII's death (1833).

The most difficult part of his task was the treatment of that vast period extending from the fall of the Roman Empire to the end of the fourteenth century. These years occupy less than seven volumes of the twenty-nine, and, from whatever aspect it may be regarded, Lafuente's treatment of them is certainly extremely defective. For the later part of the work, he zealously tracked down and studied documents in the archives, cleared up obscurities and sketched certain periods in the firmest outline, with the result that the work as a whole acquired some permanent value. Its style, in general, is somewhat redundant and tainted by the author's continual eagerness to strain after effect. At the same time it has ease and elegance, while the narrative is clear and the tone well sustained. From the purely literary standpoint, the best part of the work is the long preliminary discourse filling the greater part of the first volume, the style of which is rapid, brilliant and oratorical.

From 1800 to 1833 there were only two periods which gave an opening for political oratory : the brief parenthesis of the Cortes of Cádiz and the three-year constitutional period ushered in by the Revolution of 1820. But life in those two periods of storm and stress was a continual anxiety : every one felt that the political situation was exceptional and no one could foretell what fortune had in store for the country when it should come to an end. When the Statute was promulgated in 1834 and a representative *régime* was initiated, though somewhat timidly, the old word-wrestlers appeared once again in the political arena. Martínez de la Rosa, Argüelles, Alcalá Galiano and the rest had all been worn by the exigencies of their exile and they

came back with little faith in liberty and still less in the
aptitude of the people to understand and make use of it.
They spoke well, but they acted badly, suffered new and
bitter disillusionments and little by little lost their prestige.
Not a single speech by any one of them, nor even a memorable phrase, can be said to have survived to save their
eloquence from oblivion.

Joaquín María López (1798–1855) and Salustiano
Olózaga (1805–1873) were the first of their successors to
rise to great heights in Parliamentary oratory. Then in turn
came Cortina, González Bravo, Ríos Rosas and Pacheco :
the last named of these was the most literary, the others being
advocates, like Cortina, or journalists, like González Bravo,
who improvised oratory in order to promote or justify the
various *coups d'état* or *pronunciamientos* of generals.

The speeches of López, like those of Olózaga, have been
collected in book form, but to-day they hardly stand the
test of being read, nor can López's non-political speeches
(such as his oration over the body of Espronceda) be said to
justify the reputation given him by his contemporaries. At
one critical moment in his life Olózaga had occasion to make
a really great speech of more vivid and pathetic interest than
any mere verbal skirmish of party warfare. As Prime
Minister, he had obtained the signed consent of the Queen
(at that time a girl of thirteen) to the dissolution of the
Cortes ; and, when he believed his triumph to be secure, he
found that his adversaries, who led the parliamentary
majority, were in possession of an official statement in which
the Queen solemnly affirmed that her signature to the
decree of dissolution had been forcibly extracted from her
by the injudicious minister under threats of violence. No
doubt this story had been exaggerated, if not invented, by
the palace *camarilla :* but, if true, the crime was one of
*lèse-majesté* which the offending minister could atone for
only on the scaffold. The parliamentary majority, having
no desire for a dissolution, was hostile to Olózaga, and,
knowing his character, believed him perfectly capable of
having carried indiscretion to this extremity. Olózaga
defended himself, if not with the combination of vigour,
temperance and pathos that characterized Strafford's
speech on a not dissimilar occasion before the House of
Lords, at least with considerable skill and eloquence. His

situation was an exceedingly delicate one, for he believed
the statement signed by the Queen to be false, yet he could
not aggravate his position by openly challenging his adversaries to prove its authenticity.  There came a moment
in his speech when his voice failed him and emotion compelled him to pause.  But, as Strafford also found, it was
hopeless to attempt to move adversaries who were already
prejudiced against him.  At the end of the session, Olózaga
was forced to seek hiding, and eventually to leave Madrid
for France, until time had appeased the wrath of the
supporters of Narváez and González Bravo.  The latter,
on this occasion, played the part of prosecuting counsel in
the Cortes in a speech which was the greatest of all his
oratorical triumphs.

The most truly Romantic orator of this period was **Juan
Donoso Cortés,** with whom we have already dealt as an
essayist.  His speeches might well be re-published as so
many chapters of the *Ensayo sobre el Catolicismo*, while the
reader of that book will have no difficulty in picturing it as a
series of speeches, and supplying for himself the gestures and
the intonation of the orator and the applause and acclama-
tions of the crowd.  Even when treating prosaic and complicated subjects, Donoso's writings abound in magnificent
images.  He found himself continually and enthusiastically
applauded alike by friends and foes, all of whom were carried
away by his astounding eloquence and found it difficult to
resist the power and sincerity of his convictions.

A number of other orators, such as **Antonio Aparisi y
Guijarro** (1815–1872), modelled themselves on the style of
Donoso Cortés ; but to find his true successor—an orator
who equals him in wealth of imagery and surpasses him in
facility, variety of technique and amplitude of opinion and
sentiment—we must go to the Republican field and study
**Emilio Castelar** (1832–1899). This great statesman,
however, can hardly be brought within the limits of the
present study.

Around Espronceda there gathered a little group of
interesting writers, who inherited some of his popularity and
shared some portion of his spirit.  With two of these, Gil y
Carrasco and García de Villalta, we have already concerned
ourselves : there remain two more.

**Miguel de los Santos Álvarez** (1818-1892) made an ineffective attempt to continue *El Diablo Mundo ;* it seems that he had so lively a respect for the memory of his illustrious friend that he was wont to seek inspiration by visiting the woman of whom Espronceda had written, in a famous poem, as "Jarifa." She became to Álvarez the living memory of the departed poet, who was so incomparable a friend :

> ¡ En ti le encuentro yo, Jarifa mía !
> En ti le encuentro yo, yo que le adoro
> Con más dolor del alma cada día
> Y hago de su recuerdo mi tesoro.

These lines, like the remainder of Álvarez' productions, cannot be said to go far beyond mediocrity. Espronceda himself did more than all of them to keep green his friend's name by printing one stanza of Álvarez' *María* as an epigraph to his "Canto a Teresa," and in the following canto of *El Diablo Mundo* quoting it in the well-known lines :

> ¡ *Bueno es el mundo !* ¡ *bueno !* ¡ *bueno !* ¡ *bueno !*
> Ha cantado un poeta amigo mío,
> Mas es fuerza mirarlo así de lleno,
> El cielo, el campo, el mar, la gente, el río,
> Sin entrarse jamás en pormenores
> Ni detenerse a examinar despacio,
> Que espinas llevan las lozanas flores,
> Y el más blanco y diáfano topacio
> Y la perla más fina
> Manchas descubrirá si se examina.

This, it is to be feared, is the only line of Miguel de los Santos Álvarez which is likely to recall his work to a remote posterity.

His prose is better than his verse, and one of his *Cuentos en prosa* entitled "La Protección de un Sastre" has passages of real elegance, and, as Valera put it, "candoroso desenfado."* Its unaffected irony alone will give it a place in anthologies and make it always worth reading.

**Patricio de la Escosura** (1807-1878), a somewhat rebellious young officer, of a type quite common in the last century, rose to the rank of colonel, and became the bio-

---

* Juan Valera : *Florilegio de Poesías castellanas* (Madrid, 1904), Vol. V, p. 214.

grapher and relative by marriage of Espronceda, who had once been his schoolfellow. He wrote lyrics, some of them famous in their time, and certainly Romantic enough. Among these we may class "El Bulto vestido de negro capuz," a verse *leyenda* of unequal merit which first appeared in the Romantic review *El Artista* and is now forgotten. He also wrote some dramas which in their day were not unsuccessful, such as *La Corte del Buen Retiro* (1837), *Bárbara Blomberg* (1837) and several more of no importance. In verse he is nearly always careless and incorrect, much more so than in his novel-like prose, though this, too, is by no means free from the same defects. On the whole it was in the novel that he showed the greatest talent. *Ni Rey ni Roque* (1835), to which we referred in dealing with Zorrilla's treatment of its subject, that of the *pastelero* of Madrigal, was written when he was still young and is fresh enough to be read to-day without any great effort. As one closes the last of its tiny volumes one cannot help feeling that its author might have gone far had he given more attention to the plan of his book and polished his style. At a later date Escosura imitated Eugène Sue less happily in *El Patriarca del Valle* (1846–7) and after a silence extending over many years he began to publish some interesting reminiscences of his own life under the title *Memorias de un Coronel retirado* (1868).

Zorrilla, who took no part in politics and had not Espronceda's personal charms and advantages, never gathered around himself so numerous a group of literary disciples or friends as did the "Spanish Byron." Mention, however, must be made of the Venezuelan **José Heriberto García de Quevedo** (1818–1871), who lived on terms of intimacy with Rafael María Baralt, his successful rival in a literary contest organized by the Liceo de Madrid in honour of Columbus.

García de Quevedo took Zorrilla's place in the composition of the *Corona poética de la Virgen María*, and also finished several other pieces of work which Zorrilla had begun, such as *Un cuento de amores* and *Pentápolis*. More than three-quarters of *María* is the work of García de Quevedo. He learned by practice to imitate the style and language of Zorrilla so skilfully that, unless one knows where the break occurs in their joint works, it is extremely difficult to discover it by internal evidence. The two are no less alike in their bad passages than in their good.

The best work of García de Quevedo is that which we owe to his pen alone ; though neither his plays nor his novels are of great merit, his lyrics are often excellent. Worthy of mention are the ode *A Italia*, written in a metre recalling that of Manzoni's *Cinque Maggio*, and some parts of the poem *Delirium*, which as a whole is a confused narrative truer to its title than its author perhaps realized.

It would not be fair to omit all mention of **Jose María Diaz**, who wrote the best scenes in Act II of Zorrilla's *Traidor, Inconfeso y Mártir*. Díaz was the author of *Elvira de Albornoz*, an early Romantic play of some merit. He wrote many other such plays in verse, some Romantic, others semi-Classical, the latter recalling the indeterminate *genre* favoured by Delavigne rather than the type of tragedy associated with Ponsard and the clamorous and ephemeral reaction which followed the performance of *Les Burgraves*. Díaz hesitated between the two extreme ideals, never declaring himself definitely for either and always seeking the favour of the public, which he obtained only to a very limited degree. Nevertheless, he was an indefatigable worker and carefully avoided any prostitution of his powers.

Miguel de los Santos Álvarez died only two months before Zorrilla. Thus the last of the great Romantic writers and the last survivor of the second generation disappeared almost simultaneously. The Romantic movement, in the sense usually given to this phrase, had, of course, passed away long before. A full half-century had elapsed since it had fallen from its temporary throne and nearly forty years since it had been publicly described as "belonging only to history." To-day, though in one sense romanticism as understood by Zorrilla and his contemporaries still lives, it is generally considered as an outworn mode, a ridiculous pose and a curious mania. The qualities which charmed and dazzled the eighteen-thirties, and seemed like the burgeoning of an abundant spring, too soon shed their brilliant colours, faded with incontinent rapidity and reached the last dead days of autumn after displaying all too little of the beauties of summer.

# SELECT BIBLIOGRAPHY*

(See p. vii, above)

CHAPTER I. MARIANO JOSÉ DE LARRA

**Bibliography.** A fairly complete and convenient list of editions and critical studies will be found in *Seis Artículos de Larra,* ed. Reginald F. Brown (Liverpool, 1933).

**Collected Works.** There is as yet no really complete edition. The editions generally used are the Madrid (Yenes) edition of 1843 (4 vols.), the undated and substantially identical Paris (Baudry) edition (2 vols.) and the Paris (Garnier) edition (4 vols.).

**Selections.** The three volumes by J. R. Lomba y Pedraja ("Clásicos Castellanos" : Madrid, 1923-7) contain Larra's principal articles broadly classified according to their subjects. Details of articles not included in the collected editions, and of selections for school use, will be found in R. F. Brown's bibliography.

**Critical Studies.** The best are : J. R. Lomba y Pedraja : *Mariano José de Larra: I. Como escritor político ; II. Como escritor literario* (Madrid, 1918, 1920 : reprinted from *La Lectura*) ; "Azorín" : *Rivas y Larra* (Madrid, 1916 : to be read with caution) ; M. Chaves : *D. Mariano José de Larra ; su tiempo, su vida, sus obras* (Seville, 1898) ; E. McGuire : "A study of the writings of D. Mariano José de Larra (1809-1837)," in *University of California Publications in Modern Philology* (Berkeley, 1918), Vol. VII, pp. 87-130 ; J. Nombela y Campos : *Larra (Fígaro)*, Madrid, 1909. Professor F. Courtney Tarr, the author of a number of short studies on Larra, has an edition of his articles in preparation.

On Scott's influence in Spain (discussed on pp. 15 ff., 48, above), see P. H. Churchman and E. Allison Peers : "A Survey of the Influence of Sir Walter Scott in Spain," in *Revue Hispanique*, 1922 (Vol. LV, pp. 227-310), and E. Allison Peers : "Studies in the Influence of Sir Walter Scott in Spain," in *Revue Hispanique*, 1926 (Vol. LXVIII, pp. 1-160).

* [The historical study of the Romantic movement which the translator hopes shortly to publish contains a full bibliography of general works on the period as well as of all its chief authors. Here only a few notes can be given as an aid to the further study of individual authors.]

CHAPTER II. ANGEL DE SAAVEDRA, DUQUE DE RIVAS

**Bibliography.** A good and full critical bibliography, useful also for the period in general, is Gabriel Boussagol's "Le Duc de Rivas, essai de bibliographie critique," in *Bulletin Hispanique,* 1927 (Vol. XXIX, pp. 5–98).
**Works.** The current collected edition (*Obras completas,* Madrid, 1894–1904, 7 vols.) has several omissions, the most serious of which is *El Desengaño en un Sueño,* which, with *La Sublevación de Nápoles* and Rivas' other prose works, can be studied in the Barcelona (1884–5) edition, consisting of two large and cumbrous volumes. An earlier edition still is that of Madrid, 1854–5 (5 vols.). There are modern editions of *El Moro Expósito* and *Don Álvaro,* and (in the "Clásicos Castellanos" series) a volume of *Romances Históricos* (Madrid, 1912).
**Critical Studies.** Two full-length studies are : E. Allison Peers : "Angel de Saavedra, Duque de Rivas, A Critical Study" (New York, Paris, 1923 : *Revue Hispanique,* Vol. LVIII, pp. 1–600) and Gabriel Boussagol : *Angel de Saavedra, Duc de Rivas, sa vie, son œuvre poétique* (Toulouse, 1927). The former has a concise bibliography, fairly comprehensive as far as Rivas' life is concerned, but not attempting to go outside those limits.
**Shorter Studies.** M. Cañete : *Escritores españoles e hispano-americanos* (Madrid, 1884), pp. 3–148 ; L. A. de Cueto, Marqués de Valmar : "Discurso necrológico, etc.," in *Memorias de la Academia Española* (Madrid, 1870), Vol. II, pp. 498–601 ; Juan Valera : *Crítica literaria, 1887–9* (*Obras,* Vol. XXVII), pp. 71–196 ; "Azorín" : *Rivas y Larra* (Madrid, 1916) and *Clásicos y Modernos* (Madrid, 1919), pp. 55–63, 268 72 ; E. Allison Peers : *Rivas and Romanticism in Spain* (Liverpool, 1923).


CHAPTER III. ANTONIO GARCÍA GUTIÉRREZ

**Bibliography.** A useful and fairly complete bibliography of García Gutiérrez' works will be found at the end of N. B. Adams' study, noted below.
**Works.** Most of García Gutiérrez' important plays are reprinted in the *Obras escogidas* (Madrid, 1866). There are many modern editions of *El Trovador,* some of them with vocabularies and notes ; *Venganza Catalana* and *Juan Lorenzo* are reprinted (with introduction and notes by J. R. Lomba y Pedraja) in the "Clásicos Castellanos" series (Madrid, 1925). The remaining works are available only in contemporary editions. Students will find a particularly full collection of these in the library of the University of Valencia.

**Critical Studies.** N. B. Adams : *The Romantic Dramas of García Gutiérrez* (New York, 1922) is a somewhat slight but useful and interesting treatment of its subject. E. Funes : *García Gutiérrez, estudio crítico de su obra dramática* (Cádiz, 1900) is somewhat difficult to obtain. The only other critical material is contained in histories of literature and in such contemporary articles as an appreciation by Ochoa in *El Artista* (Vol. III, p. 121) or Larra's critique of *El Trovador*, which may be found in his collected works.

## CHAPTER IV.   JUAN EUGENIO HARTZENBUSCH

**Bibliography.** Eugenio Hartzenbusch : *Bibliografía de Juan Eugenio Hartzenbusch* (Madrid, 1900).

**Works.** The most important plays will be found in *Obras* (Madrid, 1887–92, 5 vols.). Other collections of selected works are those of Paris (Baudry), 1850, and Leipzig, 1863 (2 vols. : biographical sketch by Ferrer del Río). There are numerous editions of *Los Amantes de Teruel*, some annotated. The editions of the other plays can be consulted only in libraries.

**Critical Studies.** A. S. Corbière : *Juan Eugenio Hartzenbusch and the French Theatre* (Philadelphia, 1927) ; E. Cotarelo y Mori : *Sobre el origen y desarrollo de la leyenda de los Amantes de Teruel* (Madrid, 1907) ; A. Maseda : *Estudios de crítica literaria* (Bilbao, 1915).

## CHAPTER V.   JOSÉ DE ESPRONCEDA

**Bibliography.** Philip H. Churchman : "An Espronceda Bibliography," in *Revue Hispanique*, 1907 (Vol. XVII, pp. 741–77).

**Works.** None of the numerous editions of Espronceda's collected works is complete. Those generally used are *Obras poéticas y escritos en prosa* (ed. Escosura, Madrid, 1884), *Obras poéticas* (Valladolid, 1900), and *Obras poéticas* (ed. Cascales Múñoz, Madrid, 1923). The 1884 edition was reprinted in 1926. Some "Páginas olvidadas" have been published under that title (Madrid, 1873) and others as "More Inedita" in the *Revue Hispanique*, 1907 (Vol. XVII, pp. 704–40). There are two volumes of selected poems (*Poesías, El Estudiante de Salamanca, El Diablo Mundo*) in the "Clásicos Castellanos" edition, with a preface by J. Moreno Villa (Madrid, 1923).

Of individual works, *Blanca de Borbón* was made available to students by Professor Churchman in the *Revue Hispanique*, 1907 (Vol. XVII, pp. 549–703) ; copies of *El Diablo Mundo* (Madrid 1841, 2 vols.) and the *Poesías* of 1840 (ed. J. García de Villalta) are fairly accessible in Spanish libraries ; and *El Estudiante de Salamanca* has frequently been reprinted, notably with annotations by G. T. Northup (New York, 1919), and as a plain text (Cambridge, 1922). The first edition (1834, 6 vols.) of *Sancho Saldaña* is rarer, but there is also a two-volume edition (Madrid, 1869) and a modern edition (Madrid, 1914).

**Critical Studies.** Espronceda has attracted a number of serious workers, though a definitive biographical and critical study has still to be written. The chief biographies are those of J. Cascales Múñoz (*Don José de Espronceda*, Madrid, 1914), A. Cortón (*Espronceda*, Madrid, 1906) and E. Rodríguez Solís (*Espronceda : su tiempo, su vida y sus obras*, Madrid, 1883). Representative shorter studies are : A. Bonilla y San Martín : "El Pensamiento de Espronceda," in *La España Moderna*, 1908, (pp. 69–101) ; G. Brereton : *Quelques précisions sur les sources d'Espronceda* (Paris, 1933) ; Philip H. Churchman : "Byron and Espronceda," in *Revue Hispanique*, 1909 (Vol. XX, pp. 5–210) and "Some Espronceda Miscellany," in *Revue Hispanique*, 1922 (Vol. LVI, pp. 508–21) ; J. Fitzmaurice-Kelly : "Espronceda," in *Modern Language Review*, 1908 (Vol. IV, pp. 20–39) ; Angela Hämel : *Der Humor bei Espronceda* (Halle, 1922) ; Ch. Tisserand : "Pour une édition d'Espronceda," in *Revue Hispanique*, 1919 (Vol. XLVI, pp. 269–80) ; Juan Valera : "Del Romanticismo en España y de Espronceda," in *Obras Completas*, Vol. XIX, pp. 7–46 (reprinted from *Revista Española de Ambos Mundos*, 1854).

### CHAPTER VI. JOSÉ ZORRILLA

**Works.** Representative editions are those of Paris, 1864 (3 vols. : at that time "la sola reconocida por el autor") ; and Madrid, 1905 (4 vols.). A good selected edition is the "Clásicos Castellanos" volume of *Poesías* (ed. N. Alonso Cortés, Madrid, 1925). There is a small collection of *Composiciones varias* in the "Biblioteca Universal." Editions of individual works are too numerous to mention. *Granada* was reprinted in Madrid, 1895. See also *Últimos versos inéditos y no coleccionados* (Madrid, 1908) and *Recuerdos del Tiempo Viejo* (Madrid, 1882, 3 vols.).

**Critical Studies.** The most important is N. Alonso Cortés : *Zorrilla, su vida y sus obras* (Valladolid, 1916–20, 3 vols.). Others are : J. W. Barlow : "Zorrilla's indebtedness to Zamora," in *Romanic Review*, 1926 (Vol. XVII, pp. 303–18) ; C. Eguía Ruiz : "Un poeta patriótico : D. José Zorrilla," in *Razón y Fe*, 1917 (Vol. XLIX, pp. 61–79, 320–38) ; I. Fernández Flórez : *Zorrilla, Estudio biográfico* (Madrid, n.d.) ; J. Hazañas : *Génesis y desarrollo de la leyenda de Don Juan Tenorio* (Seville, 1893) ; D. Ibáñez Garrido : "El *Don Juan Tenorio* de Zorrilla. Estudio crítico," in *Ciudad de Dios*, 1921 (Vols. CXXIV–CXXVIII, *passim*), together with various shorter articles in the same review for 1920, 1922,

16

1923, 1926 and 1927 ; J. F. Menéndez : "Apuntes para la biografía del poeta Zorrilla," in *Boletín de la Biblioteca Menéndez y Pelayo*, 1923 (Vol. V, pp. 117–41) ; R. Menéndez Pidal : *L'Epopée castillane*, Paris, 1910, pp. 258–78 ; E. Ramírez Ángel : *José Zorrilla, Biografía anecdótica* (Madrid, n.d., 1915 ?).

Numerous articles called forth by the centenary of Zorrilla's birth will be found in the Spanish periodicals for 1917 ; few of these, however, are of much value. A recent *homenaje* of greater merit, containing articles by specialists in the period, is *Amigos de Zorrilla. Colección de artículos dedicados al poeta* (Valladolid, 1933).

### Chapter VII.  Manuel Bretón de los Herreros

**Bibliography and Works.**  A catalogue of Bretón's works will be found in the "definitive" edition (*Obras*, Madrid, 1883–4, 5 vols.) which also has some reliable biographical notes, and, though not complete, supersedes the two-volume edition of *Obras escogidas* (Paris, 1853).

Of individual works, convenient modern editions are : *La Independencia* (ed. J. Geddes, New York, 1924) ; *Marcela, o ¿A cuál de los tres?* (Madrid, 1920 ; ed. W. S. Hendrix, Chicago, 1922) ; *Muérete ; ¡y verás!* (Madrid, 1919 ; also, with *El Pelo de la dehesa*, as *Teatro*, ed. N. Alonso Cortés, Madrid, 1928).

**Critical Studies.**  The best work on Bretón is G. Le Gentil : *Le Poète Manuel Bretón de los Herreros et la société espagnole de 1830 à 1860* (Paris, 1909).  Previously the standard authority, which is still of value, was M. Roca de Togores, Marqués de Molíns : *Bretón de los Herreros, recuerdos de su vida y de sus obras* (Madrid, 1883).  The remainder of the scanty Bretón literature consists of articles and essays, mostly of little importance.

### Chapter VIII.  Ventura de la Vega

**Works.**  *Obras poéticas* (Paris, 1866) ; *Obras escogidas* (Madrid, 1874) ; *Obras escogidas* (Barcelona, 1894–5, 2 vols).  *El Hombre de Mundo* is reprinted in the series of "Autores Dramáticos Contemporáneos" (Madrid, 1881, Vol. I, pp. 253–345), with a preface by Juan Valera.  With the other plays mentioned in the text it may also be read in *Obras poéticas*.

**Critical Studies.**  For Pezuela's obituary oration, see p. 152, note. (The volume in which it appears (pp. 5–15) also contains Vega's own inaugural address to the Spanish Academy.) See also J. Güell y Renté : *Estudio . . . y juicio crítico sobre "La Muerte de César" de D. Ventura de la Vega* (Madrid, 1866) ; M. Menéndez y Pelayo : *Antología de poetas hispano-americanos* (Madrid, 1895, Vol. IV, pp. cxlvi–clxi).

CHAPTER IX. GERTRUDIS GÓMEZ DE AVELLANEDA

**Works.** The two chief editions are : *Obras literarias* (Madrid, 1869–71, 5 vols.) ; *Obras* (Habana, 1914–18, 4 vols. : Edición nacional del centenario). Modern editions of plays are : *Baltasar* (ed. C. Bransby, New York, 1908) ; *El Donativo del Diablo* (Habana, 1914) ; *Leoncia* (Madrid, 1917). For *La Avellaneda*'s life and letters, see : *Autobiografía y cartas* (ed. L. Cruz de Fuentes, Huelva, 1907 ; Enlarged edition, Madrid, 1914) ; *Cartas amatorias* (ed. L. Cruz de Fuentes, Habana, 1914) ; *Cartas inéditas y documentos, etc.* (ed. J. A. Escoto, Matanzas, 1911) ; *Memorias inéditas* (ed. D. Figarola-Caneda, Habana, 1914).

**Critical Studies.** M. Aramburo y Machado : *Personalidad literaria de Doña Gertrudis Gómez de Avellaneda* (Madrid, 1898) ; E. Bernal : "G. G. de A., su vida y su obra," in *Cuba contemporánea*, 1925 (Vol. XXXVII, pp. 85–111) ; Aurelia Castillo de González : *Biografía de G. G. de A. y juicio crítico de sus obras* (Habana, 1887) ; E. Cotarelo y Mori : "Doña G. G. de A. Indicaciones bibliográficas, etc.," in *Boletín de la Academia Española*, 1915 (Vol. II, pp. 362–83) ; E. Cotarelo y Mori : *La Avellaneda y sus obras* (Madrid, 1930) ; E. Cotarelo y Mori : "Una tragedia real de la Avellaneda," in *Rev. Bibl. Arch. Mus.*, 1926 (Vol. III, pp. 133–57) ; L. Cruz de Fuentes : *La Avellaneda. Autobiografía y Cartas, etc.* (Huelva, 1907) ; J. M. Chacón y Calvo : *G. G. de A. : las influencias castellanas : examen negativo* (Habana, 1914) ; D. Figarola-Caneda : *G. G. de A. Biografía, bibliografía e iconografía, etc.* (Madrid, 1929) ; J. A. Rodríguez García : *De la Avellaneda* (Habana, 1915) ; E. B. Williams : *The Life and Dramatic Works of G. G. de A.* (Philadelphia, 1924).


CHAPTER X. RAMÓN DE CAMPOAMOR

**Works.** The fullest of the "complete" editions is that of Madrid, 1901–3 (8 vols.). There are numerous other collected editions, of which it suffices to mention a convenient thin-paper edition in one volume (Madrid, Aguilar, 1929). Selections also abound ; handy and representative ones are *Las Mejores Poesías de Campoamor* (Madrid, 1913) and *Poesías escogidas* (Biblioteca Universal : Madrid, 1879 ; reprinted, 1925). There is an annotated edition of *Poesías* in the "Clásicos Castellanos" series (ed. C. Rivas Cherif, Madrid, 1921). Editions of single works run into many hundreds.

**Critical Studies.** Azorín : "El segundo Campoamor," in *Clásicos y modernos* (Madrid, 1919), pp. 171–6 ; A. González Blanco : *Campoamor : biografía y estudio crítico* (Madrid, 1911) ; Emilia Pardo Bazán : *Retratos y apuntes literarios*, in *Obras com-*

*pletas* (Madrid, n.d.), Vol. XXXII, pp. 5–62 ; H. Peseux-Richard : "Humoradas, Doloras et Petits Poèmes de D. Ramón de Campoamor," in *Revue Hispanique*, 1894 (Vol. I, pp. 236–57) ; S. Pulpón : "El 'Personalismo' de Campoamor," in *Revista Calasancia*, 1915 (Vols. III, IV, *passim*) ; M. Romera-Navarro : "Campoamor," in *Estudio*, 1917 (Vol. XX, pp. 390–406). There are innumerable articles on Campoamor in periodicals besides those here mentioned.

## CHAPTER XI

### TWO PROSE-WRITERS : DONOSO CORTÉS AND BALMES

DONOSO CORTÉS. **Works.** Three editions of *Obras* are readily available in libraries : Madrid, 1854–5 (5 vols.) ; Madrid, 1891–4 (4 vols.) ; Madrid, 1903–4 (4 vols.). These reprint an important article "El Clasicismo y el Romanticismo" from the *Correo Nacional* for 1838. There is a modern edition of *Discursos parlamentarios*, edited by J. Burell and J. B. Catalá (Madrid, 1915). Of the *Ensayo sobre el catolicismo, el liberalismo y el socialismo* (Madrid, 1851) an English translation was published in Dublin, 1874. Many translations of this and other works by Donoso Cortés were made in French and Italian. **Critical Studies.** Baralt's *Discurso* will be found in *Memorias de la Academia Española*, 1860 (Vol. II, pp. 5–53). See also : C. de Mazade : "M. Donoso Cortés, ses écrits et ses discours," in *Revue des Deux Mondes*, 1850, pp. 142–69 ; G. Tejado : *Noticia biográfica*, etc. (reprinted from *Obras*), Madrid, 1854.

BALMES. **Bibliography.** A. Palau : *Bibliografía cronológica de Balmes*, Barcelona, 1915. **Works.** *Obras completas*, ed. P. Ignacio Casanovas (Barcelona, 1925–7, 3 vols.). Editions (even modern editions) of individual works are too numerous to mention. **Critical Studies.** In all large Spanish libraries there is much ephemeral material on Balmes. The principal studies are : M. Arboleya Martínez : *Balmes periodista* (Barcelona, 1914) ; A. de Blanche-Raffin : *Balmès, sa vie et ses ouvrages* (Paris, 1849) ; E. Bullón Fernández : *Jaime Balmes y sus obras* (Madrid, 1903) ; J. Collell : *Balmes : Discurso biográfico* (Vich, 1890) ; C. de Mazade : "Don Jaime Balmes, sa vie et ses œuvres," in *Revue des Deux Mondes*, 1853, pp. 319–51 ; M. Menéndez y Pelayo : *Dos palabras sobre el centenario de Balmes* (Vich, 1910) ; J. Elías de Molíns : *Balmes y su tiempo* (Barcelona, 1906) ; N. Roure : *La Vida y las obras de Balmes* (Madrid, 1910) ; N. Roure : *Las Ideas de Balmes* (Madrid, 1910) ; J. M. Ruano y Corbo : *Balmes apologista, estudio crítico* (Santiago, 1911) ; E. Ugarte de Ercilla : *Acerca de la filosofía de Balmes* (Madrid, 1922), and *Balmes el polígrafo* (Madrid, 1923).

CHAPTER XII

DII MINORES—I

MARTÍNEZ DE LA ROSA. **Works.** *Obras completas* : Paris, 1844–5, 5 vols. ; Paris, 1853–4, 5 vols. ; *Obras literarias* : Paris, 1827–30, 5 vols., and various reprints ; *Obras dramáticas*, ed. J. Sarrailh, Madrid, 1933 ("Clásicos Castellanos." Comprises *La Viuda de Padilla, Aben-Humeya, La Conjuración de Venecia*). There is an annotated text of *La Conjuración de Venecia*, ed. A. L. Owen and J. T. Lister (New York, 1917). **Critical Studies.** N. Alonso Cortés : "Retazo biográfico," in *Viejo y nuevo*, Madrid, 1916, pp. 123–64 ; M. Menéndez y Pelayo : *Martínez de la Rosa. Estudio biográfico*, Madrid, n.d. (and in *Estudios de crítica literaria*, Madrid, 1893–1908, Vol. IV, pp. 237 ff.) ; J. Sarrailh : *Un Homme d'état espagnol : Martínez de la Rosa* (Bordeaux, 1930) ; L. de Sosa : *Martínez de la Rosa* (Madrid, 1930 : A popular account).

GIL Y ZÁRATE. **Works.** *Obras dramáticas*, Madrid, 1840, 2 vols., and Paris, 1850 (with biographical notice). There are many contemporary editions of individual plays and of the *Manual de Literatura*. **Critical Studies.** A. Ferrer del Río : "Necrología, etc.," in *Memorias de la Academia Española* (Madrid, 1870), Vol. I, pp. 413–21 ; F. Gonzalo Morón : "Juicio crítico de las tragedias de D. Antonio Gil y Zárate," in *Revista de España y del Extranjero*, 1842 (Vol. II, pp. 90–6, 185–92, 203–24) ; S. A. Stoudemire : Short articles in *Modern Language Notes*, 1931, pp. 171–2 and 1933, pp. 321–4 ; *Studies in Philology*, 1931, pp. 325–9.

GIL Y CARRASCO. **Works.** *Obras en prosa* (with biography by Eulogio Florentino Sanz : Madrid, 1883, 2 vols.). *Obras* (Madrid, 1873 : Vol. I only published : *Poesías líricas*. Biography by Eugenio Gil). Modern edition of *El Señor de Bembibre*, ed. R. D. Perés (Barcelona, 1907). **Critical Studies.** J. R. Lomba y Pedraja : "Enrique Gil y Carrasco : su vida y su obra literaria," in *Revista de filología española*, 1915 (Vol. II, pp. 137–79). E. Allison Peers : Chapter III of "Studies in the Influence of Sir Walter Scott in Spain" (p. 238, above : on *El Señor de Bembibre*).

GARCÍA Y TASSARA. **Works.** *Poesías*, Bogotá, 1861 (see p. 205, above) ; *Poesías* (Madrid, 1872 : authorized edition) ; *Poesías* (Madrid, 1880). **Critical Studies.** Biographical notes by F. de la Puente y Apezechea in *Corona poética*, etc. (Seville, 1878) ; M. Méndez Bejarano : *Tassara, Nueva biografía crítica* (Madrid, 1928).

RODRÍGUEZ RUBÍ. **Works.** Contemporary editions of the principal plays are fairly common in libraries. **Critical**

**studies** are few. See A. M. Fabié : *Discurso de recepción en la Academia Española* (Madrid, 1891) ; A. Flores García, in *Esfera*, 1915 (Vol. II, No. 98) ; J. O. Picón, in *Autores dramáticos contemporáneos* (Madrid, 1881–2), Vol. II, pp. 65–81.

FLORENTINO SANZ. **Works.** Besides contemporary editions of the plays, there is an annotated edition of *Don Francisco de Quevedo*, ed. R. Selden Rose (Boston, 1917) and a plain text (Madrid, 1919). The former has a useful introduction.

## CHAPTER XIII

### DII MINORES—II

Of many of the writers treated in this chapter no bibliography can be compiled other than a list of contemporary editions : these writers can only be studied in such editions and in the well-known histories of Blanco García, Hurtado y González Palencia and Mérimée (trans. Morley, New York and London, 1930) and others. The remaining writers are noted below in order of their treatment in the text.

FERNÁN CABALLERO. **Works.** *Obras completas* (Madrid, 1893–1913, 17 vols. ; Madrid, 1921–24, 16 vols. ; and several earlier collections). Of individual works some modern editions (mainly school texts) are : *Cartas*, ed. P. Diego de Valencia (Madrid, 1919) ; *Cartas . . . a D. Manuel Cañete*, ed. A. López Argüello (Santander, 1924) ; *Cuentos populares andaluces*, escogidos y anotados por T. Heinermann (Frankfurt, 1923) ; *Deudas pagadas*, etc. (Madrid, 1921) ; *Epistolario*, ed. A. López Argüello (Barcelona, 1922) ; *La Familia de Alvareda*, ed. W. S. Hendrix and E. H. Hespelt (Boston, 1928) ; *La Gaviota*, ed. G. W. Umphrey and F. Sánchez Escribano (Boston, 1930) ; *Un Servilón y un liberalito*, ed. N. L. Weisinger (Philadelphia, 1924). *Un verano en Bornos. Lady Virginia*, ed. E. Olloqui (Madrid, 1923). There are many translations of individual works into English, French and German. **Critical Studies.** J. M. Asensio y Toledo : *Fernán Caballero* (Madrid, 1893) ; L. Coloma : *Recuerdos de Fernán Caballero* (Bilbao, n.d.) ; N. González Ruiz, in *Bulletin of Spanish Studies*, 1928 (Vol. V, pp. 15–20) ; A. Hämel : "Zum Realismus Fernán Caballeros," in *Iberica*, 1925 (Vol. III, pp. 121–128) ; J. F. Montesinos : "Un esbozo de Fernán Caballero," in *Volkstum und Kultur der Romanen*, 1930 (Vol. III, pp. 232–57) ; A. Morel-Fatio : "Fernán Caballero d'après sa correspondance avec Antoine de Latour," in *Études sur l'Espagne*, III (Paris, 1904), pp. 279–370 ; C. Pitollet : "Les premiers essais littéraires de Fernán Caballero," in *Bulletin Hispanique*, 1907 (Vol. IX, pp. 67–86, 286–302).

TRUEBA. **Works.** *Obras.* Madrid, 1905–24, 11 vols., and several other editions. There are many editions of all the *Cuentos* and of most of Trueba's other works. **Critical Studies.** A. González Blanco : *Antonio de Trueba, su vida y sus obras* (Bilbao, 1914) ; M. Milá y Fontanals : "Antonio de Trueba." In *Obras Completas* (Barcelona, 1888–96), Vol. V, pp. 163–7.

ESTÉBANEZ CALDERÓN. **Works.** Modern editions are : *Cristianos y Moriscos* (Hamburg, 1922 and Liverpool, 1933 : the latter edited by A. Parker, with bibliography of the author). *Escenas Andaluzas* (Madrid, 1883 ; Madrid, 1909 ; Madrid, 1926). *Poesías* (Madrid, 1888). *Novelas, cuentos y artículos* (Madrid, 1893 ; Madrid, 1919). **Critical Studies.** "*El Solitario*" y su Tiempo, Madrid, 1883, 2 vols.

AROLAS. **Works.** *Poesías,* ed. J. R. Lomba y Pedraja (Madrid, 1929 : "Clásicos Castellanos"). **Critical Studies.** J. R. Lomba y Pedraja : *El P. Arolas, su vida y sus versos* (Madrid, 1898).

PASTOR DÍAZ. **Works.** *Obras,* ed. A. Ferrer del Río (Madrid, 1866–8), 6 vols. **Critical Studies.** F. de la Puente y Apezechea : "Necrología, etc.," in *Memorias de la Academia Española,* Madrid, 1902 (Vol. VIII, pp. 151–75) ; J. del Valle-Moré : *Pastor Díaz : su vida y su obra* (Habana, 1911) ; J. Valera : "Necrología, etc.," in *Obras completas* (Madrid, 1905–13), Vol. XXII, pp. 241–78.

CABANYES. **Works.** *Poems of Manuel de Cabanyes,* ed. E. Allison Peers (Manchester, 1923). **Critical Studies.** C. Oyuela : *Estudio sobre . . . Manuel de Cabanyes* (Buenos Aires, 1881) ; E. Allison Peers : "The 'pessimism' of Manuel de Cabanyes," in *Modern Philology,* 1923 (Vol. XXI, pp. 49–52).

ALCALÁ GALIANO. **Critical Studies.** *Memorias de D. Antonio Alcalá Galiano* (Madrid, 1886), 2 vols. ; *Apuntes para la biografía de D. Antonio Alcalá Galiano, escritos por él mismo,* Madrid, 1865 ; F. K. Lloyd : *Antonio Alcalá Galiano* (Liverpool, 1933).

# INDEX

References are not given to the Bibliography. Heavy type denotes the principal reference to a given work or author. The order of letters followed is English, not Spanish : ñ comes immediately after *n*.

248

THE END

PRINTED IN GREAT BRITAIN BY WILLIAM CLOWES AND SONS, LIMITED,
LONDON AND BECCLES.